Canada: The State of the Federation 1994

Edited by
Douglas M. Brown
and Janet Hiebert

Institute of
Intergovernmental
Relations

Institut des
relations
intergouvernementales

Canadian Cataloguing in Publication Data

The National Library of Canada has catalogued this publication as follows:

Main entry under title:

Canada, the state of the federation

1985-
Annual.

ISSN 0827-0708
ISBN 0-88911-573-7 (1994)

1. Federal-provincial relations - Canada - Periodicals.* 2. Federal government - Canada - Periodicals. I. Queen's University (Kingston, Ont.). Institute of Intergovernmental Relations.

JL27.F42   321.02'3'0971   C86-030713-1

The Institute of Intergovernmental Relations

The Institute is the only organization in Canada whose mandate is solely to promote research and communication on the challenges facing the federal system.

Current research interests include fiscal federalism, constitutional reform, the reform of federal political institutions and the machinery of federal-provincial relations, Canadian federalism and the global economy, and comparative federalism.

The Institute pursues these objectives through research conducted by its own staff and other scholars through its publication program, seminars and conferences.

The Institute links academics and practitioners of federalism in federal and provincial governments and the private sector.

L'Institut des relations intergouvernementales

L'Institut est le seul organisme canadien à se consacrer exclusivement à la recherche et aux échanges sur les questions du fédéralisme.

Les priorités de recherche de l'Institut portent présentement sur le fédéralisme fiscal, la réforme constitutionnelle, la modification éventuelle des institutions politiques fédérales, les nouveaux mécanismes de relations fédérales-provinciales, le fédéralisme canadien au regard de l'économie mondiale et le fédéralisme comparatif.

L'Institut réalise ses objectifs par le biais de recherches effectuées par son personnel et par des universitaires de l'Université Queen's et d'ailleurs, de même que par des conférences et des colloques.

L'Institut sert de lien entre les universitaires, les fonctionnaires fédéraux et provinciaux et le secteur privé.

CONTENTS

Part III

Part IV

INTRODUCTION

This is the ninth volume in the annual series of the Institute of Intergovernmental Relations entitled *Canada: The State of the Federation* appearing early each fall.

The federal election of October 1993 has changed significantly the political landscape of the federal Parliament. The election produced a national Liberal government with strong representation from all parts of the country. The election also produced two strong regional parties in Parliament — the Bloc Québécois in Quebec and the Reform Party in the west — which ensure a lively if not certain quality to the Canadian political debate. This volume addresses some of the consequences of the transformation of Parliament as well as the effects on intergovernmental relations generally of the election in Quebec. Part I includes an overview commentary on the more significant developments in the year from September 1993 to September 1994. Alain Nöel in his chapter "Distinct in the House of Commons: The Bloc Québécois as Official Opposition" outlines the paradox of a party that is determined to be treated with respect in Ottawa as the official opposition while taking on the role as the chief promoter, outside Quebec, of Quebec sovereignty. Thérèse Arseneau, in "The Reform Party of Canada: Past, Present and Future" illustrates the difficulties the Reform Party has faced in adapting to the challenges of becoming a parliamentary party and mounting an effective opposition to the Liberal government while attempting to adhere to populist methods.

Challenges to governance in Canada have also arisen from fiscal pressures on the Canadian state to manage and control the country's ever expanding debt. Following the successful practice of several volumes in this series, Part II contains chapters that examine important developments in individual provinces, with the common focus on how provinces are responding to ever increasing fiscal and economic constraints. The chapter by David Taras and Allan Tupper, "Politics and Deficits: Alberta's Challenge to the Canadian Political Agenda" focuses on the Klein government's proposed fiscal re-ordering, as Alberta undertakes a controversial effort to balance its books in three years. The authors take a critical view of the Alberta government's deficit reduction program, an initiative that has triggered a broad socio-economic debate within the province and has been discussed broadly in other provinces. Susan

McCorquodale, in "The Fisheries Crisis in Newfoundland" also discusses social and economic change in Newfoundland as the province responds to the diverse pressures that arise from the fisheries crisis that besets the province. McCorquodale's chapter raises difficult questions about resource management in the federal state. The chapter by David Cameron, "Post-Modern Ontario and the Laurentian Thesis," emphasizes the effects of underlying economic and social changes in the country's largest province that have led to acrimonious intergovernmental relations and an unsettling reappraisal of Ontario's interests within the federation.

While the assumption by the Bloc Québécois of the status of Her Majesty's Official Opposition ensures that national unity questions will not be far removed from the national political debate, the conscious decision by the federal government to avoid engaging in yet another round of constitutional proposals to reform the federation has led us to focus in this volume on other, non-constitutional, issues of interest to the federation. In an attempt to broaden our discussion of topical issues affecting the federal system, we have included in Part III three essays that explore federalism issues that are somewhat different from those most often found in the Canadian federalism literature. The chapter by Jill Vickers, "Why *Should* Women Care About Federalism?" explains the rationale for the sustained criticism by many feminist groups in Canada on the traditional territorial politics of Canada, including the emphasis on executive federalism. While some women's concerns with public policy outcomes and with national standards in social programs have led to suspicion that federalism imposes barriers to progressive changes, other women's groups, particularly francophone groups in Quebec, have greater confidence in the provincial state to protect and promote their interests and needs. In her chapter on "The Charter and Federalism: Revisiting the Nation-Building Thesis," Janet Hiebert questions the expectation, made at the time the Charter was entrenched, that the Charter would have a centralizing effect on public policy. Hiebert argues that the structure of the Charter, as well as Supreme Court jurisprudence in federalism/rights issues, allows the provinces considerable room to promote policies that reflect community or collective values that are different from the priorities of other jurisdictions. Kathryn Harrison's chapter "Prospects for Intergovernmental Harmonization in Environmental Policy" examines developments in the interdependent and overlapping field of environmental policy, to show how federal unilateralism of the late 1980s has given way to harmonization and, more recently, to rationalization of environmental policies and programs through intensive intergovernmental relations. Taken together these three chapters provide continuing evidence of the complex ways in which territorial and societal values interact in the Canadian federation.

The preparation of this book would not have been possible without the superb team effort at the Institute. We wish to thank in particular Mary Kennedy and

Alice McLafferty for text preparation, Valerie Jarus for publication formatting, Scott Nelson for cover design, Mireille Duguay for the sommaires, Marilyn Banting for copyediting, and Patti Candido for cheerful coordination of all of the above. We also thank the anonymous reviewers of the chapters in this volume for their timely and critical evaluations.

Janet Hiebert
Douglas M. Brown
September 1994

CONTRIBUTORS

Thérèse Arseneau is Assistant Professor of Political Science, St. Mary's University, Halifax, Nova Scotia.

Douglas M. Brown is the Executive Director of the Institute of Intergovernmental Relations, Queen's University, Kingston, Ontario.

David R. Cameron is Professor of Political Science at the University of Toronto, Toronto, Ontario.

Kathryn Harrison is Assistant Professor of Political Science, University of British Columbia, Vancouver, B.C.

Janet Hiebert is Assistant Professor of Political Studies, Queen's University, Kingston, Ontario.

Susan McCorquodale is Professor of Political Science, Memorial University, St. John's, Newfoundland.

Alain Nöel is Professeur adjoint, département de science politique, Université de Montréal, Montreal, Quebec.

Anne Poels is Librarian, Institute of Intergovernmental Relations, Queen's University, Kingston, Ontario.

David Taras is Professor, Faculty of General Sciences, University of Calgary, Calgary, Alberta.

Allan Tupper is Professor, Department of Political Science, University of Alberta, Edmonton, Alberta.

Jill Vickers is Professor of Political Science, School of Canadian Studies, Carleton University, Ottawa, Ontario.

Part I

1

Overview

Douglas M. Brown

Ce chapitre présente un survol des principaux événements à être survenu au sein de la fédération en 1994. La nature de la politique fédérale a été profondément affectée par deux élections : l'élection fédérale d'octobre 1993 et l'élection québécoise de septembre 1994. Les deux résultats démontrent l'ambiguïté canadienne. L'élection fédérale a amené une forte majorité libérale, mais également le potentiel de division que représentent les politiques du Bloc québécois et du Parti réformiste. L'élection québécoise a donné une majorité au Parti québécois, mais sans pour autant donner un élan à son objectif de la souveraineté québécoise.

L'auteur souligne également les tentatives par le gouvernement fédéral et les provinces — éclipsées par l'imminente élection québécoise — d'entreprendre des réformes dans une variété de secteurs, dont le fédéralisme fiscal, la révision des politiques sociales, le commerce intérieur et les efforts pour réduire le chevauchement et le dédoublement des programmes gouvernementaux. Cet ordre du jour des réformes fédérales est jusqu'à maintenant incomplet et posera un important défi à la fédération et 1995. Cet ordre du jour devra, pour obtenir l'attention du public, faire concurrence à l'ordre du jour de la souveraineté québécoise, dont le gouvernement du Parti québécois à Québec et le Bloc québécois à Ottawa feront la promotion pendant la période préparatoire du référendum. Celui qui réussira à établir les termes du débat aura une longueur d'avance pour déterminer lequel de ces ordres du jour prévaudra.

In the preceding year we have witnessed both change and continuity in the state of the Canadian federation. The federal election of October 1993 had been widely expected to be a watershed — as also was the Quebec election, anticipated to take place as early as April 1994. Now that both have passed one can see classic Canadian ambiguity in the results and in the nature of the change that they signify for Canada. The ambiguity rests in the fact that the federal election brought back to power the Liberal Party of Canada with a strong majority and credible representation from all parts of Canada — an indicator of Canadian unity. But, at the same time, voters from Quebec gave a majority of their seats to the Bloc Québécois and voters in western Canada sent to Ottawa almost as strong a contingent of Reform Party MPs. In the process, the Progressive Conservative and New Democratic parties have been devastated as institutions of national integration — an indicator of disunity.

Similar ambiguity is revealed in the results of the Quebec election of September 1994, in that the election brought to power the Parti Québécois, which is committed to Quebec sovereignty, but followed a campaign during which voters indicated that their main goal was to elect a new provincial government and where support in opinion polls for sovereignty had declined over a three-month period before election day.[1] The strong vote for the Liberal Party also indicated that the PQ would face a credible opposition in the National Assembly and that the promised referendum campaign would be closely contested.

These ambiguities will continue to dominate the federal system in the year to come. This overview chapter sets out the conflicting agendas. On the one hand the Quebec sovereigntists hope to create a climate whereby a sufficient number of Quebecers will vote to leave the federal system behind. On the other hand, the federal government will have to move beyond its relative caution and inactivity to assert its agenda to revive the federal system, to make it more efficient and effective, and to deal with major fiscal, economic, and social pressures facing Canadians. This conjuncture makes 1995 a crucial year for Canada. We have been at critical crossroads before and have had a way of surviving crises. Nonetheless the potential for a crisis of national unity in 1995 is sufficiently large to characterize it as a year of living dangerously.

This chapter addresses the consequences of the two key elections and surveys the most important intergovernmental issues, and then returns to examine the clash of agendas that will occur in the months to come.

THE FEDERAL ELECTION — AMBIGUOUS RESULTS

The election results of 25 October 1993 demonstrated the volatility of Canadian voters. The election of a Liberal majority for the thirteenth time this century was not a new experience for Canadians, but the transformation of Parliament with two regionally-based parties all but displacing two established national parties marks a fundamental break with the past.

In reaction to both the style and substance of the Mulroney government of nine years, Canadians delivered a complete defeat to the national Progressive Conservative Party. Even before the campaign began, the Conservatives could have expected trouble. The Liberals under Jean Chrétien had positioned themselves at the centre, with tougher stands on the deficit and similar issues than they had held for some time.[2] The Reform Party was eating into Conservative support in the west and the Bloc Québécois under popular leader Lucien

Bouchard seemed poised to consolidate gains made in the 1992 referendum campaign. And yet other factors were important to the result. The Canadian economy, while technically out of recession, was just barely growing, and unemployment levels in the "jobless recovery" remained high. The new Conservative leader, Kim Campbell, had the potential to attract new voters to the PCs, but also carried the blame for nine years of Conservative rule and did not appeal to Quebec voters in the same way that Mulroney had (or indeed her major party leadership contender, Jean Charest, would have).[3] Once the election was called, the Conservative campaign never caught fire, while Chrétien's Liberals seemed more confident as the campaign proceeded. A crucial national poll following the Thanksgiving Day weekend projected a Liberal victory countrywide, while also predicting a strong Bloc showing in Quebec. The result of such expectations, according to some analysts, was a strategic vote by the other side of the Conservative electoral coalition, potential Reform voters, to counterbalance votes for the Bloc Québécois with votes for Reform. Thus was the electoral coalition of the Conservatives shattered.[4]

Many have interpreted the election results as the inevitable "second shoe dropping" after the 1992 referendum, with winning coalitions representing an extension of the victory of the diverse "no" forces. While detailed analysis does not seem to bear out such sweeping conclusions, it is clear that the Bloc Québécois benefited from the disenchantment of Quebec voters with the Charlottetown Accord, and with the experience of a joint campaign with the Parti Québécois to defeat it.[5] For the first time, Quebecers had the choice of voting for a sovereigntist party at the federal level. The Bloc attracted not only the support of sovereigntists (estimated at approximately 40 percent of the electorate), but also of francophone voters not committed to sovereignty, but who wanted to protest Conservative rule (and for whom Chretien's Liberals were beyond the pale). Similarly, analysis of public opinion during and just after the election campaign indicates that Conservatives outside Quebec who voted "no" in 1992 were most likely to switch to Reform. The trend ends there, however, for there is no indication that how one voted in the referendum mattered in terms of Liberal support in 1993 or, for that matter, support for the NDP.[6]

In any event, the electoral results were striking in their regional concentration. The Liberals gained a majority of 177 seats with MPs elected from every province. Moreover they took all but one seat in Ontario, every seat in all four of the Atlantic provinces, and 12 of 14 seats in Manitoba. While the Liberal showing in the three westernmost provinces and Quebec was respectable enough for them to boast the broadest victory for their party since 1968, the chief difference between Chrétien's winning coalition and those of the Trudeau Liberals, is that the party's support among francophone Quebecers all but disappeared. The Bloc — running only in Quebec — got enough seats to form the official opposition, while Reform, despite a strong second-place showing in many Ontario ridings, took seats concentrated in Alberta and British Columbia. Thus the new Parliament is more regionally divided than it has ever been.

THE EFFECT OF THE REGIONAL PARTIES

This reduction of the number of national parties in the House of Commons to one has led some to predict a fractious and divisive House of Commons, with dire consequences for Canadian unity. There have been signs of such division at several points in the session of Parliament that began in January 1994, particularly late in the session as the Quebec election approached. However, for reasons unique to each party, neither Reform nor the Bloc have been able to fully realize their potential.[7] In the case of Reform, their own party ethic has been to downplay competitive party games in the House. While they have demonstrated regional preferences on many issues, they have also avoided opportunities to exacerbate differences between themselves and the Bloc, and the governing Liberals. Only in the last few weeks of the session, perhaps in response to their supporters' concern over Lucien Bouchard's tour in western Canada to profile Quebec sovereignty, did the Reform leadership confront more assertively the Bloc agenda and pressure the Liberal government to be tougher towards separatists.[8] In so doing the Reform continues to position itself as the pure voice of "English Canada," although with the more important effects of this positioning yet to be demonstrated.

The Bloc has also had its reasons to be less than single-minded in its parliamentary strategy. The Bloc could not simply go to Ottawa as obstructionists. They had to be seen to form a responsible opposition party if they were to benefit from the media profile and resources as Official Opposition. This has led to the party's ironic position of defending Canadian social programs and Canada's role as peacekeeper against incursions from Reform. Nonetheless, through the daily question period and in special debates, the Bloc has kept up a steady stream of provocative questions on such issues as aboriginal rights, cutbacks to the military college at St-Jean, the cancellation of the helicopter contract, proposed amendments to the pharmaceutical patents legislation, and tobacco taxes. The Bloc strategy has been to work away at the difficult compromises necessary to govern the federation, hoping to score a major hit prior to the Quebec election. Yet, in my view, such a blockbuster issue failed to materialize, thanks in part to the caution of the Liberal government (of which, more below).

The Bloc has not shrunk from raising the sovereignty issue both within Parliament and more broadly. Bouchard's first speech in the House as Opposition Leader on 19 January 1994 surprised many Canadians outside Quebec (judging by the media reaction at least) with his sovereigntist intent. Yet the biggest effort by the party to raise the profile of its goals was in the extra-parliamentary campaign on sovereignty, through trips to Washington, Paris, Toronto, and Vancouver, among other cities. In combination with statements from Parti Québécois leader Jacques Parizeau, Bouchard's activities succeeded in sparking wide-ranging debate in the media and among many (but not all) political leaders both inside and outside Quebec. Bouchard's action's forced Reform Leader Preston Manning to enter the fray with the latter's 20 questions on sovereignty to Prime Minister Chrétien on 8 June 1994[9] and the engagement of a fractious debate on national unity in the House on 22 June.

In a similar vein, Bouchard's and Parizeau's statements provoked reactions from some provincial leaders. Premiers Michael Harcourt of British Columbia, Ralph Klein of Alberta, and Roy Romanow of Saskatchewan all spoke in order to question sovereigntist assumptions, and perhaps to outflank less moderate sentiment within their provinces. Other premiers, and Prime Minister Chrétien, remained silent for the most part, preferring not to be drawn into the debate before the election in Quebec was held. As muted as it was, the debate did succeed in alerting the Canadian public to the stakes in the coming Quebec election, and to prepare them for a potentially emotional and highly political debate on Quebec independence if the PQ were to win. What sovereigntists may not have counted on was that the debate also served to show that "English Canada" may react with more passion than Quebecers expect to the prospect of Quebec independence.

In summary, the election to the federal Parliament of two strong regional parties with such opposing viewpoints is already having an unsettling effect on the state of the federation. And yet this effect must be measured against the more stabilizing effect of the government by the Liberal majority. The Liberals hold neither the strongly centralist positions of Pierre Trudeau, nor the left of centre anti-free trade position of John Turner. Instead, Jean Chrétien leads a Liberal Party with a more moderate position with respect to federalism and a more centrist position with respect to social and economic issues than the Liberal Party has held for many years. Underlined by Chrétien's commitment to maintain a moratorium on constitutional reform, the Liberal government promised a period of calm, following the sharp debates of the past five years. The Liberal majority will not be able to prevent the emergence of a divisive debate on unity issues led to a large degree by the Bloc and Reform, but its presence provides a much more stable — and therefore less destructive — environment for these debates to take place.

Nonetheless, the federal government, which the Liberals now lead, faces enormous challenges — economic, fiscal, and social — which have deep implications for the future of the federation. The successful tackling of these challenges depends on effective intergovernmental relations. And such success or failure will ultimately effect whether the lasting legacy of the new federal government is to maintain stability in the federation or to contribute to its demise. We turn next to these challenges.

INTERGOVERNMENTAL CHALLENGES

The Liberal government pledged itself to cooperative, pragmatic federalism and to keep its electoral promises of working with the provinces. While the Liberals may not feel bound by the Charlottetown Accord agenda, in particular the institutional and symbolic agenda of constitutional reform, many policy-oriented challenges underlying the Accord continue to form part of the federal government's workplan. This includes such difficult issues as: more sustainable fiscal transfers; a more harmonized tax structure; a long overdue review of social programs; the implementation of aboriginal self-government; the improvement of the economic union; and more generally agreement with the provinces on a more efficient federal system.

Current intergovernmental relations are also responding to a broader and more fundamental set of challenges that strike at the very practice of governance. Governments must respond to fundamental changes in economic and financial circumstances, in particular the restructuring of the Canadian economy forced by globalization and the debt-ridden public finances of both the federal and all of the provincial governments. Thus many of the initiatives underway in the past year have responded to imperatives from taxpayers, business and voters in general, to harmonize policies and rationalize government programs, to bring greater efficiencies to government spending and regulation and to remove the obstacles to the restructuring of the private economy. Not all the governments in Canada share the same perspective, or sense of urgency, on the nature and extent of the reforms required. Political developments in Alberta and Ontario illustrate the range of perspectives and approaches adopted. Underlying economic circumstances also differ markedly, for example, from British Columbia where the recession barely mattered, to Quebec where the recession is not quite over.

Despite the variety of experiences, however, there is sufficient common ground to sustain a number of intergovernmental efforts to create more "efficient governance." Four of the most important initiatives have been the review of fiscal arrangements, the closely linked review of social programs, the internal trade negotiations, and the variety of measures to reduce overlap and duplication. Each of these merits a brief discussion.

The first important intergovernmental issue is fiscal relations. The consensus of a wide range of analysts and commentators, including Canada's federal and provincial ministers of finance, is that the current set of fiscal arrangements cannot be sustained, and in fact, is set to "self-destruct" in this decade if unreformed.[10] The system no longer delivers what it was designed to deliver

— whether measured by means of policy harmonization, equity, national standards, or economic efficiency. Nor does it respond to the current demands for revised social programs and balanced federal and provincial budgets. To illustrate the different problems: the richer provinces, led by Ontario, have been emphatic that the Liberal government should lift the unfair cap on the Canada Assistance Program payments; the poorer provinces were alarmed at projected cuts in equalization announced in the last days of the Conservative government; and social policy activists have been worried about the inexorable trend towards zero in the federal cash infusions to health care and education. And yet, to respond to any one of these demands is to potentially reduce the resources available to satisfying the others. Meanwhile, Finance Minster Paul Martin faced the urgent task of reducing the federal deficit.

Since its election, the Liberal government has bought time, by freezing all major transfers except equalization (which is to increase by 5 percent per year for five years), sustaining the cap on CAP, and signalling that budget deficit reduction over the next three fiscal years will demand a dividend of $2 billion from the review of social programs. Federal and provincial ministers and officials continue to meet to discuss the parameters and details of the reform of fiscal relations — including the issue of harmonizing federal and provincial sales taxes.

The second major intergovernmental issue — the social security review — is intricately linked to the review of fiscal arrangements, given that major aspects of social programs are currently funded by federal-provincial transfers, (i.e., EPF and CAP). The logic of making social policy and program delivery choices first, and sorting out fiscal arrangements second, has great appeal. But, in fact, the reverse has happened over the past five years, as incremental fiscal transfer changes made for budgetary reasons have driven social policy outcomes, and exacerbated any efforts to overhaul social programs that have been in place for decades. This time around it is the apparent goal of governments to set appropriate social policy goals first, establish new programs in a more cost effective way, and leave decisions on the final shape of fiscal transfers to the end. The federal minister of human resource development, Lloyd Axworthy, has launched a far-ranging review of most federal and federal-provincial social programs (the notable exceptions being seniors' benefits and health care). The social security review has been the focus of a parliamentary committee in the spring, of an advisory group of outside experts, of extensive consultation with interest groups, and of several meetings with provincial ministers and officials responsible for advanced education, labour market regulation and training, and social services. On the table are such federal programs as unemployment insurance, child tax benefits, job creation and training; and such provincial programs with major federal funding as social assistance and postsecondary education, among others, for a total of 26 percent of total federal program expenditures.[11]

The results from the social policy review thus far are disappointing. On the one hand, press accounts reveal that there has been much initial confusion and continuing controversy within the federal government about its goals. On the other hand, both the provinces and social policy interest groups have complained that the review has been moving too quickly.[12] In the meantime there are indications that Finance Minister Martin will have to make even deeper cuts in program expenditures — with or without reform — by late fall or at the latest, the next federal budget. Finally but perhaps most telling, the federal government's process seems to have been put on hold over the summer in the lead-up to the Quebec election.[13] A proposed white paper, since downgraded to a discussion paper, had been expected in the late spring, only to be delayed now until late September 1994. In the meantime, various provincial efforts to reform welfare and to proceed with pilot projects for training and related programs continue, with the possibility that progress on these fronts will forestall more comprehensive reforms coming from Ottawa.

The third and more successful major initiative has been the internal trade negotiations. A comprehensive agreement was reached among federal, provincial and territorial ministers in June, following months of intense effort. A final text was signed by first ministers on 18 July 1994 at a meeting in Ottawa. [14] The agreement is to come into effect on 1 July 1995. Although press accounts were relatively cynical about this apparent pre-election "gift" to Premier Johnson of Quebec, and scornful of the many reservations and exceptions in the agreement, a more balanced appraisal would recognize the agreement as a significant and long overdue achievement. On the surface the agreement resembles international trade agreements, reflecting the cumulative experience of the army of federal and provincial trade bureaucrats in the series of trade negotiations leading to the Canada-U.S. FTA, NAFTA, and the Uruguay Round agreements of the GATT. But beneath the surface is a more purely domestic accord which recognizes that many barriers are in place for sound social and cultural reasons, and that the main goals are to improve, over time, what is already a highly integrated economic union. Therefore, the enduring achievement of the internal trade agreement may not be the substance of specific commitments for liberalization, but the foundation of interprovincial trade on a rules-based regime, with a clear process for building more liberalization in the future.

The fourth set of initiatives is more difficult to define and has not to date yielded substantial results. This consists of efforts to rationalize federal and provincial programs, to reduce the overlapping and duplication of programs, and to improve citizen access and client service where more than one government is involved. "Overlap and duplication" is a favourite foil of critics of the federal system, particularly in Quebec where intergovernmental competition has been intense since the 1960s. Despite somewhat inconclusive evidence of the effects and extent of such duplication, practically all levels of governments have seized on it as part of broader efforts to achieve a more efficient federalism.[15] Such initiatives are likely to have more lasting value if they are conceived as part of a broader-based effort to streamline government and to respond to fiscal and other pressures for reform. It is perhaps not surprising that such efforts are well advanced in Alberta and New Brunswick, where broader public sector reforms are also high on the public agenda. Federal efforts may also be more effective in the extent to which they are tied into the more fundamental review of government programs underway by the federal minister responsible for government renewal, Marcel Massé.

The results to date from intergovernmental initiatives seem relatively modest: the most significant result was the "Action Plans" for "Improving the Efficiency of the Federation" announced between the federal government and seven provinces at the first ministers' meeting on 18 July.[16] Given that such issues seem to have greater salience in Quebec, it seems strange that Quebec (and Alberta) are *not* among the signatory provinces. Agreements with these provinces are apparently in the works, but the lack of early progress is worth noting (and is dealt with further below). In any case none of the content of the plans seems very dramatic; they cover a host of service and regulatory programs in the environmental, wildlife, fisheries, agricultural, housing, justice and business development fields, among others. None of these items have been major intergovernmental irritants or generators of great public controversy. Nonetheless if the action plans are fully implemented as advertised then a myriad of daily interactions between governments and citizens will be improved, with long-term results in terms of governmental efficiency, cost effectiveness, and legitimacy to the federal system.

In reviewing these four initiatives as a whole, judgement on success or failure must be put off until a later date. Ten months is not a long time to put together major reforms of the federal system, and the fiscal arrangements and social security reform likely require two or three years of sustained action to produce results. Nonetheless, progress on administrative reform is disappointing compared with the expectations generated in certain quarters (Quebec and elsewhere). There had been much discussion, particulary in Ottawa about administrative agreement and bilateral deals, to demonstrate to Quebecers in particular that the constitutional status quo need not mean the status quo in terms of policy outcomes.[17] Indeed Ottawa sources had, early in 1994, confidently predicted six or more administrative agreements with Quebec by June. Obviously plans were changed, but why? A likely explanation for the lack of success is that the Quebec government led by Daniel Johnson was not interested in agreements that would be attacked as accomplishing too little in Quebec, while Chrétien's government feared the criticism of pandering to Quebec from other provinces. The strategy of administrative agreements must have seemed too risky, given the rising stakes of the upcoming election.

Indeed, this pre-election climate had its impact on many aspects of the state of the federation. Long-anticipated elections have a way of suspending political developments and constraining political actors; caution prevails as every act is scrutinized for its effects on the polls. Many major intergovernmental developments, and much long-term planning about the future of the federation itself has been on hold pending the results of the Quebec election. This sclerosis is thus the first outcome of the Quebec election — to which we now turn.

THE QUEBEC DECISION

The pre-election period began with the resignation — during the 1993 federal election campaign — of Quebec Premier Robert Bourassa. In theory the premier left office with sufficient time to allow the Quebec Liberal Party to renew itself, but, it must be said, with little real prospect that this could occur in practice. His successor was saddled with the inevitable discontent with a government long in power, presiding over the tail-end of a stubborn recession, and the failure of two attempts to achieve Quebec's demands for constitutional reform. Daniel Johnson, elected leader of the Liberals by acclamation in December and sworn in as premier on 11 January 1994, quickly attempted to put his own stamp on the government. In the months leading to the election campaign his government undertook measures to spur the provincial economy, brought some new blood into the Cabinet and, in general made a virtue of the necessity of living with the Canadian federal system.

While federalists outside Quebec may have been cheered by Johnson's unadulterated commitment to federalism as compared to the conditional support and vacillation of Robert Bourassa, the new Johnson government never succeeded in pulling ahead of the Parti Québécois in the polls. By May 1994 the PQ still enjoyed a healthy lead. With the election approaching, the media both inside and outside Quebec began to give considerably more attention to the PQ program.[18] This scrutiny was also brought on by the PQ/BQ publicity campaign of May-June, with an attendant reaction, as noted above, from Canadians outside Quebec. It is worth re-emphasizing that the debate that occurred during this period demonstrated that "English Canada" remained divided and ambivalent in its response to the prospect of a sovereigntist government in Quebec. There seemed to be genuine angst about whether or not to confront the sovereigntists with detailed responses to their plans, or to maintain a wall of silence.[19] In the meantime the issue was blamed by many financial analysts as being partially responsible for driving up interest rates and, perhaps most importantly, woke many Quebecers to examine just what was at stake in the upcoming election.

The election campaign began officially on 25 July 1994 and within two weeks the Liberals succeeded on putting the PQ on the defensive by castigating the sovereignty program. As a result, Liberal support increased marginally. The PQ was forced — most media analysts credited Lucien Bouchard for intervening in early August — to change its tack and downplay the sovereignty issue, and to appeal to the view of an apparent majority of Quebecers that the election should be about who is best able to govern the province.[20] More importantly, this change of tactics was reinforced by the slow but steady decline in support for sovereignty as shown by polls since June.[21] It is too early to know, if one can ever know, to what extent the decline in public opinion support for sovereignty was determined as a result of the Liberal campaign or of more general causes. But the change in the emphasis of the campaign to other issues had the effect of significantly reducing the stakes in the election — and of raising therefore the probability of a PQ victory.

All that seemed to be left for the decision on 12 September was the extent of the PQ win. Most analysts were surprised with the result which, while giving a solid majority of 77 seats to the PQ, deprived them of the larger victory that many had expected. Had the PQ won 85 or more seats, for example, they would have held virtually every majority francophone seat and would have been able to interpret the vote as endorsing "Québécois" support for an accelerated movement to sovereignty. Even more distressing for the PQ strategists was that total popular votes gained by the Liberals, at 44.3 percent, practically tied the vote of the PQ at 44.7 percent.[22] As for the Liberals, they can claim a moral victory, can congratulate themselves on a successful campaign, and — more significantly — are unlikely to face a challenge to Daniel Johnson's leadership. Outside Quebec, the results have been largely interpreted by the financial markets and by political leaders as lowering the probability of Quebec secession and confirming the election as a "business as usual" transition of government.

THE YEAR AHEAD: CONFLICTING AGENDAS

It is understandable that those who do not share the sovereigntist goal would downplay the significance of the PQ win and to emphasize the declining support for sovereignty and the strong Liberal showing. Yet the election of the Parti Québécois will not mean business as usual. Canada is much more likely to face a difficult and conflictual year as the promised deadline for a referendum on sovereignty approaches. The date of the referendum itself is in doubt, with Parizeau already indicating that it could be held as late as autumn 1995, and Bouchard musing that it would not be held at all unless the sovereigntists could win.[23] The underlying uncertainty about the future of the federation will continue and intensify. The issue of Quebec independence can be expected to rise again to the top of the public consciousness after the first few months of a new government in Quebec.

One can also expect that the PQ will take on an agressive stance towards intergovernmental relations. The Quebec stance will be akin to "work-to-rule," resisting any federal intrusions into provincial jurisdiction, and avoiding cooperative solutions. It is also likely to boycott many intergovernmental meetings and any reform processes that do not have as an objective the achievement of Quebec's traditional autonomist demands. Thus if the Chrétien government had any illusions about launching a new era of "cooperative federalism," these hopes seem dashed with the defeat of the Liberals in Quebec. And while Ottawa could proceed on any number of fronts to reach agreement with the other nine provinces, it would do so at the peril of isolating Quebec.

The Quebec election result underscores other difficulties facing the Chrétien government. The Liberals' long post-election honeymoon must soon come to an end if they are not to find themselves in serious difficulties. The key items on the federal agenda, such as the need to significantly reduce the deficit in the next federal budget and the social policy review noted above, are bound to bring Ottawa into direct conflict with the new government in Quebec and other provinces. A tough budget in Ottawa will be intensely scrutinized by the Bloc and the PQ government, as will proposals to reform social programs. Yet the Liberal government, and to a lesser degree the governments of the other provinces, will also want to demonstrate to Quebecers the continued legitimacy and credibility of the federal system, and to bring out federalism's vaunted virtues of adaptability and flexibility.

Debate on these issues will be joined as vigorously by other governments and by non-governmental actors, moderating the profile of the Ottawa-Quebec conflict. Nonetheless, in the next year the federal government will have to execute a difficult balancing act between aggressive reform and cautious movement towards Quebec. Progress must be made on the intergovernmental issues of reducing fiscal deficits and social program reform as well as to continue with the less dramatic but important agenda related to "efficient governance" that was outlined above. Yet the costs and conflicts of that change will likely be exploited by the sovereigntists as evidence of the costs of the federal system itself. The PQ will argue at the same time that the federal system cannot work for Quebec, while attempting to ensure that it does not work with its "work-to-rule" tactics.

In the meantime, one can also expect movement from the new regime in Quebec on its program[24] to build the case for sovereignty, to restore its momentum going into a referendum, and — perhaps most crucially — to restore the sense of inevitability of Quebec independence at home and abroad. The timing of this program will undoubtedly change as a result of the election results, but the apparent schedule is for a process moving from a solemn declaration in the National Assembly, to a committee to prepare a new constitution for a sovereign Quebec, to studies to demonstrate the costs of the federal system — and all of these steps may be expected in the coming months. In this campaign to "trigger" Quebec sovereignty, the PQ will continue to benefit from its partnership with Bouchard's Bloc. There will no doubt be tensions between these two camps on tactics and strategy, if not the ultimate goal.[25] Nonetheless, the Bloc can be expected to assist enormously in the "work-to-rule" tactics in intergovernmental relations, both in the House of Commons and in Bouchard's extraparliamentary role. The debate during May-June 1994 may have been a foretaste of what will come in 1995: defending Quebec's interests without moderation in Parliament, keeping the issue of sovereignty at the front of Canadian consciousness, and provoking and polarizing Canadians as a result.

This leads me to speculate about the likely reaction to all of this activity from outside Quebec. In the immediate aftermath of the election there appeared to be at least some degree of coordination in the statements by the prime minister and the premiers of the other provinces. The general line was to warn Parizeau against interpreting his mandate as leading to sovereignty, and to reassure voters and financial markets that the election represented a normal democratic transition of power and that the polls indicated no majority support for sovereignty. Will this solid party line continue to hold? This seems unlikely, given the differing political pressures brought to bear on the different premiers. Some federal and provincial political leaders will likely continue to refuse to be drawn into the debate; while others will likely be quick to condemn the sovereigntists and cast doubt on their plans. The disengagement strategy will undoubtedly prevail among most federalist leaders if the polls on sovereignty stay where they are in September 1994. Others will likely be forced by domestic pressure to oppose the sovereigntists more directly. Despite the different nuances of the debate outside Quebec, moderate leaders outside and inside Quebec are not likely to rise to the bait of PQ "triggering" activity, and will not engage in "pre-negotiation" with the PQ. This would remain the case as long as the outcome of a Quebec referendum remains in doubt — and short of some catastrophic development for federalists, this seems as certain an uncertainty as any in 1995.

To conclude, the year ahead is likely to resemble an intense duel between the two big agendas: that of the federal government and (at least in part) the other provinces for a revitalized federal system through nonconstitutional means, and that of the PQ/BQ for sovereignty. The sovereigntist agenda will potentially distract from Ottawa's agenda, and cast doubt on the ability of the federal government to achieve its goals. On the other hand, success for the federal agenda would also contribute to the defeat of the sovereigntists in a referendum. The conflict between the two will likely be exploited by Reform and other political forces, if they see Quebec obstructionism as blocking the way to their own priorities. Such political manoeuvring will probably come, however, amidst a growing debate about the future and value of Canada itself, as the referendum approaches.

In short, Canada is entering, not for the first time, a year of living danger-ously. Many unforeseen factors could intervene to help determine the course of events: global developments, the state of the Canadian economy, the rise and reaction to unexpected political crises. The stage is nonetheless set for a classic confrontation. Many Canadians may try to put off the inevitable, fearing the consequences of irreversible choices. But many other Canadians, including many Quebecers, are determined that a generation of questioning must soon end in some answers. In 1995 they may get their wish.

NOTES

1. Author's reading of poll results from June to August 1994. For example, a Leger and Leger poll in June 1994 found support for Quebec "sovereignty" to be 42 percent; the response to the same question in early September received only 36 percent.

2. This conclusion is based on research in progress by Richard Johnston, political scientist at the University of British Columbia, and presented at a seminar held at Queen's University, 2 December 1993.

3. Based on comments made by Hugh Segal and André Blais at a post-election symposium held on 27 October 1993 at Queen's University.

4. Comments by Richard Johnston and André Blais.

5. See chapter in this volume by Alain Nöel.

6. Comments by Johnston.

7. For further details see the chapters by Alain Nöel and Thérèse Arseneau.

8. For the media discussion of Reform's ambivalent role see *The Globe and Mail,* 9 and 11 June 1994; *Financial Post,* 23 April 1994.

9. For the full text, see House of Commons, *Debates,* 9 June 1994.

10. See Peter M. Leslie, Kenneth Norrie and Irene Ip, *A Partnership in Trouble: Renegotiating Fiscal Federalism* (Toronto: C.D. Howe Institute, 1993); Paul Hobson "Current Issues in Federal-Provincial Relations" in R.L. Watts and D.M. Brown (eds.), *Canada: The State of the Federation, 1993* (Kingston: Institute of Intergovernmental Relations, Queen's University, 1993); and Keith G. Banting, Douglas M. Brown and Thomas J. Courchene (eds.), *The Future of Fiscal Feder-alism* (Kingston: School of Policy Studies, Queen's University, 1994), esp. pp. 3-81.

11. See House of Commons, Standing Committee on Human Resources Development, *Interim Report: Concerns and Priorities Regarding the Modernization and Restructuring of Canada's Social Security System* (Ottawa: Minister of Supply and Services, March 1994).

12. For an overview commentary see *The Globe and Mail* for 8 April 1994; and 9 June 1994; also Human Resources Development Canada *News Release* 94-64, 7 July 1994.

13. *The Globe and Mail*, 10 June 1994.

14. See "Agreement on Internal Trade," 18 July 1994. The main text contains 18 chapters and runs to 215 pages; a summary is available.

15. See Gordon Brown, "Canadian Federal-Provincial Overlap and Presumed Government Inefficiency," *Publius: The Journal of Federalism* 24, 1 (Winter 1994): 21-37.

16. The details are available in a press release of 18 July 1994 from the Privy Council Office, Government of Canada.

17. See, for example, comment by Lisanne Gagnon in *The Globe and Mail*, 7 May 1994.

18. For a sample of such media commentary see *La Presse,* 21 May 1994; *The Globe and Mail,* 31 March, 7 April and 7 May, 19-21 May, and 3-7 June 1994; *Toronto Star,* 11 May, 25 July 1994.

19. See, for example, commentary in *The Globe and Mail*, 5 May and 19-20 May 1994.

20. For results of a poll commissioned by the *The Globe and Mail* and *Le Devoir*, see *The Globe and Mail,* 22 July 1994. The poll indicated that 51 percent of decided voters would vote for the PQ; 44 percent for the Liberals; and that a majority of voters (56%, cf. 36% for whom the goal was to move to sovereignty) said their first objective was to choose a good government for Quebec.

21. See note 1, above.

22. Unofficial results reported in several daily newspapers on Tuesday, 13 September 1994 put Liberal total popular vote at 44.3%; PQ at 44.7% and Action Démocratique Québécois at 6.5%.

23. See *La Presse*, 20-21 September 1994.

24. See The National Executive Council of the Parti Québécois, *Quebec In a New World*, translated by R. Chodos (Toronto: James Lorimer, 1994).

25. See *The Globe and Mail*, 4-5 August 1994; and *La Presse*, 20 and 22 September 1994.

2

Distinct in the House of Commons:
The Bloc Québécois as Official Opposition

Alain Nöel

Le succès électoral du Bloc québécois était prévisible. Il s'est également avéré signifi-catif à court terme et aura des implications majeures dans les mois à venir. La première section de ce chapitre explique le caractère prévisible de la performance du Bloc, en montrant que le nouveau parti représentait une part importante et stable de l'électorat québécois. La deuxième partie traite du rôle du Bloc québécois à Ottawa et souligne, en particulier, la proximité idéologique du parti et de son électorat. Enfin, la troisième partie discute des possibilités qui s'offrent au Bloc et au Parti québécois dans la bataille référendaire qui s'amorce, insistant notamment sur les perceptions des électeurs moins décidés. En conclusion, une brève discussion suggère que le Bloc pourrait demeurer un acteur important dans les années à venir, même si les souverainistes perdaient leur référendum.

In the days following the October 1992 referendum, much was said about the possible closure of Canada's constitutional debate. Peter H. Russell, in particu-lar, pleaded for an end to "mega constitutional politics," and predicted that ambitious constitutional proposals would "find no support from political lead-ers or the general public."[1] A poll conducted a week after the referendum confirmed that Canadians were unwilling to resume constitutional discussions: at the time, 69 percent of Canadians outside Quebec and 55 percent in Quebec supported the idea of a five-year moratorium on constitutional talks.[2]

The Quebec question, however, remained unaddressed. At the outset, the Meech-Charlottetown constitutional process was an attempt to accommodate Quebec within the framework established in 1982, and in this respect nothing was resolved. The simple demand for recognition included in the Meech Lake Accord was unacceptable in "English Canada,"[3] and the more elaborate com-promise ratified in Charlottetown was also rejected by a majority of Canadians. Following the 1992 referendum, there was nevertheless a widespread impression that a major crisis had been averted: Patrick J. Monahan, for instance, argued that "the prospects for convincing Quebeckers to remain within Canada appear significantly more promising at the end of 1992 than they did in the months immediately following the failure of the Meech Lake Accord."[4] Likewise, Guy Laforest noted that two months after the referendum "Robert Bourassa was still the leader of the Quebec Liberal Party and the Premier of Quebec, and nobody talked about the constitution." Even the notion of a distinct society had been set aside.[5]

The idea that Canada was ready to return to politics as usual appeared convincing. When the 1993 federal electoral campaign began, many observers, in Quebec as well as in the rest of Canada, predicted Quebecers would forget their flirt with the Bloc Québécois to vote for a party that could take power. Even the re-election of the Quebec Liberal Party seemed possible.[6] These expectations proved wrong, of course, and the Bloc Québécois became the Official Opposition in the House of Commons. But how predictable and how significant was the Bloc's success? And what did it mean in the short run for Quebec and Canadian politics? More important, can the Bloc's 1993 gains be interpreted as a first-period lead in the three-peroid game of independence envisioned by Jacques Parizeau?

This chapter takes up these three questions and argues that the electoral success of the Bloc Québécois was predictable, meaningful in the short run, and significant for the coming months. The first section deals with the 1993 elections, and suggests the outcome was predictable because the party represented an important and stable part of the Quebec electorate. The second considers the meaning of the Bloc's presence in Ottawa, and argues that the new party expresses rather adequately the vision of the country shared by its supporters. Finally, the third section discusses the role the Bloc will play in the coming months, in light of its first year as Official Opposition. The conclusion argues that the Bloc Québécois could well play an important role in the coming years, even if the Parti Québécois fails to win its referendum on sovereignty.

FROM MINOR PARTY TO OFFICIAL OPPOSITION

When the Bloc Québécois was formed, in the weeks following the failure of the Meech Lake Accord, it constituted little more than a small group of MPs disappointed with the Conservative or Liberal party.[7] Denied official party status in the House of Commons, the new party faced hostility in both the House and public opinion outside Quebec, where it was perceived as less than entirely legitimate. In Quebec, however, the Bloc was in tune with public opinion and, with the tacit support of Robert Bourassa, it reached politicians well beyond the ranks of Parti Québécois sympathizers.[8] In the years after 1990, it would almost always lead in the polls, to reach levels of support around 40 percent in the months preceding the 1993 election.[9] The 1992 referendum, with 57 percent of Quebecers voting No, demonstrated the enduring political relevance of the constitutional vision defended by the Bloc Québécois.[10] It also tested the party in action, strengthened it, and helped define its links with the Parti Québécois.[11]

Despite such steady support, and notwithstanding the referendum results, a number of observers believed the Bloc Québécois would not fare well in a general election. This prediction was based on the common perception that Quebec votes as a block in federal elections, usually for the winning party.[12] It was expected that, in the end, Quebecers would desert the Bloc Québécois and turn to the party most likely to take power. Accordingly, the Conservatives and the Liberals tried to woo Bloc supporters by arguing that a vote for a party that could not take power was a wasted vote or, worse in the minds of the Conservatives, an indirect vote for Jean Chrétien.[13]

Past elections suggest this view of Quebec is wrong. In 1979, Joe Clark failed to form a majority government largely because Quebecers remained faithful to the Liberal party, and Trudeau formed a minority government in 1972 for the same reason. Likewise, in 1957, Quebecers ignored Diefenbaker's lead and voted for the Liberals. In the past, Quebecers voted as a block less because they rallied strategically to the winning party than because they acted rather homogeneously, whether their preferred party was leading in the rest of Canada or not.[14] This homogeneity, it should be noted, cut across linguistic lines within Quebec, and cannot be attributed simply to cultural or linguistic factors.[15] The phenomenon was probably a consequence of the limited choice offered to Quebecers. In other words, it was driven by the supply (the partisan options that were offered) rather than by the demand (the autonomous preferences of voters).[16] In Canadian elections, the Conservative Party long constituted "the only serious alternative" to the Liberals. Yet, until 1984 the party remained barely "acceptable" to Quebecers, who consequently turned to the Liberals.[17] As a result, the Quebec vote was relatively stable and homogeneous, but it was also potentially volatile, not deeply anchored in partisan identifications.[18]

A supply-side interpretation of Quebec block voting helps account for the success of Lucien Bouchard's party in 1993. With the development of a new partisan option, the alleged tendency of Quebecers to vote for the leading party would be tested more clearly than ever. The apparent homogeneity of the Quebec vote would also be questioned, with the introduction of an option hardly acceptable to non-francophones. Early in the campaign, a majority of voters confirmed that, indeed, they did not wish to vote for the party most likely to win. Asked whether they agreed with the main parties' argument that a vote for the Bloc was a wasted vote, 63 percent of Quebecers disagreed.[19] Even voters who did not support the Bloc rejected the bandwagon reasoning traditionally associated with Quebec. Early in the campaign, Quebec voters located themselves according to their relatively enduring political preferences.[20] Only this time, a new option was available.[21]

There is a definite structure to the Quebec electorate, and it can be described with reference to three overlapping dimensions: language, partisan identification, and support for sovereignty. First comes language. As long as the Liberals were the only serious contender, this cleavage remained latent in federal elections. The situation changed in the 1980s, with the inroads made by the Conservatives among francophone Quebecers. In 1988, 49 percent of English-speaking Quebecers continued to identify themselves as Liberals, compared with only 27 percent for francophones.[22] More significantly, in the October 1992 referendum non-francophones voted massively for the Yes, in contrast to Quebec francophones.[23] The 1993 campaign confirmed once again the relevance of language: traditionally less significant in federal than in provincial politics, it became a key factor once a sovereigntist party appeared on the scene. Consistently, campaign polls showed "that 60 per cent of francophones (intended) to vote for the Bloc, while 75 per cent of non-francophones (would) vote for the Liberals."[24] In the end, non-francophones overwhelmingly supported the Liberals, contrary to francophones who preferred the Bloc Québécois.[25]

If we leave aside non-francophones, we are still left with almost 85 percent of the electorate. Here, a second dimension comes into play — partisan identification. Although the Conservative Party did well in Quebec in 1984 and 1988, it failed to take root. Even in 1988, the vote of francophone Quebecers reflected a disaffection with the Liberals more than an attachment to the Conservative Party. Among francophones, only 27 percent identified themselves as Liberals (mostly the older, more religious part of the electorate), but no more than 22 percent saw themselves as Conservatives: 44 percent of francophone voters did not identify with any party. "The antithesis to the Liberal party," concluded the authors of the 1988 federal election study, "was not any specific party so much as the *refus global*, so to speak, to the entire system."[26] In 1993, this large group of non-identifiers constituted the natural target of the Bloc Québécois. Not all of these non-identifiers would rally to the Bloc, however, because a third dimension came into play: support for sovereignty.

On the basis of the two dimensions discussed so far, the total electorate can be divided into three groups: non-francophones who tend to support the Liberal Party and represent about 15 percent of the electorate; francophone Liberals who in 1988 represented roughly 22 percent of voters; and the rest, about 63 percent, being non-Liberal francophones. In 1993, this last group was not entirely available to the Bloc Québécois because it was divided on the question of sovereignty. At the time, 39 percent of the total electorate supported Quebec sovereignty.[27] If we assume these sovereigntists all belonged to the non-Liberal group, we are left with two subgroups of non-Liberals: a sovereigntist group representing 39 percent of the total electorate and a group of non-Liberal federalists, who accounted for roughly a quarter of the electorate (24 percent).

To recapitulate, going into the 1993 federal campaign, four groups of voters defined the prospects of the different parties: non-francophones (about 15 percent of the total electorate); francophone Liberals (22 percent); sovereigntists (39 percent); and francophones who were federalists but not Liberals (24 percent). On election day, non-francophones and sovereigntists voted essentially as expected, respectively for the Liberals and for the Bloc Québécois. Francophone Liberals also seem to have acted predictably.[28] Most interesting was the vote of francophone non-sovereigntists, who lifted the Bloc's support by more than 10 percentage points above the solid sovereigntist vote (from 39 to 49.3 percent).

After the election, a debate ensued on the meaning of the vote between those who stressed its protest character and those who saw it as a more meaningful event that confirmed the results of the 1992 referendum. Robert Bourassa, for instance, argued the Bloc's victory in Quebec could be seen as a protest vote and would not have lasting consequences. In the same vein, Jean Chrétien explained on election night that good government would be sufficient to convince Quebecers they were wrong to distrust him and his party.[29] More systematically, Stéphane Dion stressed the electorate's high level of dissatisfaction with traditional parties and with politics, the fact that among ten issues voters were most preoccupied by unemployment and least concerned by constitutional questions, and the knowledge voters had that Lucien Bouchard could not take power.[30] Against this interpretation, others claimed the success of the Bloc Québécois meant something fundamental had changed in Canadian politics. Before the campaign was over, for instance, a *Globe and Mail* editorial stated the strong showing of the Bloc Québécois could not be reduced to a protest and was instead the outcome of a "logic built up over time."[31] In his analysis of the election results, Jean-H. Guay substantiated this view with three arguments: first, at 77.8 percent, the Quebec participation rate was the highest since the 1958 election, a fact that hardly suggested a disaffected electorate; second, since the failure of the Meech Lake Accord, Quebec polls consistently ranked the parties as they ended after the election, indicating the outcome was not a temporary upset; and third, a riding-by-riding analysis of the vote for the Bloc indicated it was strongly correlated with the the 1992 referendum No vote and strongly associated with stable characteristics of the electorate.[32] If jobs or economic dissatisfaction had been the main concern of Quebecers, added Guay, they would have voted for the Liberal Party, the party that placed these issues at the top of its platform.[33]

In his analysis of the individual determinants of the vote of non-sovereigntist francophones, André Blais offers elements that could be seen as supportive of both interpretations. On one hand, he finds that the Bloc Québécois attracted less well-off voters who considered that their own economic situation had deteriorated. This finding reinforces the impression of an economic protest vote, which would have raised Bloc support from 39 to 49 percent. On the other hand, Blais also finds attachment to Quebec or to Canada to be by far the best predictor of whether non-sovereigntists voted for the Bloc or for the Liberal Party, a finding that best fits Guay's interpretation of the vote as a consistent expression of identity.[34]

Canadian elections are always, to some extent, determined by economic conditions. A rise in the unemployment rate, in particular, is costly for the incumbent party.[35] What changed in 1993 was that new parties could capture the vote of dissatisfied Canadians. In Quebec, the Bloc was best placed to do so because it attracted the vote of both sovereigntists and non-sovereigntists who identified primarily as Quebecers. Bouchard's party may also have benefited from negative evaluations of the economic situation, but this factor explained at best a gain of a few percentage points. While some may have expressed a protest, it seems fair to conclude that most Quebecers voted rather naturally for the party that best represented their vision of themselves and of the country. The 1993 election, argues sociologist Pierre Drouilly, allowed the expression at the federal level of a Quebec electoral formation that goes back to the 1970s and that has progressed ever since. Indeed, the vote for the Bloc mirrored quite closely the regional distribution of the Parti Québécois vote.[36] The 1993 election revealed less a change in Quebec voters than a change in the options they were offered in federal politics.

A LOYAL OFFICIAL OPPOSITION

The vote had not yet taken place before much concern was expressed outside Quebec about the role the Bloc Québécois would play as the Official Opposition in the House of Commons. In the days after the election, there were discussions on the legitimacy and even legality of an Official Opposition based in a single province and dedicated to the sovereignty of that province. There were even talks of a Holy Alliance of federalist forces to counter the sovereigntist threat. These discussions were not devoid of irony: for years Canadians outside Quebec had complained Quebec had too much clout in Cabinet; now that Quebecers had massively voted for the opposition, some seemed to think Quebec had too much clout in the opposition.

Given such apprehensions, the first months of the Bloc as Official Opposition turned out rather well. Lucien's Bouchard's opening speech in Parliament outlined his vision of the country and his sovereigntist objectives, and it was badly received outside Quebec, as a confirmation that not much could be expected from the Bloc Québécois.[37] In the following weeks, however, the party took pains to play in a respectful and rather conventional way the role of the loyal opposition.

The Bloc basically cast itself as a party that would defend policies valued by all Canadians. Explaining, for instance, that his party would defend the integrity of the country's social programs, Lucien Bouchard noted it was "a strange paradox that a sovereigntist party from Quebec will be the only party fighting to preserve the main value of Canada."[38] The Bloc supported universal social programs, the elimination of family trusts and business tax loopholes, and the pursuit of Canada's peacekeeping effort in Bosnia. In the debate over the sale of Ginn Canada to Paramount Communications, a debate almost ignored in Quebec, the Bloc also stood up in defence of Canadian cultural industries. Meanwhile, Preston Manning and the Reform Party called for a withdrawal in Bosnia, taxes that were simply lower, drastic cuts in social programs, and a non-interventionist, market-driven cultural policy. On the four questions — foreign policy, taxation, social programs, and cultural policy — the Bloc Québécois stood closer to traditional Canadian values and policies than did the Reform Party. Also intriguing was the two parties' attitude towards the law and order issues. Faithful to the traditions of a country often portrayed as law-abiding, the Bloc Québécois repeatedly demanded that the RCMP intervene to stop cigarette smuggling. Preston Manning, by contrast, sounded like a Republican from California when he called, at about the same time, for nothing less than a "tax revolt"![39]

Six months after the election, the Bloc Québécois had earned respect as a credible official opposition, more effective in the House of Commons than the Reform party.[40] One journalist wrote provocatively that Lucien Bouchard could even turn "into the best opposition leader in recent memory."[41] For the Bloc Québécois, success and legitimacy as official opposition are important not so much because they may disturb the Chrétien government but rather because they give credibility to the sovereigntist project.[42] The party's position, however, is ambiguous. A Quebec columnist wrote with irony that Bloc MPs are working so hard at upholding Canadian values that they could end up nominated as honorary presidents for the Calgary Stampede.[43] The Bloc Québécois may in fact have modified Quebecers' perception of the House of Commons. The new opposition increased considerably the use of French in the House, regularly raised questions of interest to Quebecers, and brought the Quebec debate on sovereignty to Ottawa. In doing so, the Bloc unavoidably increased the House of Commons' relevance for those Quebecers who had paid little attention in the past. "I hope we are not working for federalism" mused Lucien Bouchard late in March 1994. Two months later, Jean Chrétien observed that, indeed, the presence of the Bloc Québécois in Ottawa had helped improve his image in Quebec.[44] True enough, the Liberals have progressed in Quebec since the election. These gains, however, cannot be attributed to the presence of the Bloc

Québécois. They are more likely the result of the final collapse of the Conservative Party in Quebec and of the honeymoon effect that benefits majority governments in their first six months in office.[45] Whatever the case, public opinion on sovereignty remains relatively stable and Lucien Bouchard is still among the most popular politicians in Quebec.[46]

Beyond the fluctuations in opinion polls, Lucien Bouchard and the Bloc Québécois appear quite representative of Quebec public opinion, on a wide range of issues beyond the national question.[47] In the debate on the *Young Offenders Act*, for instance, the Bloc Québécois was in tune with Quebec public opinion when it positioned itself against both the Liberal and the Reform parties, to argue that the Act was too severe.[48] Likewise, on social programs the party's defence of universality appears closer to Quebec than to Canadian public opinion.[49] More importantly, on the constitutional question the Bloc Québécois speaks not only for those who support sovereignty but also for the many Quebecers who think the Quebec government should have jurisdiction over more areas of government activity, alone or with the federal government.[50]

Herein lies the full meaning of the Bloc's presence in Ottawa. First, of course, the Bloc represents the large segment of the Quebec electorate that has unambiguously opted for sovereignty. In addition, as analyses of the vote suggest, the Bloc Québécois speaks for the sizable part of the population that remains attached to what Guy Laforest calls the dualist vision of Canada as two founding nations.[51] Following the failure of the Meech Lake Accord, many of these dualist Quebecers opted or were tempted to opt for sovereignty, but they never had an opportunity to vote on the question. A referendum was held, instead, on the Charlottetown agreement, which was clearly turned down, in a reaffirmation of Quebec's demand for some form of special constitutional recognition.[52]

"I will not talk about the constitution," repeated Jean Chrétien to Liberal militants in May 1994; "I was elected not to talk about the constitution."[53] Liberal voters may have given the government a mandate to avoid constitutional discussions, but this certainly was not the message that came from Quebec. As they supported the Bloc, Quebecers reaffirmed that in their opinion the constitutional issue was not settled. At the end of July 1994, a majority wanted a referendum on Quebec sovereignty to be held, by one party or the other.[54] Unable to get recognition and reform through the constitutional process, Quebecers voted to stand, on the constitution and on other issues as well, as distinct in the House of Commons.

THE MONTHS AHEAD:
SOVEREIGNTISTS IN QUEBEC AND OTTAWA

By definition, the position of the Bloc Québécois is ambiguous. As mentioned above, it is not inconceivable to the Bloc that their search for respectability as a loyal Official Opposition could detract from their promotion of sovereignty. More basically, the role played by the Bloc simply may not be sufficient to create a sovereigntist majority that does not exist at the moment. Among Quebec political scientists interested in public opinion, the dominant impression is that even with so many seats in Ottawa and power in Quebec, sovereigntists will lose their referendum on sovereignty. Indeed, given current public opinion, the task at hand for sovereigntists seems almost impossible. They still have a chance, however: public opinion remains mobile and with the right conditions a winning majority could emerge at the decisive moment.

Support for sovereignty climbed in 1990 — before the failure of the Meech Lake Accord — to peak above 60 percent in the fall of the same year. This shift in public opinion started before the formal rejection of the Accord and probably had as much to do with the debate as with its outcome. In the following months, support for sovereignty diminished. It remains that, at least at one point in time, a strong majority of Quebecers were sovereigntists.[55]

What governs such movements in public opinion? More specifically, what could bring the temporary sovereigntists of 1990 back to sovereignty? Commenting on the debate raised by Lucien Bouchard's visit to western Canada, *The Globe and Mail* suggested recently it was important to "state the facts" to win "the battle of Quebec." These are not "times for pulling punches," concluded the same editorial, and Michael Harcourt, Roy Romanow and others were totally right to denounce separatists when they had a chance.[56]

While it may sound sensible, this type of reasoning assumes a negotiation is about to begin, between two calculating actors pondering the respective advantages of their different options. In fact, public opinion on sovereignty has little to do with such a clear-minded, purposeful process. First, a good proportion of the Quebec electorate has already decided, one way or the other, and is unlikely to be swayed by last minute arguments, promises or threats. Second, the voters that became sovereigntists in 1990 and that could make a difference in 1995 are precisely the least consistent, least informed voters. These individuals tend to be less interested in politics and less anchored in clear positions, and they may not be moved solely by the type of calculus assumed by *The Globe and Mail* editorialists.

In a presentation at the May 1994 meeting of the Société québécoise de science politique, Jean-H. Guay summarized the results of a new, unpublished analysis that confirms a clear distinction between what could be called coherent and undecided voters. In his view, there are in fact three clusters of voters in Quebec. First, the sovereigntists, who identify themselves as Quebecers, support the PQ and the Bloc Québécois, and voted No in 1992. Second, the federalists, who see themselves primarily as Canadians, support the Liberals in Quebec and Ottawa, and voted Yes in 1992. Third, the undecided, who are more likely to identify themselves as French-Canadians, have fewer years of formal education, are less informed, and more easily change their position. This third group of voters, the primary target of political strategists, seems to be moved by two types of considerations: first and foremost, a sense of identity as Quebecers, which will be more or less affirmed according to the circumstances; and second, an evaluation of the costs and benefits of the two basic options, the status quo and sovereignty.[57]

Now, what did Harcourt, Romanow, Irwin and others do when they "stated the facts" about separatism? Consider Harcourt's statement, by far the most revealing. If Quebec separates, predicted British Columbia's premier, we will become "the worst of enemies." Such a statement is neither fact nor prediction; it establishes what amounts to a highly conditional "friendship," and can only reinforce Quebecers' sense of identity. Playing with the complex set of cost evaluations, identity perceptions, and emotions that could influence the less committed voters is tricky. A threat meant to raise concerns about costs may just as well trigger a powerful emotional reaction anchored in identity.

In a recent study of Quebec francophones' attitudes towards sovereignty, Richard Nadeau and Christopher J. Fleury show that even sizable shifts in cost-benefit evaluations of sovereignty may not be enough for sovereigntists to obtain a majority in Quebec. A provincewide majority in favour of sovereignty could be created, however, with "a heightened feeling of attachment to Quebec" (assuming cost-benefit considerations do not change). This, argue Nadeau and Fleury, is what happened around 1990, at the end of the Meech Lake debate. For sovereigntists, these findings imply a majority can best be created not by discussing costs and benefits, but rather "by strengthening francophones' attachment to Quebec and weakening their attachment to Canada."[58] If the emotional fuss that accompanies every step Lucien Bouchard takes out of Quebec or Ottawa is an indication of what is to come in the coming months, the chances of sovereigntists are not insignificant. A coast-to-coast emotional debate on the place of Quebec in Canada could move one-time sovereigntists back to sovereignty and create the majority the Parti Québécois and the Bloc Québécois need.

Only sovereigntists need movements in public opinion. In light of current polling, it is unclear why politicians outside Quebec would want to stir up controversies, except for local electoral advantage. Aware of the fact, federal ministers and provincial premiers refrained from intervening in Quebec's 1994 electoral campaign.[59] Given the issue at stake and the state of public opinion in Canada, however, such restraint appears unlikely in a referendum campaign.[60] We just do not know how far the debate will go, and how acrimonious it will become.

CONCLUSION

The presence of the Bloc Québécois in the House of Commons is more than a temporary aberration. When the Meech Lake Accord failed in 1990, a new phase began in Quebec politics, marked by a heightened sense of identity and a strong resurgence of support for sovereignty. The No vote in the 1992 referendum, the Bloc's strong showing in October 1993, and the election of the Parti Québécois in September 1994 were all consistent expressions of Quebecers' perception of their province within Canada. These results were unprecedented because the options offered to voters were also unprecedented. They were predictable, however, given the existing political attitudes and the recent shifts in public opinion that brought a number of francophone non-sovereigntists into the sovereigntist camp, at least for a while.

In Ottawa, Lucien Bouchard and the Bloc Québécois worked hard to function as a respected loyal opposition and, overall, they succeeded. The fact that they will never be a government-in-waiting may have helped them insofar as it made criticism easier. It could also have encouraged exaggerated claims, however. Excesses were avoided and the Bloc represented rather well enduring Canadian values and current Quebec public opinion. Lucien Bouchard even worried that the Bloc could hurt the cause of sovereignty in Quebec. If this was ever the case in the House of Commons, however, Bouchard's trips did much to compensate. As he promoted sovereignty, at home and abroad, the Bloc leader opened up heated debates, which seemed all the more incongruous because polls kept indicating sovereignty was in difficulty in Quebec. Such debates are the best hope of sovereigntists, as they need to awaken strong feelings about Quebecers' identity to win a referendum.

On sovereignty, the three electoral outcomes discussed above did not change basic attitudes all that much. Quebecers demand more autonomy and more powers for their province. They want the referendum on sovereignty promised by Robert Bourassa, but they remain reluctant sovereigntists.[61] Without a major shift in public opinion, sovereigntists cannot win what Jacques Parizeau calls the third period. For such a shift to take place, sovereigntists must to some extent count on the rest of Canada. Canadian politicians and pundits may wish to raise concerns about costs to reduce the support for sovereignty. In doing so, however, they also risk triggering powerful perceptions of identity that could matter more than evaluations of costs and benefits.

Much has been written, in both Quebec and Canada, about the possible consequences of a positive vote on sovereignty.[62] Given the lacklustre victory of the Parti Québécois on 12 September 1994, thoughts must also be given to the possibility that sovereigntists might fail in the last round. What would happen, then, with the Bloc and the Parti Québécois, with Lucien Bouchard and Jacques Parizeau? Some would argue that the two leaders would no longer have a purpose and mandate, would be demoralized, and be bound to quit, leaving a political vacuum behind them. I think these predictions are exaggerated. Granted, there would be disappointment and a sense of loss. There would also be important departures and calls for revisions and realignments. All the same, one should keep in mind that the two parties have the support of almost half the province, including many non-sovereigntists. This support would not disappear with a negative referendum result.

The Parti Québécois and the Bloc Québécois stand for sovereignty but, at the same time, they represent the nationalist and the social-democratic elements in Quebec public opinion and society. This explains in part why the two parties reach beyond committed sovereigntists during elections. It also implies that they represent more than the sovereignty project. The two parties incarnate Quebecers' demands for autonomy as well as a left-of-centre vision of governance. Following a referendum defeat, these two visions would be weakened, but not abolished. We cannot exclude the possibility that both the Bloc and the PQ would redefine their roles and work for an autonomous but not sovereign Quebec. "I am there for better or for worse," explained Jacques Parizeau a few days before the Quebec election, stressing he would complete his mandate regardless of the referendum result.[63]

In Quebec, there is a strong perception that following a federalist victory in the referendum, Jean Chrétien would move to redefine and centralize Canadian federalism. There is no doubt that a great opportunity would be offered to him. The prime minister might be tempted, however, to go too far. This, argues Guy Laforest, is what Pierre Elliott Trudeau did when he refused to let the Meech Lake Accord seal definitively his 1982 reforms.[64] If this perception of a centralist offensive is given credence by early, confrontational moves on the part of the federal government, a resurgence of the Bloc and of the PQ as autonomist parties cannot be excluded. After all, a year after the 1980 referendum, Quebecers re-elected the Parti Québécois, which had reduced its program to a simple but powerful idea: "Faut rester forts au Québec."[65] A number of reasons certainly motivated voters in 1981, including their strong dislike of Liberal leader Claude Ryan. Still, it should be kept in mind that even in 1981, following an unambiguous referendum defeat, Quebec's traditional autonomist discourse continued to be a relevant political currency.

NOTES

Some of the arguments presented here have been discussed first in *Canada Watch*, a publication of the York University Centre for Public Law and Public Policy and the Robarts Centre for Canadian Studies of York University. I am grateful to Douglas M. Brown, Stéphane Dion, Pierre Martin, Allan Tupper, and two anonymous reviewers for their comments on earlier drafts, and to Pascale Dufour for research assistance. This research was supported by grants from the Fonds FCAR and the Social Sciences and Humanities Research Council of Canada.

1. Peter H. Russell, "The End of Mega Constitutional Politics in Canada?" in Kenneth McRoberts and Patrick J. Monahan (eds.), *The Charlottetown Accord, the Referendum, and the Future of Canada* (Toronto: University of Toronto Press, 1993), p. 218.

2. Julian Beltrame, "Majority Want Canada to Stay United," *The Gazette*, 7 November 1992, p. A1.

3. André Blais and Jean Crête demonstrate with public opinion data that the English Canadian public rejected the Meech Lake Accord and did so essentially because of the distinct society clause. This analysis has never been refuted. André Blais and Jean Crête, "Pourquoi l'opinion publique au Canada anglais a-t-elle rejeté l'Accord du lac Meech?" in Raymond Hudon and Réjean Pelletier (eds.), *L'engagement intellectuel: mélanges en l'honneur de Léon Dion* (Sainte-Foy: Presses de l'Université Laval, 1991), pp. 385-400.

4. Patrick J. Monahan, "The Sounds of Silence," in McRoberts and Monahan (eds.), *The Charlottetown Accord*, p. 246. See also Russell, "The End of Mega Constitutional Politics," p. 218.

5. My translation. Guy Laforest, *De la prudence* (Montréal: Boréal, 1993), pp. 22 and 152-53.

6. See, for instance Russell, "The End of Mega Constitutional Politics," p. 219.

7. Lucien Bouchard left the Conservative government on 21 May 1990 and the Bloc Québécois was officially founded on 25 July.

8. Ibid., pp. 79-88; Lucien Bouchard, *A visage découvert* (Montréal: Boréal, 1992), pp. 344-45.

9. Edouard Cloutier and Diane Carignan, "L'opinion politique québécoise," in Denis Monière (ed.), *L'année politique au Québec 1992* (Montréal: Département de science politique de l'Université de Montréal, 1993), p. 244; Edouard Cloutier and David Irwin, "Les tendances de l'opinion publique," in Denis Monière (ed.), *L'année politique au Québec 1993-1994* (Montréal: Fides, 1994).

10. I have argued elsewhere that the referendum results are politically coherent and cannot be reduced to a protest vote: Alain Noël, "Deliberating a Constitution: The Meaning of the Canadian Referendum of 1992," in Curtis Cook (ed.), *Constitutional Predicament: Canada after the Referendum of 1992* (Montreal and Kingston: McGill-Queen's University Press, 1994), pp. 64-81. See also: Richard Johnston, André Blais, Elisabeth Gidengil and Neil Nevitte, "The People and the Charlottetown Accord," in Ronald L. Watts and Douglas M. Brown (eds.), *Canada: The State of the Federation 1993* (Kingston: Institute of Intergovernmental Relations, Queen's University, 1993), pp. 19-43.

11. Jean-François Lisée, *Le naufrageur: Robert Bourassa et les Québécois, 1991-1992* (Montréal: Boréal, 1994), pp. 610 and 614.

12. Paul G. Thomas, "Parties and Regional Representation," in Herman Bakvis (ed.), *Representation, Integration and Political Parties in Canada*, Research Studies of

the Royal Commission on Electoral Reform and Party Financing, vol. 14 (Toronto: Dundurn Press, 1991), pp. 199-200.

13. Denis Monière, "Le déroulement de la campagne électorale," in Monière and Jean H. Guay (eds.), *La bataille du Québec. Premier épisode: les élections fédérales de 1993* (Montréal: Fides, 1994), p. 32.

14. Herman Bakvis and Laura G. Macpherson, "Quebec Block Voting and the Canadian Electoral System," paper presented at the annual meeting of the Canadian Political Science Association, Calgary, 12 June 1994, p. 15; Richard Johnston, André Blais, Henry E. Brady and Jean Crête, *Letting the People Decide: Dynamics of a Canadian Election* (Montreal and Kingston: McGill-Queen's University Press, 1992), pp. 199-200.

15. Bakvis and Macpherson, "Quebec Block Voting," p. 15.

16. This argument is to some extent inspired by Maurice Pinard's supply-side interpretation of class voting in Quebec: "Working Class Politics: Interpretation of the Quebec Case," *Canadian Review of Sociology and Anthropology* 7, 2 (1970): 87-109.

17. Johnston, Blais, Brady and Crête, *Letting the People Decide*, pp. 70 and 199.

18. Bakvis and Macpherson, "Quebec Block Voting," p. 7.

19. André Pratte, "Sondage SOM: un vote pour le Bloc n'est pas un vote perdu," *La Presse*, 17 September 1993, p. A1.

20. In 1993, concludes one of the contributors to the Canadian election study, there was "no trace" of a bandwagon effect in Quebec. André Blais, "Quebec: Raising the Stakes," paper presented at the annual meeting of the Canadian Political Science Association, Calgary, 12 June 1994, p. 13.

21. Of course, the availability of a new option is not in itself sufficient. In 1945, for instance, a poorly organized, ideologically divided Bloc populaire failed to attract voters that were still attached to Mackenzie King and the Liberal Party. See Paul-André Comeau, *Le Bloc populaire, 1942-1948* (Montréal: Québec/Amérique, 1982), pp. 129, 318-40, and 432-39.

22. Johnston, Blais, Brady and Crête, *Letting the People Decide*, p. 91.

23. André Blais, "The Quebec Referendum: Quebeckers Say No," in McRoberts and Monahan (eds.), *The Charlottetown Accord,* pp. 202-3.

24. André Picard, "BQ Still the One to Beat in Quebec," *The Globe and Mail*, 13 October 1993, p. A5.

25. Blais, "Quebec: Raising the Stakes," p. 4.

26. Johnston, Blais, Brady and Crête, *Letting the People Decide*, p. 92.

27. Blais, "Quebec: Raising the Stakes," p. 5.

28. Ibid., pp. 4-5. At 33 percent, the Liberal share of the vote was not out of line with the results obtained in 1984 and 1988, 35 and 30 percent respectively. Jean-H. Guay, "Les résultats électoraux au Québec," in Monière and Guay (eds.), *La bataille du Québec*, p. 134; Pierre Drouilly, "L'élection fédérale du 21 novembre 1988 au Québec: une analyse des résultats," in Denis Monière (ed.), *L'année politique au Québec, 1988-1989* (Montréal: Québec/Amérique, 1989), p. 112.

29. Gilles Lesage, "Bourassa heureux du gouvernement majoritaire," *Le Devoir*, 27 October 1993, p. A4; Jean Dion, "Les priorités de Chrétien: les hélicoptères et l'aéroport Pearson," *Le Devoir*, 28 October 1993, p. A1.

30. Stéphane Dion, "La sécession du Québec: évaluation des probabilités," *Relations internationales et stratégiques*, 13 (printemps 1994), pp. 216-17.

31. "The Referendum Is Not Over," The *Globe and Mail*, 1 October 1993, p. A22. This editorial was quoted approvingly by Lucien Bouchard in his March 1994 Washington speech ("Towards Quebec's Sovereignty," Notes for a Speech to the Center for Strategic and International Studies, Washington, DC, 2 March 1994, pp. 14-15).

32. Guay, "Les résultats électoraux au Québec," pp. 128-73. See also Alain Desruisseaux and Alain-G. Gagnon, "Le succès du Bloc québécois dépasse le vote de protestation circonstanciel," *La Presse*, 10 novembre 1993, p. B3.

33. Guay, "Les résultats électoraux au Québec," pp. 149-73.

34. Blais, "Quebec: Raising the Stakes," pp. 6-13; Guay, "Les résultats électoraux au Québec," p. 173.

35. Richard Nadeau and André Blais, "Explaining Election Outcomes in Canada: Economy and Politics," *Canadian Journal of Political Science* 26, 4 (December 1993), pp. 775-90.

36. Pierre Drouilly, "L'élection fédérale du 25 octobre 1993: une analyse des résultats," in Monière (ed.), *L'année politique au Québec 1993-1994*.

37. "No one," wrote the *Toronto Star*, "can force a proud and patriotic people — French and English, native and immigrant — to indulge endless propaganda from a self-professed prophet of national rupture." "Bouchard Begins by Trying to End Canada," *Toronto Star*, 21 January 1994.

38. Susan Delacourt, "Bloc Plans to Defend Safety Net," *The Globe and Mail*, 13 January 1994, p. A1.

39. Edward Greenspon, "Tax Revolt Brewing Manning Warns Ottawa," *The Globe and Mail*, 2 February 1994, p. A4; Don Gillmor, "Lucien in the Sky with Diatribes," *Saturday Night*, June 1994, pp. 71-72.

40. Tu Tranh Ha, "Bouchard's Bloc: Official Opposition Knows How to Play the Game," *Calgary Herald*, 4 May 1994; Susan Delacourt, "Reform's Show Ain't Got that Zing," *The Globe and Mail*, 5 April 1994, p. A6; and Susan Delacourt, "Coach to Sharpen Reform's House Act," *The Globe and Mail*, 20 April 1994, p. A1.

41. Gillmor, "Lucien in the Sky with Diatribes," p. 38. See also Warren Caragata, "Stars on the Hill," *Maclean's*, 6 June 1994, pp. 10-12.

42. Chantal Hébert, "Les artisans du succès du Bloc," *La Presse*, 2 April 1994, p. B5.

43. Jean Dion, "Le Canada de Lucien Bouchard," *Le Devoir*, 29 January 1994, p. A1.

44. Chantal Hébert, "Le Parlement canadien à l'heure du français," *La Presse*, 29 January 1994, p. B4; Susan Delacourt, "Bouchard Says Quebec Starting to Care About Ottawa," *The Globe and Mail*, 25 March 1994, p. A1; and Susan Delacourt, Edward Greenspon, and Hugh Windsor, "Thriving in Quebec, PM Says," *The Globe and Mail*, 21 June 1994, p. A1.

45. Richard Nadeau, "L'effet lune de miel dans un contexte parlementaire: le cas canadien," *Canadian Journal of Political Science*, 23, 3 (September 1990), pp. 495-96.

46. Cloutier and Irwin, "Les tendances de l'opinion publique;" Angus Reid Group, "The National Angus Reid/Southam News Poll: Canadians' Reaction to the Re-Emergence of the National Unity Debate," 3 June 1994, p. 5.

47. According to CROP president Alain Giguère, Lucien Bouchard "incarnates the very personality of the typical francophone Quebecer, or at least the one to which the latter identifies." Quoted in Don Macpherson, "Reflection: Pollster Finds Bouchard an Archetypal Quebecer," *Gazette*, 2 February 1994, p. B3.

48. Marie-Claude Lortie, "Ottawa durcit la loi sur les jeunes contrevenants," *La Presse*, 2 June 1994, p. A1; Jean-Paul Soulié, "Jeunes contrevenants: des experts contredisent le ministre," *La Presse*, 8 June 1994, p. A6; Gilles Normand, "Lefebvre contre le projet de loi sur les jeunes contrevenants," *La Presse*, 9 June 1994, p. B1; "Les Canadiens aimeraient une loi des jeunes contrevenants plus sévère," *La Presse*, 23 June 1994, p. A17.

49. Quebecers, found Baer, Grabb and Johnston on the basis of early 1980s surveys, "have apparently evolved into the most consistently liberal population in the two countries (Canada and the United States)." While a line can be drawn between "a left-liberal Quebec" and the rest of Canada, note these authors, the Canada-United States border does not define "distinguishable cultural communities." Outside Quebec, only the American south appears distinctive, being more conservative than the rest of North America. Douglas Baer, Edward Grabb, and William Johnston, "National Character, Regional Culture, and the Values of Canadians and Americans," *Canadian Review of Sociology and Anthropology* 30, 1 (February 1993): 28. See also Richard Johnston and André Blais, "Meech Lake and Mass Politics: The 'Distinct Society' Clause," *Canadian Public Policy* 14, Supplement (September 1988), p. S38. More recent survey data that point in the same direction are presented in Jean-François Lisée, "Bons vivants, tolérants, pantouflards...," *L'actualité*, January 1992, pp. 20-26.

50. Richard Mackie, "Quebeckers Want Power Shift, Poll Finds," *The Globe and Mail*, 20 May 1994, A1; and Hugh Windsor, "Provincial Role More Important to Quebeckers," *The Globe and Mail*, 20 May 1994, p. A2. See also Jean-François Lisée, *Le tricheur: Robert Bourassa et les Québécois, 1990-1991* (Montréal: Boréal, 1994), pp. 111-13.

51. Guy Laforest, *Trudeau et la fin d'un rêve canadien* (Sillery: Septentrion, 1992), p. 13.

52. Noël, "Deliberating a Constitution," p. 76.

53. Chantal Hébert, "La question du Québec fait grincer des dents au PLC," *La Presse*, 14 May 1994, p. G1; Lise Bissonnette, "Un psychotronique au sommet: derrière la raillerie, un mépris de la légalité," *Le Devoir*, 17 May 1994, p. A8.

54. Louis Falardeau, "Les Québécois veulent un référendum," *La Presse*, 6 August 1994, p. B1.

55. Richard Nadeau, "Le virage souverainiste des Québécois, 1980-1990," *Recherches sociographiques* 33, 1 (January-April 1992): 9-28.

56. "Time to Be Honest About Quebec," *The Globe and Mail*, 20 May 1994, p. A18.

57. On the latter point, see André Blais and Richard Nadeau, "To Be or Not to Be Sovereigntist: Quebeckers' Perennial Dilemma," *Canadian Public Policy* 18, 1 (March 1992): 89-103.

58. Richard Nadeau and Christopher J. Fleury, "Cross-Pressured Nationalists and the Sovereignty Decision: Evidence from the Quebec Case," paper presented at the annual meeting of the American Political Science Association (New York, 1-4 September 1994).

59. Anthony Wilson-Smith, "Keeping Their Counsel: Canada's Political Leaders Fight Separatism with Silence," *Maclean's*, 12 September 1994, pp. 20-21.

60. Angus Reid Group, "The National Angus Reid/Southam News Poll: Canadians' Reaction to the Re-Emergence of the National Unity Debate," 3 June 1994.

61. Richard Mackie and Rhéal Séguin, "Quebec Wants Charter Settled," *The Globe and Mail*, 22 August 1994, p. A1.

62. See, in particular: Commission d'étude des questions afférentes à l'accession du Québec à la souveraineté, *Exposés et études, Volumes 1-4* (Québec: Assemblée nationale, 1992); Alain-G. Gagnon and François Rocher (eds.), *Répliques aux détracteurs de la souveraineté du Québec* (Montréal: VLB éditeur, 1992); and Daniel Drache and Roberto Perrin (eds.), *Negotiating with a Sovereign Quebec* (Toronto: Lorimer, 1992).

63. Michel Venne, "Si c'est non, Parizeau reste," *Le Devoir*, 6 September 1994, A4. At about the same time, Bloc Québécois MPs started to suggest they would also remain in Ottawa following a referendum defeat. Wilson-Smith, "Keeping Their Counsel," p. 21.

64. Laforest, *Trudeau et la fin d'un rêve canadien*, pp. 168-70.

65. Graham Fraser translated this slogan as "We gotta stay strong in Quebec." *PQ: René Lévesque and the Parti Québécois in Power* (Toronto: Macmillan, 1984), p. 268.

3

The Reform Party of Canada:
Past, Present and Future

Thérèse Arseneau

L'élection de 51 députés réformistes lors de l'élection de 1993 a soulevé de nombreuses questions. De quelle façon leur plate-forme populiste affecterait-elle leur performance à la Chambre des Communes? Le Parti réformiste influencerait-il l'ordre du jour politique et l'unité nationale? Le Parti est-il là pour de bon? En réponse en ces questions, on avance ici, premièrement, que le populisme du Parti de même que ses efforts pour être un parti peu conventionnel ont eu un effet sur sa performance en Chambre qui fut au mieux terne. Mais plus important encore fut l'inexpérience du Parti réformiste de même que son incapacité à tirer profit d'occasions pour embarrasser le gouvernement ou pour faire progresser ses propres politiques. Deuxièmement, le Parti, contrairement au Bloc, n'a eu, jusqu'à maintenant, que peu d'effet sur l'ordre du jour politique. Ceci s'explique par l'absence de focalisation de la part du Parti réformiste ainsi qu'à sa perte de crédibilité en ce qui a trait à la retenue fiscale. Troisièmement, en ce qui a trait à l'effet du Parti réformiste sur l'unité nationale, on avance que bien que le Parti n'ait pas attisé le feu de l'aliénation de l'Ouest, il s'est laisser aller à fustiger le Québec, un passe-temps qui pourrait s'avérer dangereux pour l'unité nationale. Le Parti réformiste a aussi lancé une importante critique de la stratégie adoptée par Trudeau en matière d'unité nationale et a tenté d'articuler une nouvelle vision du Canada. Ceci toutefois pourrait s'avérer à long terme plus utile que nuisible à l'unité nationale. Enfin, l'avenir du Parti réformiste est loin d'être assuré. Il repose sur l'aptitude du Parti à conserver les votes récoltés en 1993 et à élargir son soutien sur une base plus nationale.

In November 1987, at a convention of 306 delegates in Winnipeg the Reform Party of Canada was formed, Preston Manning was elected party leader and a platform emphasizing fiscal responsibility, populist political reforms and more power for the west was adopted. The year-old party fielded 72 candidates in the four western provinces in the 1988 federal election and garnered 275,000 votes. It was most successful in Alberta where it received 15 percent of the popular vote, mostly in rural constituencies and in the south.[1] Elsewhere in the west the party's performance was disappointing; in British Columbia the Reformers managed 5 percent of the popular vote while in Saskatchewan and Manitoba the party's support was negligible. Some federal politicians described the Reform Party as merely another regional fringe party made up of cranks and malcontents which would fizzle out without consequence.[2] The major parties' initial strategy was to treat the Reform Party as a temporary phenomenon which would run its course and, inevitably, disappear.[3]

Five years later, in the general election of October 1993, much had changed: the Reform Party received 19 percent of the *national* popular vote and 52 seats in the House of Commons. The party that was meant to quietly disappear was suddenly the third largest party in the House, supplanting both the Conservatives and the New Democrats. Even though Reform has been around since 1987, and has had an elected Member of Parliament since 1989, it is still widely viewed as an unknown entity. Many questions have been raised about the likely impact of the election of the Reform MPs on Canadian politics. Four such questions are the focus of this chapter. How has the party's populist platform affected its performance in the House of Commons? What effect has Reform had on the policy agenda? Has Reform had an impact on the issues of national unity and Quebec separatism? Is Reform here to stay? The purpose here is to focus on Reform's performance since the election and to speculate about the party's future.

POPULIST REFORMERS IN THE HOUSE OF COMMONS

The platform adopted by the Reform Party incorporates fundamental populist themes: sweeping political reforms that promise to give more power to the "common people" and to all MPs, and that promise to significantly alter the tone and the *modis operandi* of the House of Commons. Reformers champion direct democracy in the form of binding referenda, voters' initiatives, and the recall of MPs who have not upheld their oath of office — fundamental allegiance to their constituents and to the Queen. The party manifesto also supports a "direct democratic process" on moral issues such as abortion and capital punishment and on matters that "alter the basic social fabric such as immigration, language, and measurement."[4] They campaigned in 1993 on the promise to shun many of the conventions of the House, vowing to foster a more cordial atmosphere there, to reduce party discipline, and to allow more free votes. Connected to this is Reform's proposed change to parliamentary rules so that the defeat of a government measure would not automatically lead to the defeat of the government; in order for the government to fall there would have to be a formal vote of non-confidence. Such rule changes would also be meant to decentralize power from the executive to all MPs. Similarly, Reform's

"Triple-E" Senate proposal should be seen as an elaborate political reform designed not only to increase provincial input but also to reduce the Cabinet's power. The Reformers envisage an "effective" Senate, devoid of Cabinet ministers and free from partisan voting, which would act as a counterweight to the executive-dominated, highly partisan lower house. Within the Reform Party caucus, before party discipline would be applied on any issue, the party promises to conduct a free vote to determine whether or not the party wishes to vote *en masse* and, if so, what the party's common position will be. These caucus votes are to be made public. The party also supports "more stringent and more public ratification procedures for Supreme Court Justices in light of the powers our legislators are handing to the courts."[5] Reformers also call for a popular ratification process, similar to the one employed in Australia, for all future constitutional reforms.

Given the magnitude of what the Reform populist package promises, the election of the 52 Reformers sparked much speculation as to the likely effect of their populism on the operations of the House, and on the party's performance there in particular.

Reformers have made attempts to carry through with their promise to make the House a more courteous place. Their parliamentary style has been low-key and less confrontational than that of the other parties, treating MPs, including government MPs, with more respect. These attempts have, in the early days of the first session at least, affected the operations of the House in a general way. In the lead up to the election of the Speaker, for example, the candidates were "campaigning" on Reform's themes of raising the level of decorum in the House. Similarly Reform's calls for some rule changes in the House were met, initially, with some tacit approval from other parties. But in terms of the party's own performance in the House, their attempts to distance themselves from the behaviour of the "traditional" disciplined parties have been damaging. The party has failed to make use of opportunities to embarrass the government and/or to push its own policy agenda. Party Leader Preston Manning, for instance, failed to respond in the House to Finance Minister Paul Martin's first budget for nearly two weeks, and by the time he did it was old news. This was a surprising move from this self-appointed fiscal watch-dog. A second example was the party's response to the alleged improprieties of MP Jag Bhadurian, a prime opportunity for the party that pushes for honest government and the power of recall. For a week the party did not attempt to use the incident to make a case for recall for fear of looking like one of the "old-line" parties taking advantage of the government's misfortunes.[6] In short, it is not behaving like a conventional Opposition party.

Similarly, the party has not made effective use of two of the key weapons of the Opposition: Question Period and the media. Manning admits that in Question Period Reformers have been caught off-guard by the government's ability to avoid questions. This can be attributed to MP's relative inexperience. Only two of the 52 have ever held public office and the leader is not one of the two. Manning admits that the parliamentary party has not made effective use of the media. He attributes this to the fact that Reform is not behaving the way the media expected or wanted them to: "we did not come riding into parliament on horses and shooting guns ... we are dull, which makes bad copy."[7] It is also due again to inexperience and missed opportunities.

In sharp contrast the performance of the Bloc Québécois MPs has been emotional, fiery, and focused. While Reform has stumbled in Question Period, the Bloc has made good use of these sessions to put the Quebec question on the agenda and *has* caught the attention of the media. The result is that the Bloc is seen to be the dominant Opposition party, while Reform's performance has been deemed lacklustre. To be fair to Reform, the standards by which it has been judged have often been the media's standard of good news copy. In making a fairer judgement one must recognize that Reform was tried to be different, to carry through with its promise of more genteel behaviour and to refrain from automatically opposing the government, as compared to the traditional party standards of disciplined parties fighting from opposite sides of the House. This raises questions about whether it is possible for an unconventional party to operate effectively in the very convention-driven House of Commons.

Arguably, populism is not the cause of the party's lacklustre performance. A common criticism of Reform is that it has not been exceedingly populist. Reform's brand of populism has been described as "top-down" populism and is similar in style to the Albertan Social Credit's authoritarian populism.[8] In practice, the Reform party structure is less "populist" than described in party rhetoric. Complaints have arisen that the party's grassroots base has been replaced by a "Calgary clique" and by a dominant leader who is described as "the populist who wants to be in control."[9] Party members have admitted that the "party's vision" is actually "Manning's vision."[10] This was evident at the party's 1991 convention; delegates were keenly aware of their leader's wishes and anxious to oblige him. Manning made it clear that while he was opposed to running provincially, he was eager to expand the party in the east. From all accounts, delegates confirmed both of these more from a sense of loyalty to their leader than from a spontaneous change of heart. Stephen Harper, Chief Policy Officer for the party at the time, was quoted as saying, "it's amazing what you can persuade them to do once you convince them that it's the leader who is telling them."[11] As John Dafoe states, "the freedom to do what the leader wants you to do is not supposed to be a fundamental tenet of democratic populism."[12] The party's candidate recruitment package and Manning's requirement that all members of the national campaign organization sign a confidentiality of information agreement are seen by some as further examples of the party jettisoning its populist spirit.[13]

The party's internal tensions over its populists instincts has also been demonstrated in its conduct in the House. Manning's sitting in the backbenches of his party, the highly visible caucus meetings, holding a public forum on doctor-assisted suicide to guide members on the issue are examples of populist initiatives. In the backrooms, caucus has overruled Manning on a number of occasions. For instance, when the party was trying to decide what perks members should reject, Manning, as he did so often in the past, produced a proposal and asked caucus to ratify it. The caucus refused and voted instead to set up a committee to develop its own plan. Similarly, caucus voted to reject both Manning's proposal to merge the party executive and caucus and his nominee for the party's representative on the House Board of Internal Economy Committee.[14] Perhaps the most public example of Reform MPs employing the right to express their differences of opinion with the leader was the debate over Manning's party-funded expense account. This came to light largely due to Reformers bringing it to the public's attention. When the group of eight Reformers who did this were chastized by the party's executive council, the caucus came to the MPs' defence claiming they had the right, even the obligation, to speak out. While this incident did serve to assert the power of caucus, and hence the image of Reform as a populist party, it also made Reform look divided. In a sense Reform cannot win in this type of situation: if it does not act as a populist party it is condemned for abandoning its principles; when the party does decentralize power and allows MPs to express differences of opinion, it appears divided.

Are these instances of internal party populism meaningful examples of decentralization and direct democracy or just a superficial veneer? Manning is still known to be a "hands-on" leader who controls the party to a great extent. His style is paternalistic, and, with respect to telling his MPs how to act, *more* controlling and intrusive than the leaders of the "traditional" parties. Manning's "Code of Ethics," which advises Reform MPs on how to avoid problems with alcohol and marital disputes, is an example of one such intrusion. Even more telling in respect to the party's true commitment to populism is the fact that in terms of party discipline in the House, the party is not unlike the much berated traditional parties. In practice, there is not much difference in outcome between the traditional party's practice of caucus votes that precede the automatic imposition of party discipline in the House, and Reform's policy of having a caucus vote on whether party discipline will be imposed on each particular policy, a vote that is passed with amazing regularity. In sum it seems that Reform has struck its own balance between populism and party discipline, and its behaviour in the House may be characterized as a half-hearted attempt at decentralization, direct democracy and populism.

REFORM'S EFFECTS ON THE POLICY AGENDA

Reform is a party with a right-wing fiscal and social policy agenda. In the 1993 federal election campaign, Reform promised to be the fiscal conscience of the House by championing economic libertarian fiscal reforms. It seeks, for example, the elimination of the federal deficit within three years. This would be achieved through a combination of economic growth and a slew of cost-cutting measures. Reform promotes a competitive free market, reductions in subsidies to agriculture, business and special interest groups, and the freezing of transfer payments to the provinces. Reform is the party of limited government. It promises the elimination of "thick layers of middle management" in federal administration, regional-development grants, and federal "pet projects" such as bilingualism and multiculturalism. It also advocates the privatization of most Crown corporations, including Petro-Canada. The party would cut parliamentary spending by reducing the size of Cabinet, tightening regulations concerning MPs' pensions and expense accounts, and by freezing MPs' salaries.

In terms of social-welfare policy, Reform's position is one of limited government involvement. The party promotes alternatives to the present welfare state, such as encouraging families, communities, non-governmental organizations and the private sector to "reassume" their responsibility in social service areas. Reformers also oppose state-run daycare and even any "expenditure-increasing" childcare initiative. They plan to return Unemployment Insurance to the private sector, making it employee-employer funded and managed. Reform both emphasizes the need for the individual to do for him- or her-self, and attacks the concept of universality in social welfare, largely due to the fact that it is bankrupting Canada.

During the 1993 federal election campaign, Reform also worked hard to portray itself as *the* "law and order" party. In *The Blue Book* the party states that it "supports a judicial system which places the punishment of crime and the protection of law-abiding citizens and their property ahead of all other objectives."[15] During the campaign the party fleshed out its law and order policy which included the promise of tougher sentences for criminals and the tightening up on early parole. A central feature of the party's justice platform was the commitment to crack down on young offenders. Among Reform's promises were that repeat young offenders would be tried in adult courts, the age at which young offenders could be charged with certain crimes would be reduced from 12 to 10 years, and the media would be allowed to name young offenders and to cover their trials. A Reform government would, Manning promised, hold a binding referendum on the question of reinstatement of capital punishment, a referendum the "yes" side expects to win. Manning also promised to abolish automatic parole and to deport any non-citizens convicted of serious crimes.

The party's views on immigration policy, as outlined in *The Blue Book*, is based on economic criteria, namely, the immigrants' ability to adjust quickly and independently to the needs of the Canadian job market and society. Reform also supports the restricting of sponsorship privileges to immediate family members. While "genuine" refugees would still be accepted by Reform, "bogus" refugees would be immediately deported, the inference being that Canada is currently accepting too many refugees from the latter category. Reform campaigned in 1993 on the promise of freezing immigration levels at roughly 150,000 per year, down from the current rate of 250,000.

The official position in *The Blue Book* is that the party supports the establishment of "a new relationship" with native peoples, one with reduced "economic dependence of the aboriginal peoples on the federal government and the Department of Indian Affairs" and "the replacement of the current economic state of aboriginal peoples by their full participation in Canada's economic life and achievement of a state of self-reliance."[16] Reform is opposed to "special" status for natives and supports instead the "federal government enabling aboriginal individuals, communities or organizations to assume full responsibility for their well-being."[17] *The Blue Book* states the Reform Party's desire for the "early and mutually satisfactory conclusion of outstanding land-claim negotiations" but is not more specific about what they would deem to be "satisfactory." Reform opposed the Charlottetown Accord's aboriginal self-government package, partly on the grounds that the details of the package were so vague that agreeing to it was tantamount to signing a blank cheque.

Reform opposes multiculturalism on several grounds. The first is financial: deficit-ridden Canada cannot afford to fund multicultural groups. Reform calls for both an end to such funding and the abolition of the multiculturalism bureaucracy. The second is based on the theme of limited government — the protection of one's culture is a private rather than a public matter and therefore not the proper domain of government. In essence what Reform argues here is that it is not opposed to multiculturalism per se, but to state-driven multiculturalism specifically. Hence *The Blue Book* states "the Reform Party supports the principle that individuals or groups are free to preserve their cultural heritage using their own resources. The Party supports their right to do so."[18] This position seems to be immediately contradicted, however, by a further plank in *The Blue Book*: the party stands for the "integration" of immigrants into Canadian society and opposes the concept of "hyphenated Canadianism." The very idea of multiculturalism is opposed on the grounds that it divides rather than unites Canadians. It is this third stance, perhaps most commonly identified with the party's opposition to the wearing of turbans and other religious or ethnic dress in the RCMP, that most frequently leads to the charge that Reform's views on multiculturalism reflect intolerance.

Some Reform-oriented policies have found their way onto the national policy agenda. The Liberal government, for example, has proposed tightening up the *Young Offenders Act* and is currently reviewing the social security net. The federal government is also proposing changes to Canada's immigration policy, including, possibly, the deportation of landed immigrants who commit serious crimes. But the most noticeable shift towards a Reform-type agenda has been in the area of fiscal policy. There has been a definite move away from free spending federal governments to more frugality. Fiscal restraint and deficit reduction have become the norm in Ottawa.

But what has been Reform's role in causing this shift? Although cause-effect relationships are extremely difficult to prove in politics, a number of points are worth making. Reform, from its formation in 1987 through to the 1993 federal election, stressed the need for economic restraint, bringing the issue to the forefront of the public stage and keeping it there. Arguably, though it was the financial reality of Canada's debt situation more than Reform's powers of persuasion that led federal political parties to the conclusion that the need to check the national debt is now a necessity. Interestingly, in the House itself, Reform has not emphasized the economy to the extent the party claimed it would. Despite promises not to get distracted by the Quebec issue, it nevertheless has become a major focus of the party. Manning and Reform campaigned, for example, during the Charlottetown Accord debate and the 1993 election, to place a moratorium on constitutional issues and to focus on the economy instead of Quebec. Yet while Chrétien has taken this approach, Manning has criticized him for it and contends that the prime minister should be doing more to lead Canada towards a "new federalism." Critics have argued that Manning has done an about face, that his new federalism is reminiscent of Trudeau's renewed federalism promise of 1980 and presumes more constitutional negotiations.[19]

Another difficulty is that while Reform promised to lead by example in the House in terms of fiscal restraint, mainly by eliminating its MPs' perks, members have found that giving these up is more difficult than they thought. The caucus considered a 10-percent pay cut and a slight reduction in their tax-free expense account, but decided to make these cuts voluntary. Caucus members are still free to fly Business Class and to eat in the subsidized parliamentary restaurant. No Reformer has found it more difficult to give up these perks than has Preston Manning himself. Although he appeared to be willing to "do without" when he returned the keys to the government-provided car at an orchestrated media event, the public later discovered that the party is providing him with an allowance for a car instead. Manning also accepted the extra salary as leader of the party, to bring his annual taxable income, with expense accounts, to $149,500. As these details became public they undermined Manning's credibility with the public and his own party on the frugality issue.

Reform's influence on the policy agenda has been limited, of course, by the fact that the party is not the government. Given the Liberal's healthy majority and the disciplined nature of the House, there are definite limitations placed on what Reform can achieve. Still, it is fair to ask whether Reform has been as successful as can be expected for a programmatic Opposition party in a majority government situation. The answer here is "no," mostly due to the reasons already discussed: Reform's performance in the House has been lack-lustre, unfocused, and largely ineffectual; the party has missed prime opportunities to promote its policy agenda and has failed to make effective use of the media and Question Period; contradictions between the party's emphasis on and the acceptance of perks and other financial privileges had undermined the party's credibility and, along with this, its ability to emphasize a key policy plank.

REFORM AND THE NATIONAL UNITY QUESTION

One of the most noted, and, for some people, most ominous outcomes of the 1993 federal election was that, in terms of seats in the House, the Liberals alone maintained a national base; the Bloc Québécois and the Reform Party between them have distinctly regional bases of support, while the Progressive Conservatives and NDP were all but eliminated. This fact alone has led to some anxiety concerning Reform's possible negative impact on national unity — another regional party exacerbating sectionalism in Canada. This concern is based on the characterization of Reform as a party of western Canada. The second and more troubling concern is that the Bloc-Reform division will heighten Quebec-English Canadian tensions thereby giving a boost to the separatist cause in Quebec. In which case, Reform is categorized as an anti-Quebec, pro-English Canadian party. These two characterizations of Reform and the party's likely affect on regionalism and Quebec separatism bear closer examination.

When the Reform Party burst onto the political scene it was immediately branded as yet another western, protest party, the latest in a long line of western third parties to articulate the traditional grievances of the region and to seek more power for the west. This categorization of Reform is not unfounded. The party was formed in the west and is still dominated by activists there. Furthermore, it was the party's continuing popularity in the west, and, in particular, in Alberta, that sustained it through the five years between federal elections. There is also no denying that initially the party's main aim seemed to be that of a western party. Its founding slogan was "The West Wants In" and a resolution, later revoked in 1991, limited the party to running candidates west of the Ontario-Manitoba border.

This pro-western stance is evident in the party's early manifestos, the 1988 and 1991 *Blue Books*. The party's reason for being was to fight for more effective representation of western interests in Parliament and to secure economic and constitutional equality for the west. These objectives were to be achieved primarily through a "Triple-E" Senate; Reformers wanted to counterbalance an all-powerful House of Commons dominated by Ontario and Quebec, with an equally powerful elected Senate with equal representation from each province. Similarly, the call for reduced discipline in the House of Commons was meant to ensure, among other things, that western MPs can represent western interests even in parties dominated by Ontario and Quebec MPs. The party supported more "adequate" western representation on the Supreme Court of Canada. Certain economic reforms in the early platforms also reflected the party's regional perspective, such as support for a regional fairness test, the inclusion of economic rents from hydroelectric schemes in the public revenue of provinces for the purpose of calculating federal-provincial transfer payments, and the elimination of federal taxes and pricing policies on the natural resources of the provinces. Reform supported the upgrading of transportation facilities, the removal of discriminatory freight rates, and expressed opposition to the Bank of Canada's policies, all in response to traditional western grievances.

The most obvious and recent proof of the party's western base is found in the results of the 1993 general election where 51 of the party's 52 seats were won. In a preliminary report of the 1993 National Election Study, Johnston, Nevitte and Brady describe Reform as a party with a strong regional base, a small party with an optimal geographic concentration and a geographically thin base of support.[20]

How does this regional base affect national unity? The concern is that regionalism is pulling the country apart and what is needed in Canada are national parties that help to breach the sectional cleavages. It is feared that regional parties exacerbate the already strong centrifugal forces. Alan Cairns, for instance, has argued that the party system, importantly conditioned by the electoral system, rather than merely reflecting sectionalism, is actually responsible for intensifying it. For Cairns sectional politics lead to instability and ultimately threaten the nation's unity by encouraging regions to call into question the very nature and legitimacy of the political system. Regions, unlike classes, can choose to secede.[21]

Do Cairns's concerns apply to the Reform Party? The answer depends on whether it is accurate to describe Reform as a western/ regional party promoting a sectionalist agenda that pulls Canada apart. Granted, the party is mainly based in the west in terms of party organization and seats in the House of Commons, but when the west is examined province by province one difficulty becomes apparent: while the Reform Party *was* extremely popular in Alberta and B.C. in the 1993 election (46 of the party's 52 seats were won there), Saskatchewan and Manitoba only elected five Reformers between them. Significantly, Ontario elected as many Reformers as did Manitoba. Another difficulty with the western label is that, as is often the case in Canada's first-past-the-post system, looking at the 1993 election results in terms of seats alone overstates the party's regional base. For example, more people voted for reform in Ontario than in Manitoba and Saskatchewan; the party even did well in parts of Atlantic Canada. As David Cameron points out "the party was a serious contender in many of the seats it lost, particularly in Ontario, where it came second in no fewer than 56 seats (57 percent of the available seats)."[22] Yet according to the Cairns argument, this does not negate the legitimacy of the regional label for Reform and merely highlights the electoral system's complicity in heightening the regional nature of the Canadian party system.

More important is the fact that the party does not stress regionalism or western alienation the way it did when it was formed in 1987. There has been a definite shift in the policy emphasis of the party; it has developed into something more than a purely western party. This shift is only partially apparent in *The Blue Book*; some of the specific references to enhancing "western" interests and representation found in the earlier versions are either absent from or toned-down in the 1991 *Blue Book*. The shift is more apparent in Manning's leadership. In early speeches Manning stressed the regional side of the movement and focused on the west's traditional grievances. But Manning intended that the new party would learn from the mistakes of its predecessors: it would not be narrowly regional or based on a single issue, but rather, well-organized with a broad-based platform and a potentially *national* mandate.[23] From 1991 onwards he has preached the importance of a balanced federal budget, decreasing the deficit and empowering the people. Significantly, the themes the party emphasized during the 1993 campaign, populist political reforms, fiscal libertarianism, social conservatism, a hard line on Quebec nationalism and opposition to "special status" for minorities, while popular in the west, were not exclusively western. Manning carefully honed his message when travelling in Atlantic Canada, rural Ontario, and the north, regions he referred to as "other hinterlands" since they too were alienated from the existing political system.[24] Here the speeches were designed to attract anyone disenchanted with high taxes, unresponsive politicians, the traditional political parties, and "the myriad of confusing sociological changes that are threatening their sense of well-being."[25] Manning therefore portrays Reform as a party of "alienation," but not specifically of "western" alienation.

As Jeffrey Simpson points out, "the Reform Party is the first protest group from western Canada that has not called for a substantial transfer of power from Ottawa to the provinces."[26] Instead, Reformers support a new strategy, a commitment to what they call "systemic change" aimed at setting Canada's fiscal, parliamentary and constitutional houses in order.[27] At the heart of this strategy is the claim that by focusing on strengthening federalism for all, the west will ultimately be better represented. As Whyte states:

> It is no small moment for Confederation that a decade of adversity shifted disenchanted westerners from a decidedly provincial mentality to a strategy intended to strengthen the federal union. There is no demand for retribution in the Reform agenda, no request for extraordinary consideration, no blunt assertion of one region's interests over another's. The goal is simply a balanced federalism.[28]

Manning regularly expresses his support for "decentralization." But what he is advocating is something quite different from the traditional use of the word. He seeks increased power to constituents and more influence for the provinces, but through a greater input in the federal government, especially in a reformed Senate, rather than increased authority to provincial governments. What he and the Reformers support therefore is a regionally sensitive but *limited* federal government since it is their belief that all governments have grown too large and must be constrained and slimmed down.

Significantly, then, although the Reform Party is western in terms of seats in the House of Commons, it aims to be more than simply a western phenomenon that expresses only the traditional grievances of western Canada. This reduces the risk that the party will heighten regionalism in the west. According to Cameron, the party "perceives itself to be, and presents itself as, a national party."[29] He goes on to argue that whether or not the Reform Party is a national party is dependent on how one defines national, or more specifically, which "nation" is being represented. At most, says Cameron, Reform can claim to represent English Canada, or at least some part of it. Even though the party has begun to organize in Quebec, in terms of its base of operations, membership and general outlook, Reform remains a party of English Canada.[30] Most important to understanding the identification of Reform as a party of English Canada is its policies on bilingualism, the two founding nations theory and Quebec's status in the federation.

In *The Blue Book* the party expresses its support for the removal of "enforced bilingualism" except in key federal institutions and federal services where numbers warrant. Instead of nationwide bilingualism, which, according to Manning, no longer relates to the ethnic reality of most of Canada, the party champions the recognition of French in Quebec and English in the rest of Canada. As part of this opposition to bilingualism, and as a cost-cutting measure, the Reform Party advocates the removal of bilingual bonuses in the federal civil service. On the other hand, the party does support the protection of minority language education, which includes English-language education in Quebec, "personal bilingualism," and the asking of "the people" through referendum to develop a new language policy.

Reformers also oppose the concept of Canada as "a meeting of two founding races, cultures, and languages." It highlights the two very different and mutually exclusive visions of Canada: one of Canada as a partnership of two founding nations and one of Canada as a partnership of ten equal provinces and the federal government. While the former is seemingly enshrined in the constitution and federal government policies such as the *Official Languages Act*, the latter is the view that has long been popular in the west and has been articulated by the UFA, Social Credit, the Lougheed and Diefenbaker Conservatives, and now by the Reform Party.

Reform attacks what it perceives as Quebec's "special" status; the party opposed both the Meech Lake and the Charlottetown Accords since their distinct society clauses would have entrenched this special status. Moreover, in future constitutional negotiations the party promises to take a "hard-line" with Quebec and asserts that:

> Confederation should be maintained ... by a clear commitment to Canada as one nation in which ... all regions are entitled to equal status in constitutional negotiations.... Should these principles of Confederation be rejected, Quebec and the rest of Canada should consider whether there exists a better political arrangement which will enrich our friendship, respect our common defence requirements, and ensure a free interchange of commerce and people, by mutual consent and for our mutual benefit.[31]

In essence, Reform promises to take on the role of defender of the rest of Canada, and, given its position on bilingualism, more specifically the rest of "English" Canada, against Quebec in constitutional negotiations. This raises the question of how the Reform Party views the rest of Canada. For example, does it include all non-francophones, including non-English-speaking Canadians and minorities generally? At first it may appear so. Manning, speaking in 1991, stated:

> English speaking Canada [is] more and more becoming a society with many heritages.... A Canada which gives special constitutional status to the French and the English as "founding peoples" also automatically relegates the nine million Canadians who are of neither French nor English extraction (including aboriginal peoples) to the status of second-class citizens.[32]

This statement echoes an argument made by minority groups during the Meech Lake debate that to elevate one group's status but not another's leads to a relative downgrading of the latter. Although Manning's speech would be welcomed by those referred to as "Charter Canadians," it seems unlikely that these groups are being targeted, electorally, by the Reform Party. As was previously stated, Reformers are opposed to the concept of multiculturalism, state financing or administration of daycare, special rights for native peoples, and changing the RCMP uniform for the free expression of religious or ethnic differences. The party's position on these policies would not be popular with ethnic minorities, women's groups, aboriginals, and the listed categories in section 15 of the Charter respectively. Furthermore the tone of Reform Party vocabulary is unlikely to appeal to these groups. Minority groups are referred to as "special interest groups forcing their agenda on government," and bilingualism is characterized as "enforced bilingualism."

In actual fact, Manning's opposition to the entrenchment of the French-English duality is designed to champion English-speaking Canadians who do not define themselves as "Charter Canadians." In part, Manning focuses specifically on English-speaking western Canadians:

> [O]uter Canadians, especially western Canadians, were beginning to fully realize the real significance of the "two nations" theory of Canada. A Canada built on a union of the English and the French is a country built on the union of Quebec and Ontario. And in this union the other provinces are, in a fundamental sense, little more than extensions of Ontario.[33]

With its criticism of bilingualism, multiculturalism, the two founding nations theory, and special status for Quebec and minority groups, the Reform Party is articulating the concerns of a broader group perhaps best described as non-Charter Canadians. Alternatively, this group has been called Canadians of "majoritarian" background, a group that thinks it no longer dominates but rather feels "assaulted by demographic, linguistic and economic changes"[34] and believes that the rights of the majorities are being sacrificed for the rights of well-organized minorities.[35]

More fundamentally though, the Reform Party is attacking the national unity strategy and the vision of Canada developed by Trudeau and continued, despite its seeming failure, since then. In its place, the party offers its own vision of Canada based on three fundamental principles:

- That the demands and aspirations of all regions of the country are entitled to equal status in constitutional and political negotiations;
- That freedom of expression is fully accepted as the basis of any language policy;
- That every citizen is entitled to equality of treatment by governments, without regard to race, language, or culture.[36]

According to Reform, the old Canada, based on two founding nations, multiculturalism and group rights, is dead and a "New Canada," based on Diefenbaker's vision of "One Canada," equality and individualism, is ready to take its place. The key feature of this new "Reformed" Canada would be the party's particular version of "equality": treating every province and individual exactly the same. Instead of "special status" for Quebec, in the New Canada there would be equality of provinces. Instead of "special status" for minorities and women there would be "equality" for each individual Canadian. For Manning in this new "colour blind" Canada "citizens [would be] treated equally in ... law and the constitution *regardless* of race, language and culture, rather than ... some citizens [being] granted special status *because* of race, language or culture."[37]

Thus, rather than attacking the "big" interests like its populist predecessors, the Reform Party is attacking the little interests which it believes have undue influence in Canada.[38]

Given the above discussion, how disruptive has it been to the House — and national unity — having large numbers of Bloc and Reform MPs together in the Opposition? Ironically, despite Reform's vocal criticism of the Bloc's position on Quebec, rather than characterizing the two parties as bitter adversaries, it is perhaps better to view them as odd bedfellows. In a number of ways the two parties are at least compatible. For example, in terms of language policy Reform wants French in Quebec only and English in the rest of Canada; this is not incongruous with the Bloc's position. The Bloc wants to separate Quebec from Canada, Reform is the party most ready to let it leave, but on Canada's rather than Quebec's terms. Even on the constitutional front what might first appear to be irreconcilable positions may not be. The Bloc wants Quebec's powers to be greatly expanded. Since the Bloc believes this will be impossible to achieve, they advocate separatism. Reform insists that Quebec must be equal in powers to the other provinces. But, as McRoberts suggests, devolution of powers to the Quebec government, provided Quebec MPs would be precluded from being involved in these areas of jurisdiction in the House, might be acceptable to Reform since in those areas the rest of Canada would be able to control the federal government.[39] Reform and the Bloc also agree on a very central point: the obsolescence of the national unity strategy of the mainline parties. Reform and the Bloc are therefore in a fundamental sense complementary.

Although Reform promised to avoid making Quebec separation the focus of the House, the topic has become a mainstay for the party. More specifically, the denial of Quebec's traditional nationalist aspirations has become a favourite Reform pastime. According to Gibbins, there is potential political advantage to be gained for both Reform and the Bloc in attacking each other:

> If non-Quebeckers begin perceiving the need for a political leader to stand up to Quebec, Reform may be seen as the logical alternative because it has no ties to the province.... The fate of the Reform Party is yoked very closely to the BQ. The stronger the BQ looks, the better the Reform Party's position in English Canada. And the stronger the Reform Party looks, the better for Lucien Bouchard. He can point to Reform and say, "Look, this is what's coming for you [Quebeckers] in Canada."[40]

Nonetheless, the dangers to national unity of employing this strategy are apparent: by playing off each other in this manner the parties risk an escalation of tensions between Quebec and English Canada. This, of course, suits the separatist Bloc's purposes, but what about Reform's? The strategy is a potentially lucrative vote getter; the 1993 National Election Study found that the most important single factor in Reform support was attitudes towards "outgroups"

(groups other than those to which the supporters belonged), which includes wanting to do less to promote French and Quebec in Canada.[41] It remains to be seen though whether Reform supporters are happy with the party's emphasis on Quebec in the House; some may feel disillusioned and betrayed by the Reform MPs' shift of focus because, as noted above, it deflects attention from the economic issues. Also, for a party that now claims national aspirations and is attempting to organize in Quebec, the strategy of Quebec-bashing seems counterproductive.

Reform's attack of the existing national unity strategy and the vision of Canada it entails, however, need not be damaging to Canada. According to McRoberts rather than fatally fracturing the country, the success of the Bloc and Reform, complete with new visions for Canada, might unexpectedly enhance national unity:

> By seeking to articulate the distinctive interests of Quebec and the rest of Canada, rather than to incorporate them within some artificial notion of an undifferentiated Canada, the two parties can create the basis for tradeoffs and accommodations that were heretofore unthinkable... Thus Canadians might still have the opportunity and necessity to resolve their differences within the framework of federalism.[42]

For McRoberts, the fact that the major parties have lost their monopoly on defining Canada might mean that, by accepting Quebec and the rest of Canada as separate entities, Quebec separatism will be avoided and some form of national unity will actually be maintained.

THE FUTURE OF REFORM

Reform's success in the 1993 election must be put into perspective. As Johnston, Nevitte and Brady aptly quip, "contrary to a widely held western view, Reform did not win the election."[43] What they did achieve was a potentially prominent place in the 35th Parliament. But what of their long-term prospects? Many factors, some under the control of the party, others external to it, could affect its future.

Absolutely fundamental to this examination is the question of what are Reform's goals for its future? It is clear that the party intends to be a national rather than regional party. The party already identifies itself in that way and has made a concerted effort to broaden its base eastward. As was pointed out earlier, in terms both of percentage of popular votes in the 1993 election and of the party's policy emphasis, there is validity in Reform's claim of being more than a western party. But in Canada's "winner-take-all" single-member plurality system, what really counts is winning seats. By this most visible indicator of base of support, Reform is an Albertan and British Columbian party. If it is to become "national" in the most vital sense, its first goal must be to become a more national party in terms of seats in the House of Commons. Only then will Reform be able to finally shake off the title of western party.

Reform also has policy-oriented goals that it wants to have implemented. Past experience in Canada has been that ideological third parties have often had their policies adopted (or stolen) by the major brokerage parties. According to Clarke, Jenson, LeDuc and Pammet "as the two major parties recognized the validity of critiques developed by third parties and/or were frightened by their vote-getting potential, they moved to minimize the discontent by modifying their own positions"[44] thus undercutting the third parties' bases of support. But what party in this Parliament is likely to do this? In the past, it would have probably been the Progressive Conservatives; as the brokerage party slightly right of centre and therefore closer ideologically and in terms of voter base to Reform, it would have been in the best position to try to absorb Reform. But the Conservatives are not a presence in this Parliament. The Liberals are the only major brokerage party left but are ideologically too distant from Reform to adopt many of its policies.

Where this large-scale adoption of the Reform platform is taking place is at the provincial level. Mike Harris's Conservatives in Ontario are working to absorb the Reform agenda and its voters. In Alberta, Premier Ralph Klein has implemented an aggressive Reform-style budget with major cuts in health and education designed to reduce the deficit without raising taxes. Although the impact of these actions, being in the provincial rather than in the federal arena, may not be as immediately felt as would similar moves taken by a major brokerage party in the House, they may have an impact on the longevity of the federal Reform Party: specifically, will there be the same level of support for Reform in the House if its policies have been introduced at the provincial level already?

Whether it is for the purpose of implementing its platform, for securing the party's longevity, or for the more pragmatic desire of wanting power itself, it is the contention here that the ultimate goals of the Reform Party are to permanently replace the Conservatives as the major party of the right, to consolidate the votes they took from the NDP and, eventually, to govern. To achieve these goals, it will have to broaden its Alberta British Columbia base of seats, primarily by winning more seats in Ontario. This strategy sounds rather obvious and deceptively simple. For the Reform Party though, such a move is anything but: it will be difficult to achieve and there are definite risks which come with even attempting it.

Johnston, Nevitte and Brady argue that Reform's chances of becoming a major party could be hampered by the fact that the party is ideologically far from the mainstream.[45] Reform has carved out a distinctive ideological niche. The potential problem is that it is too distinctive and too remote from the average voter. The preliminary results of the 1993 National Election Study showed this to be a problem in relation to the party's position on Quebec. "For all that Reform was distinct on a dimension on which most voters were far from the traditional parties, Reform itself was not close to the typical voter. Most voters wanted less done for French Canada, but not much less."[46]

Another ideological position potentially very limiting for the party is Reform's concept of "equality," a notion at the very heart of what the party stands for. "Equality" would mean the equality of provinces, not a popular concept traditionally in Ontario. The version of "equality" promoted by the Reform Party is also very different from the equality at the heart of the Charter of Rights. For Reform, equality means treating everyone the same and the equal rights section of the Charter is a special rights section. In the Charter version the equal rights section, rather than negating equality as Reformers contend, is seen as the means to reverse past discriminations and therefore finally achieve equality for Charter Canadians. Related to this is the criticism that there is an undue emphasis on group rather than individual rights. Since there is already strong affection for the Charter in English Canada where "the Charter has taken root and generated a broad base of support,"[47] Reform's anti-Charter version of equality may limit the party's appeal.

Perhaps even more limiting than the content of the program is its very existence, especially if Reform feels compelled to adhere to it. The successful parties in Canada are the pragmatic brokers, those willing to say little and/or whatever it takes to get elected. Ideological parties have typically been relegated to the political sidelines. If Reform is to make a permanent breakthrough as a major party, it seems the platform will have to be sacrificed. It also seems likely that Reform will have to act more like a conventional party — disciplined, centralized and with limited avenues for grassroots input.

Given these difficulties, the risks of even attempting such a move to more central, traditional ground are great. The party might fail to attract new supporters *and* alienate the supporters it now has. Its attempts to attract Ontario voters could result in the loss of western support, as happened to the Conservatives after Diefenbaker. As the 1993 National Election Study observed, Reform tapped into an anti-politician sentiment; "voters who rejected the statement that politicians are no more fallen than the rest of us were nearly 10 points more likely than all others to support the party."[48] These voters could well be lost if Reform were to become a "traditional" political party. And while the party's platform is not mainstream, it was attractive to those who voted Reform. To drop the platform could lead to the loss of these votes.

The Reform Party has to make a difficult choice between now and the next election. It can remain unconventional, right-wing, and programmatic in an attempt to maintain the base it currently has. Or, it could attempt the move to the central, traditional, pragmatic ground but risk failing to consolidate a new base while losing the old one. Yet even if they choose the more cautious first route, the votes the party received in 1993 are not necessarily its to keep. They are votes only very recently parked with Reform, coming mainly from traditional Conservative voters and also, but to a lesser extent, from past NDP supporters.[49] To a limited extent, Reform has the power to consolidate these new supporters; it can emphasize its western populism to NDP supporters and its fiscal and social conservatism to the Conservative supporters. Whatever route Reform chooses, the party is bound to be a presence in this Parliament and in the next federal election. Beyond that, though, is far from certain.

NOTES

1. Peter McCormick, "The Reform Party of Canada: New Beginning or Dead End?" in Hugh Thorburn (ed.) *Party Politics in Canada,* 6 ed. (Scarborough: Prentice-Hall, 1991), p. 345.

2. See quotes from Don Mazankowski and Harvey Andre, *Western Report*, 27 March 1989, p. 15; and 6 August 1990, p. 12.

3. Hugh Windsor, "Reform Band Tunes Up for the Big Show," *The Globe and Mail*, 4 May 1992, p. A4.

4. Reform Party, *The Blue Book*, 1991, p. 10. Editor's note: "measurement" presumably refers to the controversial adoption of the metric system of measurement since the 1970s.

5. Ibid., p. 7.

6. Ibid.

7. Ibid., p. 7.

8. See John Dafoe, "Reform's Purge Not Proof of Populist Democracy," *The Globe and Mail*, 15 February 1992, p. D2; and Peter Sinclair, "Class Structure and Populist Protest: The Case of Western Canada," *Society and Politics in Alberta*, ed. Carlo Caldarola (Toronto: Methuen, 1979), p. 75.

9. Miro Cernetig, "The Paradox of Manning," *The Globe and Mail*, 20 October 1993, p. A1.

10. *Western Report*, 12 November 1990, p. 18.

11. Cernetig, "The Paradox of Manning," p. A2; and Dafoe, "Reform's Purge Not Proof of Populist Democracy," p. D2.

12. Dafoe, "Reform's Purge Not Proof of Populist Democracy."

13. *Alberta Report*, 4 March 1991, p. 15.

14. *Alberta Report*, 21 February 1994, p. 10.

15. *The Blue Book*, 1991, p. 31.

16. Ibid., p. 32.

17. Ibid.

18. Ibid., p. 35.

19. See Peter McCormick and Tom Flanagan, *Alberta Report*, 13 June 1994, p. 9.

20. Richard Johnston, Neil Nevitte and Henry Brady, "Campaign Dynamics in 1993: Liberals, Conservatives, and Reform," 1994 Annual Meeting of the Canadian Political Science Association, University of Calgary, 12-14 June 1994, p. 20.

21. Alan Cairns, "The Electoral System and the Party System in Canada, 1921-1965," *Canadian Journal of Political Science*, 1 (March 1968): 55-80.

22. David Cameron, "The Beginning of the Endgame: Canada's Recent General Election," *Queen's Quarterly*, 100/4 (Winter 1993): 763.

23. Kenneth Whyte, "Nice Guys Finish Last," *Saturday Night*, July/August 1993, p. 59.

24. Ibid., p. 59.

25. Jeffrey Simpson, "Reform Plays Well on the Road," *The Globe and Mail*, 25 January 1992, p. A5.

26. Ibid.

27. Kenneth Whyte, "Reform Works a Small Miracle," *The Globe and Mail*, 26 October 1993, p. A9.

28. Ibid., p. A9.

29. Cameron, "The Beginning of the Endgame," p. 768.

30. Ibid.

31. *The Blue Book*, 1991, p. 7.

32. Preston Manning, "An Address to the 1991 Assembly of the Reform Party of Canada," Saskatoon, 6 April 1991, p. 7.

33. Ibid.

34. Jeffrey Simpson, "Accurately Charting Reform's Movement," *The Globe and Mail*, 7 March 1992, p. C10.

35. John Dafoe, "The West's New Populism Turns its Guns on Pressure Groups," *The Globe and Mail*, 16 January 1993, p. D2.

36. Preston Manning, "Leadership for Changing Times," an Address to the 27-29 October 1989 Assembly of the Reform Party of Canada, p. 6.

37. Preston Manning as quoted in Lorne Gunter, "Manning Takes Another Crack at Ontario," *Western Report*, 1 February 1993, p. 10.

38. Dafoe, "The West's New Populism Turns its Guns on Pressure Groups," p. D2.

39. Kenneth McRoberts, "New Faces Offer Hope," *The Globe and Mail*, 4 October 1993, p. A3.

40. Roger Gibbins as quoted in Miro Cerntig, "Manning Hasn't Given Up Fiery Rhetoric on Quebec," *The Globe and Mail*, 24 September 1993, p. A8.

41. This factor also includes non-Quebecers attitudes towards immigration and how much should be done for racial minorities. See Johnston et al., "Campaign Dynamics," pp. 13-14.

42. McRoberts, "New Faces Offer Hope," p. A3.

43. Johnston et al., "Campaign Dynamics," p. 20.

44. Harold Clarke *et al.*, *Absent Mandate* (Toronto: Gage, 1991), p. 11.

45. Johnston *et al.*, "Campaign Dynamics," p. 20.

46. Ibid., p. 10.

47. Alan Cairns, "Citizens (Outsiders) and Governments (Insiders) in Constitution-Making: The Case of Meech Lake," *Canadian Public Policy*, XIV (1988), S142.

48. Johnston et al., "Campaign Dynamics," p. 14.

49. See ibid.; and Elisabeth Gidengil, "The NDP and the Prospects for Social Democracy in the 90s," 1994 Annual Meeting of the Canadian Political Science Association, University of Calgary, 12-14 June 1994.

Part II

4

Politics and Deficits:
Alberta's Challenge to
the Canadian Political Agenda

David Taras and Allan Tupper

Cet article décrit et analyse les importants changements qui se sont produits en Alberta sous le gouvernement progressiste-conservateur de Ralph Klein. Il porte sur le principal engagement de monsieur Klein, à savoir l'élimination du déficit du gouvernement albertain d'ici 1997 en opérant seulement des coupures au niveau des dépenses. Nous décrivons les circonstances qui ont généré le préoccupations de Klein, examinons la politique qui entoure les finances publiques en Alberta et discutons en particulier de la nature de ses politiques en matière d'éducation et de santé. Nous proposons un certain nombre de perspectives quant aux événements et aux forces qui sont derrière les politiques de monsieur Klein.

Nous soutenons que les initiatives de monsieur Klein créeront probablement un défi pour Ottawa et constitueront une expérience qui sera au centre du débat politique et idéologique au Canada.

This chapter examines the dramatic developments that have taken place in Alberta under Ralph Klein's Progressive Conservative government. Its focus is on the deficit elimination policies initiated by the Klein government and the sweeping changes that have been brought to virtually every aspect of the province's public life as a result of these policies. Klein's principal commitment — to eliminate Alberta's government deficit by 1997 by expenditure cuts alone — is a form of political and economic shock therapy.

To his supporters, Klein is a bold and visionary leader whose resolute policies will lead Alberta (and Canada, if only Chrétien had Klein's courage) to economic stability and prosperity. To his detractors, he is a right-wing ideologue who is pursuing regressive policies that are weakening and dividing the province. They also believe that Alberta's experience is a warning to the rest of the country of what can happen if drastic and ill-thought out "ready-fire-aim" budget cuts are made too quickly. Alberta is once again at the centre of national controversy. In the 1970s and early 1980s, Peter Lougheed's energy and constitutional politics were a major challenge to the federal government. In the 1990s, the Klein experiment — his government's efforts to eliminate the provincial deficit and sharply limit the role of the provincial government — may have the same effect.

This chapter has a number of objectives. It puts Klein's politics in context with Alberta's changing political economy. We acknowledge the impact of the Reform Party on Alberta politics. We also argue that Klein's politics are rooted in deeper changes. The policies of former premiers Peter Lougheed and Donald Getty, important changes in national politics, and international events all shape Klein's stage. We then discuss the Klein government's overarching objectives — its extraordinary emphasis on deficit elimination as a provincial government priority, its abhorrence of tax increases and its assertion that severe budget cuts are driven by economic imperatives. Our key argument is that such fiscal policies have set other policy changes in motion which, if fully implemented, will transform the role that government plays in Alberta. We also suggest several perspectives for interpreting and analyzing the Klein government and the consequences of its policies. Finally, we consider the implications of the Alberta government's agenda for Canadian politics in the 1990s. What are the intergovernmental implications of Alberta's commitment to severe expenditure cuts and *laissez-faire* economics?

Events are changing rapidly in Alberta and its politics are volatile. It is wildly premature, a little over a year after Klein's election, to speak about a "Klein revolution." We wish to be cautious. We are also aware of the difficulties of trying to write dispassionately about policies that are likely to profoundly alter the status quo in our province of residence. We believe that Klein's budget cuts and policy changes will leave Alberta a more divided and unequal society and probably less able to confront national and international economic change. We appreciate, however, the complexities of the issues at stake and the range of competing viewpoints.

ALBERTA POLITICS: THE RISE OF *LAISSEZ FAIRE*

How can we account for the rise of the Klein government, which is such a stark contrast to the Conservative governments led by former Premier Peter Lougheed? Between 1971 and 1985, Lougheed governments ushered in profound changes in Alberta's political economy. Especially after the remarkable post-1973 rise in world prices for oil and natural gas, Lougheed spearheaded a major expansion of the role and influence of the provincial government. His governments were major actors in the resource and constitutional politics of the 1970s and early 1980s. Armed with substantial budget surpluses, Alberta

pursued strategies of industrial diversification designed to transform its economy before its non-renewable resources were exhausted. Lougheed, although
resolutely pro-business, used the provincial government to extend the sway of
Alberta business abroad and build indigenous industries.

In the heady 1970s, a long-term transfer of political and economic power to
western Canada seemed to be underway. Lougheed governments undertook
programs of infrastructure improvement and presided over a significant expansion of provincial educational and health facilities. The latter activities, driven
by demographic changes, caused provincial government expenditures to grow
rapidly. The hallmark of an Alberta budget in the 1970s and early 1980s was
the assertion that oil revenues (and Conservative managerial competence!)
allowed Albertans to enjoy the finest public services at the lowest rates of
taxation in the country.

Hindsight debates now rage about the coherence of Lougheed's policies,
about the extent of public support for them, and about their effectiveness in the
area of economic diversification. Such debates cannot be resolved here. But
two things can be said with confidence. First, Lougheed's governments were
seen as unsettling forces in Canadian federalism. Second, his use of the
provincial government to promote economic diversification was not seriously
questioned by influential Albertans during the Tory heydays between 1971 and
1985. Peter Lougheed was politically dominant and his ideas, with the muted
dissent of Alberta's social democrats, were Alberta's public philosophy. This
combination of forces led Lewis G. Thomas to worry in 1981 about the national
implications of the changing views of Alberta's elite:

> The elite had moved from its role as agent of the central government in the creation
> of a national economy to the role of advocate of regional economic autonomy.
> Could such an elite find a compromise at once acceptable to the people of the
> province and consistent with the future of Canada as an undivided nation?[1]

Lougheed's last government, elected in 1982, faced significant changes in
the domestic and international political economy. The National Energy Program
(NEP), deeply unpopular in Alberta, wreaked havoc in Alberta's oil and gas
industries. And by 1985, the world's oil politics had changed dramatically as
major price drops removed oil from its exalted status as a commodity of
extraordinary significance. The worldwide price collapse resulted in substantial
reductions in Alberta government revenues and, consequently, to significant
changes in provincial politics. Alberta was humbled, as the resource boom
turned to bust and as the province's large resource royalties, the source of its
postwar political distinctiveness, receded. Another important factor was the
1984 federal election, which returned the Progressive Conservatives with a
national majority including all of Alberta's seats. Joe Clark and Don Mazankowski were senior federal ministers from Alberta in a government dedicated

to federal-provincial harmony and a reduced role for government in the economy.

Lougheed left politics in 1985, but before doing so was actively involved in picking an heir. At a leadership convention in that year he was succeeded by Donald Getty, a senior minister in Lougheed Cabinets between 1971 and 1979. The much maligned Getty bore the brunt of provincial economic decline. In the 1986 and 1989 provincial general elections the Conservatives retained power but lost ground to the New Democrats and the resurgent Liberals. A virtual one-party state had quickly become a competitive three-party system.

Two singular trends in Getty's governments paved the way for Klein and his aggressive agenda of political change. First, the Getty government presided over the collapse of major Alberta firms that had emerged and flourished with the assistance of the provincial government. A noteworthy example was the demise of the Principal Group, an Edmonton-based financial services conglomerate that was a player in Alberta's efforts to establish itself in North America's financial services sector. Equally well publicized was the government's financial loss, in excess of $550 million, in the cellular phone manufacturer, NovAtel Communications. These events undercut the Conservatives' image as a party of administrative competence. Much more significantly, such business failures eroded confidence in government-led strategies of economic diversification. As a substitute, there emerged in Alberta the well-worn notion, promoted by the new right and influenced by the examples of Ronald Reagan and Margaret Thatcher, that only the market could select "winning" industries and that government must retreat to its traditional roles as arbiter, referee, and provider of "essential" services if markets were to perform properly. A *dirigiste* provincial state had run its course in Alberta.

The other major development during the Getty years was the government's inability to deal effectively with the province's new fiscal and economic circumstances. Faced with an almost catastrophic plunge in oil and natural gas revenues and caught by the early 1990s in the undertow of a deep worldwide recession, the Getty government imposed tax increases and expenditure cuts which, even when combined, did not prevent large operating deficits and a burgeoning debt. In Alberta, such policies were accompanied by the prayer that resource prices, and hence provincial revenues, would rise substantially and thus prevent severe restraint. Between 1986 and 1992, taxes and other government fees were increased although Alberta's personal income taxes were still Canada's lowest (albeit fractionally) and a retail sales tax was avoided. Getty governments also cut public spending, but either too severely or inadequately depending on the standards employed and the politics of their critics. As Paul Boothe, an economist, argued: "The Getty government was cutting real per-capita spending right throughout its tenure."[2] Getty's first budget in 1986 yielded a $3.43 billion deficit while his last in 1992 was $2.78 billion in the red.[3]

The Getty government's failure to manage provincial finances set the stage for the Klein agenda. Controversial expenditure cuts, unpopular tax increases, the Principal and NovAtel fiascoes and the spiraling debt all contributed to the view that Alberta's public finances were in crisis and in need of radical reform. The status quo was held to be untenable after six years of incremental solutions that yielded higher taxes, reduced public services, and produced record deficits. Getty's policies also generated an "anti-cutback" constituency, centred in the public sector unions, school boards, universities, social service agencies, and many women's groups, that bitterly opposed the Klein agenda coming as it did on top of the substantial deterioration in public institutions caused by his "cuts".

The powerful commitment of Peter Lougheed and Alberta's political and business elites to bilateral (now continental) free trade is a subtle but crucial element in the province's shift to *laissez faire* in the 1990s. Deeply troubled by Alberta's economic decline and convinced that the NEP was its cause, Lougheed saw free trade as a bulwark against nefarious federal policies. He also understood that free trade might bridle the interventionist capacity of the provincial governments. But his fear and resentment of federal policy led him to accept potential restraints on "province building."[4] Free trade's core assumption that markets, not governments, best determine national and regional industrial structures now holds sway among Alberta elites.

After 1985, low oil prices, the conversion to free trade, the apparent failure of provincial industrial strategies and the growth of government debt radically altered Alberta politics. By the early 1990s, the once dominant Conservatives were divided. Battered by media criticism, they had fallen in popularity and were threatened by resurgent opposition parties. Getty's leadership was under fire and the party's future was unclear. An apparently strong faction, allegedly the disciples of Lougheed, remained. But its philosophy was far removed from Lougheed's original designs. It stressed managerial competence, fiscal conservatism, and concerns with social rights and Canadian unity. Another faction was loosely akin to the federal Reform Party with interests in tough law and order, debt reduction, and "back to basics education." In the midst of this turmoil, Ralph Klein, the minister of the environment and former mayor of Calgary, was not seen as a major player. We now turn to an examination of his unexpected rise to power.

THE KLEIN PHENOMENON

When he first entered provincial politics in 1989, after having been the popular mayor of Calgary between 1980 and 1989, it seemed unlikely that Klein would eventually become the premier of Alberta. As a reputed former Liberal who had been lured to the provincial Tories in exchange for a prominent position in the Getty Cabinet, he was viewed with suspicion by many in the Conservative Party. Observers wondered how long it would be before Klein's raucous, shoot-from-the-hip style got him into serious difficulties. Some predicted that as a former big city mayor he would have difficulty connecting with rural Alberta. He was also seen as someone who had little grasp of or interest in policy issues. In short, Klein was seen as a colourful bit player, who, while remaining a strong vote-getter for the party, would be relegated to a supporting role. In 1992, there was little indication that he Klein would remake the party in his own image and transform it and himself into the instrument and symbol of an ideological crusade.

As mayor of Calgary, Klein had an uncanny instinct for being liked and for gauging and articulating the public mood. Part of his appeal was a "tough guy" persona, exemplified by his promise made at the height of the boom in 1982 to "kick ass" and throw unwanted "creeps and bums" from eastern Canada in jail. Another was his "man of the people" populism. Klein challenged organizers of the 1988 Calgary Winter Olympics to open their meetings to the public and warned that the Olympics could not succeed unless ordinary citizens were fully involved. More importantly perhaps, Klein presided during the boom years. He became identified with the good times, years of unbridled growth and ambition. He was a cheerleader of big development. As Don Gillmor has written, "With Mr. Klein, every night was Saturday Night. Under Klein the physical city began to match the outsized spirit Calgary has always claimed for itself."[5] The city also built up a sizable debt.

His temperamental outbursts and reputation as someone who enjoyed a drink were celebrated by Calgarians as a part of the city's free-spirited and unrepentant self-image. One can argue that Klein's greatest advantage as a politician — his image as a populist street brawler — became a liability when he made the transition to provincial politics. The business and Conservative Party elites, for whom Mr. Lougheed had been such a model, appeared to be unimpressed by Klein's apparent lack of managerial skills and what many saw as his rough and ready demeanor. They, like so many others over the years, underestimated Klein's formidable political skills,

As noted earlier, much had changed in Alberta politics by the time the Conservative leadership race took place in 1992. The Getty government had fallen precipitously in the polls as a result of the Principal Affair, the NovAtel fiasco, loans to Peter Pocklington, its handling of the Treasury in general and Getty's distant and erratic management style. He did not have the prestige to anoint a successor of his choosing. The rising force in Alberta politics was the federal Reform Party founded in 1987. By 1992 it had become a formidable political power in Alberta, not only winning converts within the Getty Cabinet and the provincial Conservative Party but reshaping and focusing the public mood. In the early 1990s, many of the Getty government's actions were conditioned by the fear that the Reform Party might enter provincial politics. Whatever the Reform Party's origins in feelings of western alienation towards Ottawa, nostalgia for Social Credit and the Manning years in Alberta, evangelical Christianity and genuine populist impulses, much of its appeal was based on a crusade against spending and taxes. Indeed eliminating the deficit was a central pillar of its program. It venerated the private sector, wanted tough action on crime and a "back to basics" approach to education. One can contend that the Reform Party succeeded in setting much of the agenda in Alberta politics and much of Ralph Klein's agenda as well.

Reform's message was not lost on the provincial Liberal Party whose leader, Laurence Decore, attempted to outflank the Tories by moving the party to the right. He advocated drastic deficit reduction measures which he characterized as "brutal," legislative and educational reform, and a reduced role for government in the economy. In 1994, the Alberta Liberal Party is certainly not an ideological clone of Jean Chrétien's federal Liberal Party.

As the landscape of Alberta politics changed, Klein's populist image became an advantage. His style was in sharp contrast to that of Don Getty and he could appeal to Reformers. Klein had used his position as minister of the environment to travel the province and build a formidable rural base. Although the field of candidates to succeed Getty included five other Cabinet ministers, Klein won the endorsement of a majority of Tory MLAs.

The Conservative leadership selection process in 1993 used a universal ballot in which all party members could vote. The voting was conducted in two stages. If no candidate garnered a majority of votes on the first ballot, a second ballot would be held a week later among the top three vote-getters. Much to everyone's surprise the minister of health, Nancy Betkowski, a moderate Tory with strong support in Edmonton, led Klein in the first ballot by a single vote. When six of the seven other contenders threw their support to Betkowski, Klein's fate seemed to be sealed.

His campaign organization, however, proved to be surprisingly effective as it was able to mobilize a large number of rural voters in the period between the first and second ballots. He took a secure second ballot victory. The coalition that came together to support Klein, and perhaps more importantly at the time to stop Betkowski, became the backbone of a transformed Conservative Party. In the aftermath of the leadership race, Betkowski and her supporters were either pushed or went into exile. The absence of a more moderate wing paved the way for the development of a unified sense of purpose among remaining Conservatives. Klein undoubtedly had a keen sense of where his bread had been buttered.

The premier's supporters came disproportionately from Calgary and from rural areas and were generally less well-educated and less affluent than

Betkowski's supporters.[6] The clearest differences between the two camps, however, were ideological. Klein owed his leadership to a right-wing constituency that had strong views about the need to reduce the size and role of government, believed that many welfare programs were unnecessary and wanted grassroots problem solving and "down to earth thinking."

Klein may have been a late convert to right-wing orthodoxy (he had downplayed the importance of the debt during the leadership race, for instance), but he had a keen sense of political manoeuvre. He knew that as premier he had to distance himself from Getty's legacy and outbid the Liberals in demonstrating to voters that he and the Conservatives would be instruments of change. The crucial test of his early months in office came over the issue of MLA pensions, which had become a symbol of the waste and self-indulgence of the Getty regime. Under incessant criticism from the media and attacks from an angry public, Klein, in one fateful blow eliminated pensions for all first-term and future MLAs and forced those who were retiring to take a 10 percent cut. In doing so he robbed the Liberals of their most devastating election issue and turned the situation to his own advantage. To many Albertans, he was the hero of the day.[7]

The centrepiece of the Conservatives' election strategy in 1993 was the *Deficit Elimination Act* introduced in a pre-election budget. Impetus to take strong action on the deficit came from a budget roundtable held in Red Deer and from the report of the Alberta Financial Review Commission, a group of businessmen and accountants appointed by the Provincial Treasurer to assess Alberta's public finances. The Klein government pledged not only that it would eliminate the deficit in four years but that this would be done without increasing taxes. Alberta would become a tax haven. The linchpin of the new policy was the "Alberta advantage," a claim that low taxes would attract so much business investment that 110,000 jobs would be created.

Ralph Klein's personal popularity had much to do with the Tories' election victory. The Conservative campaign was based almost entirely on packaging his folksy charm and everyman image and in presenting the Conservatives as "Ralph's Team." The strategy was to deflect attention away from the legacy of the Getty government and make the election into a personality contest between Klein and the more austere Laurence Decore. The fact that few policy differences distinguished the Liberals from the Conservatives allowed the Tories to play the leadership card effectively.

The New Democrats, who openly called for higher taxes on wealthier citizens and on corporations, seemed to be doomed almost from the start of the election. They were poorly financed, burdened by the poor performance of the federal and Ontario New Democrats and out of step with the increasing fixation of voters on deficit controls.

During the campaign, Klein avoided detailed discussions of his proposed budget cuts. He made much of the increases in funding for education that had been granted in 1993, promised seniors that there would be no fundamental changes in their benefits, and argued that cuts to daycare funding, hospitals, and universities could be offset by monies raised from lotteries and bingoes. His message was that Albertans would be consulted about policy changes and that public opinion would shape his agenda.

The Tory campaign also stressed law and order issues. The premier wanted Ottawa to get tough with young offenders and reintroduce the death penalty. He also defended remarks made by Deputy Premier Ken Kowalski in the last week of the campaign that the opposition parties were the "enemy" of rural Alberta and the traditional family.[8]

The election results were not a surprise. The Tories won a majority of 51 seats compared to 32 seats for the Liberals. Although the popular vote was close (44.5 percent for the Conservatives as against 39.7 percent for the Liberals) the Tories swept their traditional strongholds in central and southern Alberta and won all but three seats in Calgary. The real division was between Edmonton and its environs, where the Liberals won every seat, and the rest of the province. The New Democrats were decimated, losing all of their 16 seats in the Legislature.

POLITICS AND DEFICITS IN ALBERTA

The Alberta government is dedicated to balancing its budget by 1996-97, to doing so by budget cuts alone, to cutting all areas of public expenditure, and to imposing neither new taxes nor tax increases. This program has sparked an intense controversy in Alberta about the state of the provincial public finances.

Without exception, commentators acknowledge that Alberta's public finances require reform. On four occasions since 1986, the deficit has exceeded $2 billion. Expert commentators generally acknowledge that expenditures have been reduced significantly since the mid-1980s, although this point is never mentioned by the Klein government. Finally, the debt problem is generally thought to be rooted in the post-1986 drop in provincial oil and gas royalties. From the mid-1970s until 1986, slightly more than 50 percent of total provincial revenues flowed from such levies. Since 1986, the percentage has dropped to an annual average of 21.7 percent. In this vein, the Alberta Financial Review Commission concluded that collapsing oil and gas revenues were the nub of the matter.

> The problem can be linked to the dramatic drop of $3,040 million in resource revenue in 1986-7.... The downturn in 1986 was not a cyclical move which can be expected to reverse. Indeed, it must be recognized that resource revenue will

inevitably decline over the long term owing to the natural decline in the producing fields.[9]

The Commission concluded that the real problem was "overspending," a term that it defined as synonymous with "deficit."

The Klein government is determined to reduce total government spending by at least 20 percent by 1996-97. In such large and politically contentious areas of provincial expenditure — education, health, and social services — the cuts are radical by Canadian standards. They total $1.48 billion by 1997. Health care will be cut by $734 million (17.6 percent), education (elementary, secondary) by $239 million (12.4 percent), advanced education by $175 million (14.2 percent), and family and social services by $327 million (18.3 percent). The cuts are "front loaded" — that is, largest in the first year then shrinking in the next two. In other areas of government, the cuts are much larger. For example, the province is radically changing its relationship with municipalities. Most forms of unconditional provincial assistance are being eliminated with the result that by 1996-97 the budget of the department of Municipal Affairs will be 48.2 percent lower than its 1992-93 base. In Agriculture, Environmental Protection and Federal and Intergovernmental Affairs, the comparable reductions for the period are 23.5, 30 and 21 percent respectively. Substantial further expenditure reductions are being achieved by a provincial policy that "encourages" salary reduction; 5 percent is the desired cut, for all provincial employees and all members of the "MUSH" sector (municipalities, universities, schools, and hospitals).

The Klein government's public justifications for its expenditure cuts rests on the principle that balanced government budgets are central to economic prosperity. The argument is that the ballooning debt is an unfair burden on "future generations" and that escalating expenditures on debt servicing are impediments to the province's capacity to provide new services. The Klein government's key assumption is that expenditure cuts are less harmful to the provincial economy than tax increases. As mentioned earlier, the goal is to create a tax haven — "an Alberta advantage" — in order to make Alberta a magnet for investors.

The government's absolute determination not to tax is, of course, heavily ideological as we will discuss later in this chapter. Calls for tax increases to maintain services are dismissed by Klein as "no brainers." "No society has ever taxed itself back to prosperity."[10] The assumption is that increasing taxes will inevitably lead to more government spending as governments are, by nature, almost uncontrollably expansionist, wasteful, and inefficient. Whatever the truth of this claim, it is certainly shrewd partisan politics in the context of contemporary Alberta. Opponents recognize that advocating a tax increase can be tantamount to political suicide. Thus the debate on taxes has been stifled.

Yet tax increases have been the route taken in most Canadian jurisdictions and throughout the industrial world.

The government has an interesting view about administrative efficiency. Klein portrays himself as a guardian against waste and extravagance in public spending. But his central message is that a balanced budget can only be achieved through substantial program cuts. No amount of administrative reform can achieve the sums required for fiscal freedom. Klein's government does not hold a benign view of the public sector over which it presides. To the contrary, it argues that a "burdensome" administrative class has emerged in Alberta whose high salaries and dubious contributions divert public resources from the classroom, the lecture hall, and the emergency ward. The government has also dressed traditional arguments about running government "like a business" in the garb of modern public management dogma. It is particularly impressed by the well-known ideas of David Osborne and Ted Gaebler who, with almost religious fervor, argue that government must be "reinvented" so that "empowered" public servants can "do more with less."[11] To this end, the Alberta government is now said to be operating five core "businesses."[12] These arguments about public administration have important consequences for the Klein government's program. They permit a subtle attack on public managers and, through reference to government "reinvention," define the issue of expenditure cuts as one of managerial strategy not political ideology. Critics are isolated as opponents of progressive administrative reforms in a changing world.

THE KLEIN AGENDA AND THE MAKING OF
THE NEW ALBERTA

The Klein government has used its crusade against the deficit to introduce a vast program of privatization and to implement a right-wing social agenda. The battle to eliminate the deficit is part of a larger ideological commitment. Indeed, Klein has initiated a program of social engineering, the reordering of societal institutions and priorities to fit a particular ideological mould that is virtually without precedent in recent Canadian history. Some critics argue that the government has given right-wing zealotry and demagoguery both legitimacy and a free rein. Certainly, the Klein agenda goes well beyond an adulation of the private sector and the view expressed by Jim Dinning in the 1994 Budget Speech, that government workers were "good people trapped in bad systems."[13] Klein and/or senior Conservatives have spoken in favour of scrapping the *Charter of Rights and Freedoms*, hanging young offenders, having the parents of young offenders sent to jail, dismantling or seriously eroding the provincial Human Rights Commission, and banning books such as John Steinbeck's *Of Mice and Men* from Alberta schools. Senator Ron Ghitter, a moderate Tory with a strong commitment to human rights causes, has detected what he describes as "a disturbing and insensitive attitude that mirrors views held by arch-right wingers such as Americans Rush Limbaugh and Pat Buchanan."[14] This is the ideological tone, and the political dynamic, that underpins and fuels the government's deficit elimination strategy.

So sweeping are the proposed policy changes in Alberta that we have limited our discussion to education and health care, two essential motors of the provincial state. Education was identified in the 1994 Budget Speech as one of the "core businesses of government." Klein has altered the entire landscape of educational governance. The most dramatic move was to remove from school boards the right to receive funding out of local property taxes. Tax dollars will now flow directly to the province which will also have the power, together with school boards, to select school superintendents. The minister of education, however, will be able to fire superintendents if they fail to meet provincial objectives. The government argues that these changes will permit a fairer distribution of resources across the province and break down the differences between schools in urban and rural areas. Critics claim that such policies are destroying the autonomy and local responsiveness of democratically elected school boards by imposing a centralized mandate.

Catholic school boards quickly mobilized to fight the new educational regime by threatening to take the government to court for violating their constitutional rights. After a tough battle the Klein government retreated and will now allow Catholic boards to raise taxes directly. In an interesting turn of events, Alberta's public school boards are launching legal action against the new *School Act* on the grounds that it gives Catholic boards greater power and autonomy than public boards.

One of the most controversial developments was the plan to reduce funding for kindergarten education, known in Alberta as Early Childhood Services (ECS). Claiming that cuts to ECS could be justified by expert research in the field, Klein reduced spending on ECS from $1,260 per child for a 400-hour program to $595 per child for 200 hours of instruction.[15] Many school boards responded by charging user fees of up to $600 for the additional 200 hours of instruction. The government has been unable to produce the studies on which it supposedly made its decision but experts have disputed Klein's claims citing studies which suggest that ECS can be of considerable benefit especially to those children who come from poorer and less well-educated families.[16] Educators are now worried about the beginnings of a two-tier education system, one that will give enormous advantages to wealthier children as user fees are eventually applied to more and more school programs and after school activities.

Another area of contention is the government's plans to be the first jurisdiction in Canada to establish charter schools, about 30 of which are planned in the next three years. Charter schools, which will be fully-funded public schools that must meet provincial curriculum requirements, differ from other schools in that they will be created and managed by groups of parents or community institutions that believe in alternative forms of education. These schools will be able to hire their own teachers and decide for themselves how provincial standards will be met. Schools could specialize in science, athletics, or the arts and adhere to particular educational philosophies or codes of behaviour. As these are public schools tuition will not be charged and religious instruction cannot be imposed on students.

Critics again charge that charter schools are the beginning of a two-tiered educational system. Although these schools are technically open to all students, scholars who have studied this phenomenon in the United States point out that charter schools in that country tend to serve the interests of affluent, well-educated families.[17] In some jurisdictions teachers who work for charter schools are not guaranteed a position with their old boards if they wish to return. Teachers are vulnerable and lose much of their professional authority. Indeed, preliminary indications are that if a charter school in Alberta chooses not to be affiliated with a school board, it will not be obligated to hire members of the Alberta Teachers Association.

Worries about a two-tiered system — one for the those who are well off, the other for everyone else — have been expressed most often with respect to health care. Health care, which is described as another of the "core businesses" of government, involves an amalgam of strategies including increased premiums and user fees. Health-care premiums will rise by 20 percent and fees for long-term care residence will go up sharply. Senior citizens will pay premiums for the first time. In addition, patients will be charged for treatments that are not based on "significant need." At the same time, the number of hospital beds will be reduced from 4.3 per thousand to 2.4 per thousand. This will mean a large number of hospital closings. New regional hospital superboards have been created to achieve the necessary rationalizations. They will allocate resources and make cuts among the hospitals under their jurisdiction based on a fixed budget from Edmonton. The emphasis will be on preventive medicine and promoting the "well-being" of Albertans rather than funding a "sickness care" system. Palliative and pre- and post-operative care will be shifted to the community.

Even more controversial is the Klein government's commitment to the expansion of a private health-care industry. Alberta already has private clinics that specialize in cataract surgery, abortions, and magnetic-resonance imaging. Wealthier patients can avoid the long wait for a MRI scan at hospitals by paying $1,000 at a private MRI clinic. Those who want immediate cataract surgery pay a "facility fee" of $1,275. A new initiative, the so-called Gimbel Bill, would allow medical entrepreneurs to set up charitable foundations and operate American-style medical complexes for patients who could afford to pay hefty fees. Some doctors have already discussed the possibility of building large medical industrial parks.

The argument in favour of this approach is that it would relieve pressure on government-run hospitals, thus ensuring greater access for those who are in need. Opponents see the bill as threatening the integrity of the entire health-care system and violating both the spirit and the letter of the *Canada Health Act*. Private hospitals would attract better doctors and wealthy patients would gain access to facilities and equipment that would be unavailable to other citizens. The quality of health care would depend on one's economic status.

A central chord found in Klein's policies is the notion that modern government can provide only basic services and that individuals or families that want the "extras" or "frills" will have to pay for them. There is a pervasive emphasis on individual rather than community obligations. For instance, the business plan in health care calls for the taking of "individual responsibility," while a white paper on postsecondary education states as its principal goal the need to "foster individual responsibility in a learner-centred system."[18] Self-reliance is the ultimate virtue and the Klein government has promoted the view that its great wisdom has been in deciding what "the real needs" of citizens are.

Although Klein's concept of the "Alberta advantage" rests on the promise of no new taxes, Albertans will pay new or higher user fees for virtually every service or activity that involves the provincial government in any way. Tuition for postsecondary education and health-care premiums will be more costly and almost all permits, licences, documents, tests, and inspections will be subject to new or higher fees.

The merits of privatization is a theme that runs through the business plans of Alberta government agencies. Alberta's privatization scheme is more breathtaking in its scope than similar initiatives elsewhere in the country. Almost all Crown corporations have been sold off, the retail sale of liquor has been privatized, the province's student loan program will be administered by the Canadian Imperial Bank of Commerce, and there are plans for private bailiff services. Moves may be underway to privatize foster care, group homes, and senior citizens lodges. The atmosphere is such that the city of Calgary is currently contemplating the privatization of all major city utilities including waterworks, waste disposal, and the provision and maintenance of electrical services.

On the anniversary of his first year in office Klein observed that, "These are not painful things that we are doing, and most people have bought into our programs. They support us."[19] Despite Klein's bravado his government's shock-therapy approach to cutting the deficit is likely to have serious social and economic repercussions. In its 1994 budget the government admitted that its fiscal policies would dampen the economic growth currently being propelled by natural gas exports, a rise in oil prices, and burgeoning livestock, forestry and small business sectors. Lay-offs, salary rollbacks, and the fear felt by many public sector workers that they might soon lose their jobs will certainly have a stifling effect on consumer spending. Klein's claim that his policies would produce 110,000 jobs, the hinge on which his government's economic theory and perhaps even its re-election prospects rests, may be difficult to achieve.

A deeper concern is that his policies will create a society where there is an increasing gap between rich and poor. High tuition fees for postsecondary education, a two-tiered health-care system, charter schools, and financial barriers that prevent access to daycare and kindergarten could widen the gulf between those who have the resources to take care of themselves and those who had previously depended on the state to provide opportunities for a good life.

Another important consideration is that Alberta is likely to lose some of its best doctors, scientists, teachers, and administrators as skilled professionals, who are in high demand elsewhere, find Alberta a less attractive place to live. This exodus combined with diminished resources for schools and universities are likely to limit Alberta's ability to be competitive in key industries in the twenty-first century. Investments in "human capital," it can be argued, are the real fuel of future prosperity.

Klein's policies may also have a dramatic effect on women, especially those who are economically disadvantaged. Higher costs for daycare, limited access to kindergarten, the prospect of user fees for many after-school activities, and even the cutbacks to seniors' benefits will make it more difficult for women to remain in the workforce. Although this effect may not have been intended, it fits into the image of the ideal family promoted by many in the Tory caucus. One way of solving the unemployment problem is to take a large number of women out of the workforce by pursuing policies that celebrate the virtues of the traditional family.

PERSPECTIVES ON KLEIN'S POLICIES

This section suggests four perspectives that may be helpful in understanding the Klein agenda. These interpretations have been widely debated in the Alberta media and in public forums. An opinion poll published in the *Edmonton Journal* and the *Calgary Herald* in April 1994 which probed public responses to the Klein government's policies offers some perspectives about attitudes to the Klein agenda. The poll showed relatively high levels of support for the premier and for the Conservatives but substantial concern about the government's deficit elimination policies.[20] We refer to this poll at various points in our analysis.

A first point is that the Klein government is often said to reflect a shift of political power to conservative rural and small-town Alberta, away from Edmonton and Calgary. Aided by electoral boundaries which overrepresent rural voters, the Conservative Party now advances an anti-government platform broadly similar to that of the Reform Party. Advocates of this view note major changes in education policy whereby the province now controls local school taxes so as to redistribute them from city to countryside. Similar analyses are made of the government's radical reductions in municipal government grants which are much more severe for larger cities. But even at the level of electoral calculus this analysis is lacking. Klein's electoral victory is as much based on his strengthening of the Conservatives' support in Calgary as it is in his maintenance of Conservative strength in the rural centre and south. Moreover, Alberta's cities are underrepresented in the legislature, but not so badly that a government can be formed without substantial support in at least Edmonton or Calgary. Public opinion data reveal no major differences between urban and rural dwellers in their views about the government's restraint program.

A second interpretation locates Klein's support principally in the self-interested behaviour of Alberta's politically influential upper-middle classes. John Kenneth Galbraith in *The Culture of Contentment*, Robert Hughes in *Culture of Complaint,* and Linda McQuaig in the Canadian context in *The Wealthy Banker's Wife*, all describe what they see as a central phenomenon of the 1990s — the refusal by those who are well-off to shoulder basic responsibilities for the welfare of society as a whole.[21] Robert Hughes uses the phrase "private opulence, public squalor" to describe the erosion of civic culture in the United States.[22] This analysis, applied to Alberta, sees affluent voters as adopting a cynical, highly selective view of government. They want governments to provide services from which they benefit. They bitterly oppose public expenditures that assist lower income persons. Whatever their short-term differences, the affluent are united by a virulent opposition to tax increases. They support, or at least tolerate, an erosion of public schools and health services as their income permits them to pay user fees and pursue "private" options.

Many problems plague this analysis, especially its inconsistent use of such terms as elites, social classes, and the affluent. Such niceties aside, much of the Klein agenda has little obvious appeal to wealthier, urban Albertans. A transfer of tax revenues to rural school boards and policies which "off-load" provincial responsibilities to cities are telling examples. And in a different vein, the Klein government's cuts to welfare expenditures are, according to the poll that we have cited, the sole area of his restraint program that is supported by a large majority. If welfare expenditures are opposed because they redistribute income, they are opposed by many more than upper-middle class Albertans. Upper income Albertans, especially female members of what Spiro Agnew once mocked as the "Volvo station wagon set," are likely to be defenders of well-funded, accessible kindergartens in the public schools. As this example shows, class interest is a complex phenomenon. Finally, it is fanciful to think that many Albertans, regardless of their income, have thought much about "two-tier" health and education systems let alone arrived at firm conclusions about their merits. Many of the ideas of the Klein government — overt advocacy of "for profit" medicine is a prime example — were long thought to be alien, if not offensive, to the Albertan and Canadian consciousness. Can that consciousness be changed in a matter of months?

A third interpretation sees the Klein government as a diverse coalition held together by its "populism" and by Klein's personal style. It embraces Albertans worried about public debt, conservatives fearful of the demise of "traditional values," free enterprisers excited by promises of much smaller government, and long-standing Conservatives who want to retain power even under a different ideological banner.

Severe overuse has rendered populism almost valueless as an analytical tool. The term populism now describes ideologies, a preference for particular public policies, a political movement's style and even a leader's personal idiosyncrasies. To our thinking, contemporary Conservative populism in Alberta is a "weak" variation with two dimensions — Klein's folksy, personal style and the party's commitment to debt reduction, *laissez faire*, law and order, and "family values." But unlike "strong" populism, it advances no coherent critique of society's power structure. Nor are the Conservatives interested in transcending executive-dominated indirect democracy or in eliminating secrecy or cronyism.

A fourth perspective suggests that the policies and rhetoric of Klein's populism feed and exacerbate a "politics of resentment" whose target is well-educated, public sector workers. The government's view has elements of various "new class" theories, intermittently popular among right-wing Americans, that stress the power of parasitic public employees.[23] The idea is that public sector workers are not merely overpaid shirkers but also authority figures whose status must be reduced. They are the people whose examinations, rules, and petty procedures impede the actions of the "doers" in society. Teachers, doctors, social workers, government managers, and certainly professors — a group that together can be described as knowledge workers — are threatening to and resented by those without high educational qualifications. Klein has constantly played to such sentiments. A cardinal principle governing his policy roundtables, convened in 1993 to discuss budget cuts, was that the providers of government services — educators, physicians, and managers — wielded too much policy power and had to be replaced by "average citizens." To some, his government represents the triumph of the world of street smarts and hard knocks over the world of books and abstractions.

The devaluing of the public sector also plays to the resentments of oil patch and other private sector employees who suffered badly in the many lay-offs and shakeups that occurred in the late 1980s and early 1990s, and now believe that it is the public sector's turn to feel the pain.

The future of the Klein agenda is uncertain as the impact of his budget cuts have not yet been fully felt. Alberta's politics could likely change when, for example, major hospitals close in Edmonton and Calgary and arguments about government's role move from abstractions to tough questions about the value of public services for the quality of everyday life. The contradiction in public opinion data — between Albertans' desire for balanced budgets and low taxes and their anxiety about the impact of cuts in health and education — will lose its theoretical quality. The Alberta experiment will also demonstrate the tension between "traditional values" and market capitalism. As Christopher Lasch argues, corporate capitalism, with its emphasis on materialism and private gain, is itself a potent threat to "family values."[24] Does the Klein government's policy of almost unregulated market competition in the retail sale of liquor promote happy communities and family life? Will the withdrawal of services — ESL, counselling, tutoring, and remedial attention — needed to support special needs and immigrant children foster family values?

Our final point is perhaps self-evident to Albertans but less obvious to other Canadians. The Klein agenda faces substantial opposition, but none on grounds of principle or ideology from within the legislature or the provincial party system. As noted already, the provincial Liberals campaigned in 1993 on a platform broadly similar to that of the victorious Conservatives. The Liberals have been hamstrung in their role as opposition because they have had difficulty finding ways to criticize policies that they had previously championed. Their own fiscal conservatism prevents them from capitalizing on public opposition to expenditure cuts and policy changes in health and education. Alberta's New Democrats, whose social democracy is mild even by Canadian standards, were eliminated from the legislature in 1993. The Klein government thus faces an extra legislative opposition led by senior citizens who oppose cuts to programs that benefit them, by school boards who see their autonomy as being wrongfully usurped and more meekly by public sector unions whose stake is obvious. Beyond such groups, Alberta politics also manifests various community-based groups that have grown up spontaneously to oppose budget cuts. In Edmonton, a rally attracted 15,000 people concerned about a possible hospital closure.

The longer term consequences of the clash between a unified and ideologically driven government committed to major policy changes and an oppositio composed of heterogeneous interest groups are uncertain. But in the short term the struggle is decidedly to the government's advantage. The opposition lacks organizational unity and ideological coherence. With the possible exception of seniors, it is readily portrayed as selfish and out of step with the "silent majority" of restraint supporters. Moreover, an opposition driven by interest groups ultimately critiques the government's program on grounds of detail. Its goals are to forestall or simply delay undesirable changes, to bargain for greater freedom to shape responses to restraint and to be more deeply involved in the implementation of change. By its very nature, the opposition is tactical and incremental.

THE KLEIN GOVERNMENT AND CANADIAN POLITICS

The study of Canadian federalism stresses the strains engendered by the postwar expansion of governmental activities. The consequences of public sector restraint for public policy and for intergovernmental relations have been much less systematically explored. How does Klein's program of severe budget cuts influence Canadian politics?

This question leads us onto an uncertain terrain where the behaviour and actions of the Klein government are extremely hard to predict with confidence. The Klein Conservatives see themselves as "icon smashers," harsh provincial government critics of some federal policies and national symbols. For example, the government opposes the *Young Offenders Act*, which they see as the source of rampant youth crime. Federal multicultural polices and those elements of the *Charter of Rights and Freedoms* that promote "group rights" or impede law enforcement are routinely savaged. The government of Alberta reinforces the messages of the Reform Party.

In the 1990s, government deficits at both levels create a "politics of offloading" in Canadian federalism. Governments blame each other for their problems and may devise policies that transfer the burden of expenditure responsibility to another level. This phenomenon is generally thought to have federal-provincial and provincial-municipal axes. But Klein's reforms highlight an interprovincial dimension as the governments of Alberta and British Columbia spar about the impact of Alberta's cuts and policy changes in social assistance. British Columbia asserts that Alberta is consciously exporting its welfare rolls to British Columbia where payments are higher and where "work for welfare" ideas are not in vogue. This policy dispute is intensified by the tendency of premiers Klein and Harcourt to attack each other's governments rhetorically. Each premier has publicly portrayed the neighbouring government as an advocate of an ideological crusade whose tenets must be exposed. British Columbia thus becomes a nightmare of high taxes and paternalistic socialism while Alberta is seen as an example of the disastrous consequences of policies shaped by "right-wing" economics.

The federal-provincial dimension of Klein's program also has a rhetorical flavour as Alberta delights in portraying its bold resolve as superior to Ottawa's timidity. In his 1994 provincial budget, Alberta's treasurer argued: "The (federal) Liberal government is putting off the inevitable in the hopes that things will get better. Going slow, making small changes, increasing spending and increasing the horrendous debt burden for all of us. Going slow may be comforting to some. But it's a house of cards built on false hopes."[25] In turn,

Prime Minister Chrétien has argued that Alberta's cuts are transferring problems to Ottawa. Alberta is unrepentant and continues to trumpet its policies as the model for national economic renewal. Its stance may transform federal-provincial discussion about economic policy away from controversy about the regional impact of federal policy towards intense ideological debate about the role of government.

We have discussed Alberta's health-care reforms and noted their emphasis on de-insuring certain services now covered by medicare and their acceptance of "for-profit" medicine. Many details are unclear and it is hard to judge how far Alberta will push its commitment to market principles as determinants of the provincial health-care system. Considerable debate has occurred about the growing importance of private clinics run by medical entrepreneurs which, for a "facility fee," provide much prompter access to medical services than is possible in public hospitals.

In his major television address in January 1994, Klein pointedly argued that his government's health-care reforms would respect the *Canada Health Act.* This commitment highlights a concern to avoid a frontal attack on medicare. It also tacitly acknowledges many Albertans' acceptance of a national medicare system. By the same token the federal government has been cautious in its assessment of Alberta's initiatives. Federal ministers have defended medicare and denounced moves towards "two-tier" medicine. But Alberta's health-care reforms have not yet been responded to in detail. In 1994, when it is still difficult to distinguish rhetoric from policy, Ottawa's "wait and see approach" has sensibly avoided a clash over high principles. Alternatively, as Klein weighs public opinion and partisan advantage, Ottawa may be viewing Alberta as a laboratory. How far and in what ways will public opinion tolerate alterations to the health-care status quo? Can national standards be retained as both levels of government reduce their health-care expenditures? Might Alberta's reforms generate an acceptable hybrid of public and private medicine with potential national applications?

Klein's policies intensify debates about "off-loading" and challenge key premises of the *Canada Health Act.* They are potential sources of severe intergovernmental conflict. But the story is more complex. A provincial government driven by fiscal restraint loses its authority as a critic of federal expenditure reductions — even those with adverse consequences for that province. Alberta's response to the 1994 federal budget is instructive. As noted, the main line of attack was to contrast Ottawa's gradualism with Alberta's severe budget cuts. This critique, for instance, precluded strident provincial criticism of major cutbacks to military bases in Edmonton and Calgary when such were presented as federal responses to "fiscal realities." This observation should bolster the spirits of those who see Canadian federalism as partially responsible for the degeneration of our politics into petty intergovernmental squabbles.

It must not be forgotten that the government of Alberta seems obsessed by the preoccupations of much of current public management theory to the effect that public agencies know their "businesses" and understand their "customers." Such a management philosophy may lead to friction if governments pursue different visions of administrative reform. But conflict is by no means pre-ordained.

The Klein agenda does include a critique of some federal policies but its vision is primarily limited to Alberta and is not preoccupied with debate about where Alberta "fits" in the national community. Klein's continual fretting about a possible federal "carbon" tax exemplifies the degree to which Alberta remains suspicious of Ottawa's intentions. There is little doubt that Alberta's anti-tax populism and the presence of the Reform Party opposition in the House of Commons might combine to generate an angry Alberta critique of possible federal tax reforms.

What are the implications of these developments for possible constitutional negotiations in the short and medium term? In the 1970s and early 1980s, the government of Alberta was a major player on the national stage. Lougheed was a forceful, and to his critics, bellicose, defender of provincial powers and a decisive and influential actor in intergovernmental relations. Under Getty, Alberta faded as a national player. And in one sense, Alberta's support of the Meech Lake and Charlottetown accords placed it firmly on the side of the status quo. Getty's constitutional flagship, a "Triple-E" Senate, was a substantial change in provincial policy as Alberta shifted its attention from the division of powers to strengthening national institutions as sites for regional and provincial accommodations.[26]

Under Klein, Alberta's future on the intergovernmental stage is unclear. Thus far, he shows neither interest nor expertise in the broader pattern of Canadian politics. His provincial agenda, unlike Lougheed's, does not rest on an inter-twined strategy for the national stage. He has advanced no creative views about Quebec nationalism, aboriginal issues or democratic reform to cite a few examples. But he is certainly capable of inflammatory rhetoric. He has threatened to withdraw the $310 million that Alberta has invested in Hydro Québec bonds if Quebec makes moves to secede, and has mused openly about a political alliance of the western provinces. At time of writing, he has appointed a panel of university professors to advise him on developments in Quebec.

CONCLUSION

Klein's radical program is a significant experiment in Canadian politics. In 1994, Alberta is a province-sized laboratory for testing an economic theory that sees deficit elimination through expenditure cuts alone as the sole source of job creation, investor confidence and economic renewal. The prescription is an extensive reduction of the role and influence of government. In fact, the government should base its own operations on business principles. The state's role is simply to provide "basic services" — self-reliant citizens must assume primary responsibility for their own well-being.

This economic theory has fostered radical policy change and experimentation across the provincial government and its agencies. Charter schools and privatization schemes in health care are either new in concept or untried in Canadian practice. Experts, and more importantly, Albertans who live with these policies, disagree sharply about their value and their effectiveness. The successes and failures of the Alberta "model" are likely to dominate Canadian public debate for the foreseeable future.

The breadth and depth of Klein's policy changes highlight the flexibility and resilience of Canadian federalism. The government of Alberta is able to chart a largely independent course even though its ideology challenges values that are widely accepted elsewhere in Canada. But harsh intergovernmental confrontation is possible. Alberta's challenges to the *Canada Health Act* and possible constitutional developments might create serious problems.

A paramount question — to which we have no ready answer — is why is Alberta's political landscape so different? The *laissez-faire* policies of Ronald Reagan and Margaret Thatcher seem *passé* in much of the western world. Such views have never been strongly held in Canadian federal politics and were again rejected in the 1993 federal election. Yet these ideas flourish in Alberta. Whether the Klein government will retain its ideological fervor and popular support is unclear. In 1994, it provides an example *par excellence* of the still potent force of ideology in democratic politics.

NOTES

1.   Lewis G. Thomas, "Alberta 1905-1980: The Uneasy Society," in P. A. Dunae (ed.), *Rancher's Legacy: Alberta Essays by Lewis G. Thomas* (Edmonton: University of Alberta Press, 1986), p. 211.

2.   As quoted in Dave Pommer, "The Gathering Storm," *Calgary Herald*, 11 December 1993.

3.   All figures relating to Alberta's public finances quoted in this article are taken from Alberta, *Budget '94: Securing Alberta's Future — The Financial Plan in Action* (Edmonton, 24 February 1994).

4.   G.B. Doern and B.W. Tomlin, *Faith and Fear: The Free Trade Story* (Toronto: Stoddart, 1991). Doern and Tomlin remind us that Canadian advocates of bilateral free trade saw it, probably naively, as an industrial strategy per se not as an alternative to it.

5.   Don Gillmor, "The People's Choice," *Saturday Night*, August 1989, p. 37.

6. See David K. Stewart, "Electing the Premier: An Examination of the 1992 Alberta Progressive Conservative Leadership Election," a paper presented to the annual meeting of the Canadian Political Science Association, Calgary, June 1994.

7. For an overview of the pension issue see Kenneth Whyte, "Klein of the Times," *Saturday Night*, April 1994.

8. Ashley Geddes, "Premier defends Kowalski's views," *Calgary Herald*, 10 June 1993.

9. Alberta Financial Review Commission, *Report* (Edmonton, 1993), p. 15.

10. These comments were made by Klein during a televised address to the province in January 1994.

11. D. Osborne and T. Gaebler, *Reinventing Government: How the Entrepreneurial Spirit is Transforming the Public Sector* (New York: Plume, 1993).

12. Alberta, Budget '94.

13. Ibid., p. 12.

14. As quoted in Sheldon Alberts, "Klein pulls Tory party to the right," *Calgary Herald*, 11 June 1994.

15. Lisa Dempster, "Boards ponder need for waiver," *Calgary Herald*, 27 March 1994.

16. For an overview of the debate about the impact of kindergarten on children see D. Martin, "Policy specifics escape premier," *Calgary Herald*, 25 March 1994.

17. "Alberta charter schools will likely adopt the following criteria," *Calgary Herald*, 20 March 1994.

18. Alberta, *Health Business Plan 1994-95 to 1996-97* (Edmonton, 1994) p. 1; Alberta Advanced Education and Career Development, *Draft White Paper: An Agenda for Change* (Edmonton, March 1994), p. 9; and Alberta Community Development, *Business Plan 1994-95 to 1996-97* (Edmonton, 1994).

19. Scott Feschuk, "Klein says service cuts' not painful'," *The Globe and Mail*, 14 June 1994.

20. For details see Brian Laghi, "Klein still tops polls ... but Albertans edgy about cuts," *Edmonton Journal*, 29 April 1994.

21. J.K. Galbraith, *The Culture of Contentment* (New York: Houghton and Mifflin, 1992); Robert Hughes, *Culture of Complaint* (New York: Warner, 1994); Linda McQuaig, *The Wealthy Banker's Wife* (Toronto: Penguin, 1993).

22. Hughes, *Culture of Complaint* p. 41.

23. For a valuable overview see Christopher Lasch, *The True and Only Heaven: Progress and Its Critics* (New York: W.W. Norton, 1991), especially chap. 11.

24. Ibid.

25. Alberta, Budget '94, p. 7.

26. For overviews and differing interpretations of Alberta's recent constitutional strategies see Roger Gibbins, "Alberta and the National Community" and J. Peter Meekison, "Alberta and the Constitution," in Allan Tupper and Roger Gibbins (eds.), *Government and Politics in Alberta* (Edmonton: University of Alberta Press, 1992), pp. 67-84 and 247-68 respectively.

5

The Fisheries Crisis in Newfoundland

Susan McCorquodale

Une catastrophe a frappé la région de l'Atlantique et plus particulièrement Terre-Neuve. Le moratoire imposé sur la pêche de la morue a un effet social important dans une province qui n'a que peu de perspectives d'emplois dans d'autres secteurs. Ce chapitre analyse les causes sous-jacentes à la crise des pêcheries en examinant ce qui est arrivé aux stocks de morues, qui est responsable de leur effondrement et ce qui peut être fait à l'avenir.

Trois facteurs principaux qui ont mené à la crise sont examinés : l'insuffisance de la science halieutique, l'effet de la surpêche étrangère, ainsi que l'effet de facteurs naturels comme les changements climatiques. La réponse offerte par les politiques publiques à la crise des pêcheries est examinée par le biais du contexte sous-tendant l'intense pression sociale pour l'emploi dans la pêche et la transformation du poisson, en incluant l'assurance-chômage comme incitation. Un autre élément de la problématique est le conflit fédéral-provincial sur la juridiction des pêcheries, conflit qui continue d'entraver la réforme de la gestion des pêches. Les auteurs soutiennent que les gouvernements doivent effectuer des choix difficiles dans un avenir rapproché si un réajustement positif à la crise doit se produire.

INTRODUCTION

The natural catastrophe that has struck Newfoundland has not had the suddenness of a hurricane nor the visibility of the flooding Mississippi, but it is real, widespread, and lasting in its effects. The cod fish off the northeast coast and southern Grand Banks of Newfoundland are a depleted resource, in serious danger biologically. Once one comprehends the enormity of that reality, two sets of questions arise. First, how could it happen? Who or what is responsible? Second, what is going to happen in the future? Within the region a way of life is threatened. Experts tell us that harvesting and processing capacity should be reduced by 50 percent. But for 12,000 to 17,000 individuals, alternative job opportunities are not easy to come by.[1] Historically in Atlantic Canada a crisis in the fishery seems to happen with uncanny regularity.[2] In the past traditional, industrial, political, and social pressures have succeeded in thwarting any attempt at change. The question today is different because the extent of the resource decline is so severe. It seems we face a choice: either government policymakers and individuals can use *this* crisis to set a new course or things can be allowed to drift into bitterness and endless recriminations.

To deal first with the causes of the crisis, we need to pull apart the various strands of a complex, interrelated series of issues. Did the scientists fail, if so, why? How lasting was the effect of very heavy foreign fishing in areas beyond Canadian jurisdiction? Has divided responsibility between federal and provincial governments produced conflicting policy outcomes? And, as to the future, the short answer is that no one knows, but we can at least set out current thinking about what *should* happen and make some sort of assessment of what the chances are for change versus the chance that the old forces of tradition will succeed to thwart change this time, as they have in the past.

From the fifteenth century onwards, it was the cod fish that attracted Europeans to the waters around Newfoundland. The fishery has determined the settlement patterns, the social mores, the speech, and the politics of Newfoundland ever since. Fishing is important regionally in other parts of Atlantic Canada, but much of what follows will concentrate on the province of Newfoundland because the fishery matters here more than in any other part of Canada.

Once settlement was established, the technology of fishing did not change very much over the next 150 years. It was overwhelmingly an inshore fishery, prosecuted on the populous northeast coast for only a short season due to ice conditions and the Labrador Current. The product was salt cod and it was sold into a competitive world market by local firms whose success depended on the market. Attempts at economic diversification in the last years of the nineteenth century by building a railway succeeded only in producing a large public debt. When the debt of World War I and the Depression of the 1930s were added to the colony's burdens, the result was a period of British-led appointed government between 1934 and 1949.

Pivotal change came with the social and political impacts of World War II and union with Canada in 1949. For the fishery, change meant the replacement of small wooden boats with heavy powered offshore vessels which allowed fleets to log more sea-days, and new trawls which allowed the harvest of much larger catches. Increasingly the product was frozen fish, principally frozen cod blocks, which meant little value-added processing, shipped into an American market. Newfoundlanders either could not or would not invest in the new technology, and consequently had to watch as increasing numbers of foreign vessels harvested (or maybe more accurately raped) the sea. When this era began in about 1955, Newfoundland vessels landed 97 percent of the fish caught in waters adjacent to the northeast coast. By 1975 the share had dropped to 8 percent.[3]

In one remarkable year, 1968, the foreign fleets harvested an astounding 660 million metric tonnes of cod. (Newfoundland's inshore and offshore catch that year was an additional 120 million tonnes.)[4] Gordon Munro has noted that "if this level of effort had continued unabated, inshore harvests would have been driven to the vanishing point by the early 1980s."[5] Indeed cod catches did decline from the 1960s peak to a low of 372,000 tonnes in 1974 — of which only 36,000 tonnes was landed in Newfoundland. To gain domestic control of this situation, the Canadian government acted, belatedly, in 1977 to declare a 200-mile zone of exclusive economic fisheries management. The aim was to set in place an economically sound harvest annually, and to allow the cod stocks to rebuild. At first this effort brought remarkable success for the growing Canadian fleet, as reported catches increased from the low of 36,000 tonnes in 1974 to a peak of 245,000 tonnes by 1988.

Nonetheless, a mere 15 years after the introduction of the 200-mile limit, when the Canadian Atlantic Fisheries Advisory Committee (CAFSAC) met in June 1992, it recommended a catch level in this same area of 50,000 tonnes or less. Since 15,000 tonnes of that catch had already been caught by the domestic offshore fleet, 10,000 tonnes was the estimated "by-catch," and 10,000 tonnes had also already been caught by foreign vessels, that left a meagre 15,000 tonnes for the domestic inshore fishery — not exactly a harvest of plenty.[6] Something drastic was happening to the resource itself and an immediate response was necessary. On 2 July 1992 the minister of fisheries, John C. Crosbie, announced a two-year moratorium on commercial cod fishing in fishing zones 2J3KL.[7] To assist fishers, plant workers and trawlermen adversely affected by the closure, the federal Department of Fisheries and Oceans (DFO) would implement an income support program, called the Northern Cod Adjustment and Recovery program (NCARP).

What could account for such a decline in the stocks? Different weights can be attached to different factors and the uncertainty of a clear answer serves only to exacerbate an already existing tension, principally between fishers, their union, and the provincial government on the one side; and government officials, appointed and elected, of the lead department, Fisheries and Oceans on the other.

It is not obvious where responsibility lies. Explanations as to what happened seem to fall into two groups: human and natural. On the human side, the list includes overfishing, both domestic and foreign, dumping, misreporting catches, and massive miscalculations about the size of the stocks. Competition between governments and conflicting policies served to increase the number of individuals dependent on the industry. Once in the fishery, both fishers and processors felt they had a *right* to a certain quantity of fish. The final impact of this expansion ultimately hit the resource itself.

If one looks for explanations on the natural side, it is a more puzzling list. Harsh climactic conditions and poor feeding may have caused slow growth or low rates of survival of young fish, and there may have been a disruption of spawning and migration, or perhaps higher rates of death from normal causes, including seals.[8]

The discussion in this chapter is organized as follows. Under the heading of external factors in the crisis, we examine in turn the nature of fisheries science, the problem of foreign overfishing and natural factors affecting the cod stocks. In the second part of the chapter, under the heading of fisheries management, we examine the socio-economic context for fisheries management, the problem of federal-provincial conflict and efforts for managment reform. In the conclusion, we address the continuing challenges of the fisheries crisis.

FISHERIES SCIENCE

Scientists working for the Department of Fisheries and Oceans share in the exercise of the federal government's exclusive jurisdiction over "Sea Coast and Inland Fisheries" under section 91(12) of the *Constitution Act, 1867*. They are responsible for assessing the state of the stocks of Canada's commercial fisheries and to recommend a level of fishing effort that will ensure the continued existence of what should be an infinitely renewable food resource.

A useful tool in trying to make a judgement about the difficulties of conducting marine science and the competence of the results in these particular circumstances is the report of an Independent Review Panel on the State of the Northern Cod Stock.[9] The chair of the panel was a former president of Memorial University and the members included world renowned fisheries scientists from the United States and England. The panel's 1990 report examined how and why science had failed and issued a sharp warning about the future fishing effort.

The panel's report began by noting that once Canada gained control of the 200-mile zone in 1977, the correct science policy was adopted. That is, the stocks were to be carefully monitored and each year catch levels were to be set at approximately 20 percent of the exploitable biomass (the weight of fish three years old and above). It should have meant a healthy and steadily growing stock and a growing Total Allowable Catch (TAC) in successive years.[10] Between 1977 and 1984 stock recovery seemed to be working out as anticipated. The catch levels were allowed to increase from 135,000 tonnes in 1978 to 266,000 tonnes between 1984 and 1988.

However, today it is evident that overconfidence and error underlay this scientific advice. The Harris Report says that the biologists forgot that marine science is a very non-quantifiable science, and lulled by false data signals coming from rising catch levels, they failed to recognize the high risk involved with state-of-the-stock assessments based on relatively short and unreliable data series. By early 1989, some members of the science community were becoming uneasy as new and more sophisticated statistical modelling techniques revealed that the northern cod stock had not recovered from the heavy overfishing of the 1960s and 1970s at the rate projected and confidently expected. Some excellent science and good management tactics had been less effective than they might have been because they were conceived and executed, as the Harris panel put it, as if a vast, diverse and dynamic system could be segregated into watertight compartments.[11]

While it is true that the miscalculations of DFO scientists, in respect to the growth of the northern cod stock up to 1988, might have been committed by any other scientific group given similar circumstances, the Harris panel suggested that the problem might have been identified sooner had there been a greater appreciation of the weakness of science and a greater commitment to caution.[12] Overreliance on the mathematical modelling of fish population dynamics was not counter-balanced with an adequate understanding of the interrelatedness of environmental factors, the life history, and behavioural aspects of the cod, or the characteristics of the fishing operations both inshore and offshore.[13]

After 1977, as the Canadian fishing effort replaced the foreign fishing effort, the heavy reliance on the catch rates reported by offshore vessels as a measure of abundance led to basic errors. The scientists forgot or ignored the fact that increasing catches might not be the result of increased stock size, but could also reflect increased efficiency as sea-going hunters of fish gained experience and brought sophisticated sonar technology to their tasks. A combination of an over-estimate of stock size and a fishing mortality that was higher than reported by a factor of two or three, culminated in the catastrophic depletion brought to our attention in July 1992.[14]

Another report, written by two marine biologists and an anthropologist at Memorial University, sees this history of scientific advice as an example of poor science.[15] These authors see as "dubious at best" explanations about ecological factors as the reasons for the recent declines. They point out that the small size of the area outside the 200-mile limit (i.e., approximately 5 percent of the total range of northern cod) does not warrant regarding the question of foreign fishing as anything other than "myth" or "one among several scapegoats."[16] Dealing with the issue of the role of scientists in the "black box" of government decisionmaking, Steele, Andersen and Green argue that DFO scientists are far too "imbedded in, dependent upon and subservient to the state."[17] This scepticism about the competence and independence of the government's scientists lies at the root of much of the blame about what happened.

The Harris panel balanced their criticisms by pointing out the size of the "operational" responsibilities of the Science Branch, Newfoundland Region. The territory of the branch covered perhaps 150,000 square kilometres. With only 16 scientists the region was responsible for the management of nearly 50 different commercial stocks of fish. Simply estimating their biomass and calculating the possible effects of various catch levels normally consumed about 75 percent of the science budget. Moreover, these scientists seemed to be working without adequate computer facilities or state-of-the-art electronic equipment aboard their research vessels.[18] At least in part to reduce this problem, in June 1990 the department allocated $33 million over five years to "accelerate ongoing cod-related research" in the Newfoundland Region.[19] Indeed Lee Alverson, an American biologist with worldwide experience and a member of the Harris panel, reported that there had been an erosion of the quality of scientific endeavour in much of the developed world as governments see the cost of fisheries management as possibly exceeding the economic benefits of the fishery in the circumstances of open access. In the absence of scientific advice to enlighten public controversy, the only result is the continued decline in the fisheries.[20]

FOREIGN OVERFISHING

It is well to remember that the well-being of the industry depended in the pre-1977 period on more than domestic management. At meetings of the International Commission for North Atlantic Fisheries (ICNAF) scientific information and consummate negotiating skills had to be deployed together. In making the Canadian claim for conservation the Department of External Affairs (from the point of view of the fishing community) was a rather unsatisfactory protector. With many other Canadian interests with which to concern itself, External Affairs was seen as trading off the fishery. The biologists of DFO working in the highly centralized framework of Ottawa policy felt convinced that scientific data alone should provide the base for determining quotas. In other words, so long as Canada treated the offshore fishery resource as international common property and as long as this country behaved like a Boy Scout in a thieve's den, effective stock management remained an ideal.[21] It is to this matter of the crippling effect on fish stocks of international effort that we now turn.

The Harris Report is blunt about the effectiveness of the first attempt to bring order into the international fishery off Canada's east coast. ICNAF was a "total failure" as an agency for conservation.[22] To obviate direct international conflict, the Commission set catch quotas so high that they could not possibly be met. Traditional European fishers were joined by "East and West Germans, Russians, Poles, Romanians, Danes, Norwegians, Cubans, and Japanese as fish became an increasingly valuable commodity, as domestic fisheries were depleted, and as technological advance permitted access to hitherto inaccessible resources in distant waters."[23]

After 1978 the European Economic Community, while in theory in favour of sustainable development and a member of the successor international regulatory agency, the Northwest Atlantic Fisheries Organization (NAFO), set their own unilateral groundfish quotas, allowing the EC fleets to harvest up to *twelve times* the quotas established by NAFO. In addition, countries that are not for example, members of NAFO, South Korea, Panama, and the United States did not abide by NAFO guidelines.

Apart from ignoring quotas, the accompanying misreporting of catches could lead to a chain of miscalculations about the size of the stocks, which in turn could damage them further. In 1986, for example, a TAC of 36,000 tonnes was set to be taken from the "nose" and "tail" of the Banks (those areas of the Grand Banks lying beyond the 200-mile limit). The catch that year is estimated to have ended up at landings of over 100,000 tonnes.[24] It should be added that no one in Newfoundland believes that these were the true numbers. Discarding and misreporting are widely suspected. In one assessment of foreign fishing DFO has reported that between 1986 and 1992 the EC had received NAFO quotas totalling about 120,000 tonnes and had reported catches of more than 500,000 tonnes of cod, flounder, and redfish. This is *in addition* to the more than 200,000 tonnes of these same fish taken by non-NAFO vessels, many of them Spanish and Portuguese vessels operating under flags of convenience.[25] In the eyes of most Newfoundland fishers this international irresponsibility amounted to outright piracy. Other observers add that, as noted above, in terms of Canada's trade and international concerns, for far too long the Atlantic fishery mattered very little in the federal scheme of things and could too easily become a pawn in a larger game.[26]

The problem of European overfishing outside Canada's 200-mile limit dates back to 1986, the year Spain and Portugal entered the EC with their big offshore fleets. Spanish and Portuguese fishers have been plying the northwest Atlantic for hundreds of years, but as members of the EC they successfully pressured the Community to ignore the quotas allocated by NAFO. Canada's choice in dealing with the EC has been political efforts to win popular European support for conservation, and the international diplomatic route. Something of a breakthrough in this impasse came in late-1992 when John C. Crosbie, minister of fisheries worked out what has been called the "5-percent solution." In return for open Canadian ports for EC vessels, Canada agreed that NAFO countries, mainly Spain and Portugal, could take 5 percent of the total northern cod stock, roughly the percentage that falls outside the 200-mile limit. Included in the deal was a promise of much better monitoring of EC vessels. Crosbie characterized his approach vis-à-vis the EC was "to trust, but verify."[27] Jeffrey Simpson commented about this deal: "It is doubtful anyone else in politics — including his cabinet colleagues or the nit-picking Premier of Newfoundland, Clyde Wells — could have displayed the courage and tenacity to achieve these objectives."[28]

Local reaction to this particular agreement shows the fear and anger felt in Newfoundland and the consequent condemnation of Ottawa's choice of policy. The provincial fisheries minister, Walter Carter, said the Europeans could not be trusted and that the surveillance provisions were inadequate. Carter was reported as saying "We have no reason to trust them." Likewise, the president of the Newfoundland Fisheries Association (which represents the fish processors) agreed that the Europeans had a credibility problem.[29] To those in the industry in Newfoundland, too many uncounted fish had gone out of the water. The EC's hands were certainly not clean. From the federal minister's point of view, however, the provincial government's attitudes and comments were unhelpful. In a speech to the Board of Trade in March 1992, Crosbie had said that Premier Wells spent his time assessing blame rather than helping solve problems. Likewise he rejected the call from the leader of the "Fisherpersons of Newfoundland and Labrador" who said that Newfoundlanders should follow the lead of Icelandic fishers who cut the nets of foreign trawlers at sea.[30] To Crosbie the thing to do was to persuade countries to do the proper thing, to alter world opinion.

A key factor in changing direction in EC policy was Canada's success in putting the issue of fisheries management and overfishing on the international environmental agenda. Initially overfishing had not been identified as a problem for the preparatory meetings leading to the United Nations' Conference on the Environment in Rio de Janeiro held in June 1992. But as it turned out, overfishing became one of the central issues. Rio was followed up with a meeting in St. John's where Canada and 48 other "like-minded" countries sought to coordinate their positions for a forthcoming UN conference. In New York, Canada co-sponsored a proposed Convention on Straddling Fish Stocks and Highly Migratory Fish Stocks.[31] The latest diplomatic victories in the search for international regulation of threatened fish stocks came first in September 1992 when NAFO extended the moratorium on fishing for 2J3KL cod outside 200 miles; and then in February 1994, when NAFO announced its decision to ban all fishing of southern Grand Banks (3NO) cod.[32]

It was left to Crosbie's successor as minister of fisheries, Brian Tobin, to steer Ottawa's policy in a more confrontational direction. Spurred perhaps by the example of self-denial of Canada's moratorium on cod fishing and the immediacy of the stock depletion issue, the minister began to take an increasingly "hard line" on illegal fishing. In April 1994, Canadian fishery officers boarded a fishing vessel, the "Kristina Logos" in international waters. As a Canadian-owned and registered vessel, even if flying the Panamanian flag, it was fully subject to Canadian law. The "Logos" was seized and escorted to St. John's where its holds were discovered to have $150,000 worth of undersized and illegal cod and redfish. It was the first time Canadian enforcement officers had seized a foreign-flagged ship in international waters.

In May 1994 legislation was tabled in Parliament that empowered Canada to exercise "custodial management" over stateless vessels and flag-of-convenience vessels operating outside the 200-mile limit. The federal authorities will be able to make regulations that list the straddling stocks to be protected and establish the conservation and management measures necessary to protect the listed stocks. The use of reasonable force would be permitted if necessary to arrest these "pirate" vessels. It remains to be seen if Canada can get away with what Giles Gherson calls a "creeping extension of its maritime jurisdiction" or whether the international community will see it as a step too far, setting a dangerous precedent whereby Canada abrogates to itself — in the name of conservation — the right to control the high seas beyond 200 nautical miles.[33]

NATURAL FACTORS

In the complex, interrelated world of fisheries management, there is yet another current controversy. How significant are the changes in the environment on stocks of fish? At a straight-forward level of thinking, one might expect that two years of no cod fishery might at the very least mean restoration of stable resource levels. Such is not the case. Something else appears to be at work. It is to that issue we now turn.

Two years after the moratorium was imposed the most recent scientific reports from DFO say that the number of northern cod off Newfoundland is now estimated to be only 3 percent of the 1990 level.[34] The report goes on to note that even after four years of studying the decline, scientists are unable to determine why the species is in such a precarious state. Undoubtedly fish stocks have been affected by a variety of human factors, but natural factors also appear to be present.

At the beginning of 1991 the biomass was estimated at 1.0 million tonnes. The research vessel survey in the fall of that same year indicated an almost 50 percent biomass decline in one year.[35] The fundamental debate among fisheries scientists is whether that loss of 500,000 tonnes of northern cod from the biomass can be explained or not within the normal variability of assessment. If it can, then the 500,000 tonnes of cod may indeed have been (as many fishers believe) "paper" fish, that is, they merely represented an artificial estimate of fish that were never there in the first place. The view among many Canadian fisheries scientists, however, is that the downturn between 1990 and 1991 was *sudden*. Proving it is the trick![36]

Overfishing is clearly involved in stock downturns, but there is also growing evidence that many biological events can be linked to climate change. In northeast Newfoundland the worst ice conditions in the last 35 years were experienced in 1991. Slower growth rates and lower recruitment, for example, suggest that some of the problem is environmentally driven. Species other than cod are also experiencing stock declines. American plaice in 2J, for example, has declined about 95 percent even though it has been very lightly fished.[37] Those who blame overfishing have a hard time explaining the continued decline of some stocks in the absence of a fishery.

Scientists of a contrary view point out that the fishery had sustained a catch of about 200,000 tonnes for 150 years, through periods when the environment had been just as harsh as it had been in recent years. What happened in the 1980s was the crucial difference. Buoyed by estimates that the stock might eventually support catches as high as 334,000 tonnes of cod by 1987[38] the industry built too many plants and new vessels underpinning the conditions for domestic overfishing. Undoubtedly both overfishing and environmental changes have contributed to stock decline, but not equally in all places. Those who blame environmental factors, like seals and cold water, have trouble explaining how fish have thrived despite these hazards in the past.

DFO's Northern Cod Science Group is concentrating on just such a range of scientific questions. This includes investigations into the underwater climate of the northeast Newfoundland Shelf; the presence of toxic chemicals in sea water; what determines the abundance of capelin (the food fish for cod); and what determines the abundance, diet, and physiology of seals (whose growing numbers are widely believed to detrimentally affect cod populations). It is somewhat ironic to note the formal inclusion of fishers in this science effort. Acknowledging that fishers and scientists look at the world through different windows, the group has made an effort to bridge the two solitudes. They hired a biologist to work directly with inshore harvesters. He has gathered experiential information from more than 2,000 northern cod fishermen, translated it into data that scientists can use and presented the analysis to CAFSAC in early 1992. Fishers were invited to participate in the annual trawl surveys and have returned from these trips with a much fuller understanding of survey methods.[39]

Finally, in recent years, the public in Newfoundland has become much exorcised about the offshore "dragger" fleet, that is, what the trawl doors are doing to the sea bottom itself and what effects trawling has on the spawning behaviour of cod aggregations. The scientists are therefore also taking a serious look at the effects of trawling on the sea bottom.[40] It is a pity that all this cost and effort could not have been expended a little sooner, when there were still fish in the 2J3KL zone.

We have already noted what the Harris panel has said about the need for a high degree of caution from scientists when they offer advice to fishery managers about the state of the fish stocks. The panel did not specifically deal with the issue of overfishing versus natural factors in their assessment of what happened. But one issue that they did address is relevant to the final questions to be pursued here. What can be done to better integrate biological and oceanographic information into the assessment processes? The objective should be to make better estimates of key population parameters.[41] The panel pointed to the need to differentiate the respective roles of fisheries science and fisheries management. In quoting from a report prepared 20 years earlier by J.A. Gulland, they make the point that:

> Management is a matter of making decisions and it is often as important to make a decision in time as to make the best decision. Management has to resolve a wide range of political, social or economic problems.... It is a fallacy to think that scientists, given time, and perhaps money, can produce the complete answers to management problems, e.g. the precise value of the maximum sustainable yield from any particular stock of fish.[42]

Whether or not DFO science is "subservient" to the state,[43] Gulland and Harris both suggest that scientific advice is not the only value at stake in decisionmaking. To differentiate science and management is not, however, to overwhelm one or the other. As Alverson points out we must expect that all members of the industry (fishers, processors, banks, unions) will always seek to maximize economic opportunities within constraints imposed by law. If these group pressures overinfluence those responsible for fisheries policy and fisheries regulations and their enforcement, the fault lies with the policy and decisionmakers, enforcement officials, and their political masters.[44]

If one "given" in the world of fisheries management is the factual reality of the state of the resource itself and the environment in which it swims: another equally valid reality is that of the political and social environment in which final decisions are made. Fishers, processors, banks, unions, and provincial governments all influence fisheries management. If we are to make any assessment about the fisheries crisis in Atlantic Canada, the effects of this environment must also be considered.

FISHERIES MANAGEMENT

THE SOCIO-ECONOMIC CONTEXT

The declaration of the 200-mile limit created a euphoria and gold rush mentality in Newfoundland and throughout Maritime Canada. New fishers were licensed by the federal authorities; new fish processing plants were licensed by the provincial authorities. In the words of the Kirby Task Force:

> By mid-1979 each of the Atlantic provinces and Quebec had worked up detailed fishery development plans, all overlapping, especially in the Gulf of St. Lawrence where each province had designs on the same fish. Almost all this development was to take place largely with federal dollars, mainly channelled through the

Department of Regional Economic Expansion. Provinces with no trawler fleets wanted them; provinces with trawlers wanted to add more and bigger vessels. Processing plants expanded; new ones were built. Fishermen who had left the industry since 1968 came back again. Banks loaned money with less than normal prudence.[45]

Expansion in an industry based on a natural resource, however, is not like expansion in a manufacturing industry. The Harris panel put the difference this way:

Every fisherman issued with a fishing licence expects *as a right*, access to sufficient fish to provide a livelihood; every processor who is given a plant licence expects access to sufficient fish to make the enterprise profitable; every new vessel built and every loan advanced for the purchase of fishing gear demands an increase in fish landings to justify the investments. The temptations to grant the licences or to approve the loans may be nearly irresistible. But, so may be the pressures subsequently generated to allocate the resources to justify the earlier decisions. The repercussions may be disastrous for the stocks.[46]

To illustrate the reality of these points, consider two sets of figures: the growth in the numbers of fishers and the growth in the number of processing plants. But first we should take note of a warning that it is not easy to know just how many people are employed in the fishing industry, even for the present, let alone the past. Sinclair points out that in an industry with a strong seasonal variation, a decision must be taken whether to report all who are involved, those who work at least some agreed minimum time, or perhaps those for whom fishing or fish processing is their main occupation. Official definitions have changed over time. Different agencies that collect data (e.g., Statistics Canada and DFO) use different boundaries, making intra-provincial analysis difficult.[47] An overestimate of the number for whom fishing is important can give a misleading impression of overcapacity. Moreover, the figures can vary a great deal. The Kirby Task Force, for example, estimated that there were 48,000 processing jobs in the Atlantic region in 1981.[48] This was about 5,000 less than the census figure for 1981. An annual Statistical Review produced by DFO put the 1981 figure at 23,278.[49]

That warning said, we press on to get some sense of expansion and the resulting overcapacity. The report from a 1993 conference dealing with the fisheries crisis, tells us that in 1975 there were 89 licensed plants in Newfoundland; in 1980 the figure was up to 138; in 1992 there were 173 plants. These 173 plants operate in 160 communities with 162 of the 173 plants obtaining raw material exclusively from the inshore fleet.[50] Defining 20 weeks as a full season in the inshore fishery and 40 weeks in the offshore fishery, it turns out that in the inshore sector processing plants work an average of 17 percent of their capacity; and in the offshore sector it is 49 percent.[51] Again, however, one must be careful not to jump to conclusions. Much of this level of capacity has been installed to accommodate the seasonal peak landings associated with the in-shore fishery when approximately 50 percent of the total production can occur within a one-month period. Admittedly, this leaves plant capacity redundant for most of the year.

Commensurate with growth in plant capacity was a growth in employment. In fact overall the fishery accounted for 56 percent of all employment growth in Newfoundland between 1977 and 1986; by contrast, government employment accounted for 39 percent of the growth.[52] For every 100 persons employed in the fishery in 1977, there were about 200 persons employed in 1986. These same general trends continued into 1991 and point to increasing dependency on the fishery both for employment and for employment growth.[53]

Moreover, this employment has been skewed in a couple of interesting directions. As the number of plants processing fresh fish proliferated, it made formal employment available in small communities in previously unheard of numbers. Much of this new employment went to women. In 1971 less than 19 percent of those employed in the fish processing sector were female; in 1986 employment had nearly tripled, and females were close to 50 percent of those employed. This means that in rural communities dependent on the fishery, many families are now used to two fishery-related incomes, and any suggestion of mobility is considerably constrained.

Secondly, overall the fishery workforce is both young and poorly educated. Only 8 to 10 percent of plant workers are within ten years of retirement;[54] conversely nearly 55 percent were between the ages of 15 and 34.[55] As for level of education, figures for 1986 (which would appear to be the most recent available) show that nearly 76 percent of *all* fishery workers had less than a high school education and 40 percent had less than Grade 9. Figures from the Northern Cod Adjustment and Recovery program (NCARP), a program with a strong re-education component, show that as of December 1992, of the approximately 25,000 workers eligible for benefits, more than 70 percent had less than Grade 10.[56] This lack of formal education adds a significant impediment to both occupational and geographical mobility.[57]

Finally, to complete this picture, it should be noted that the fishery in Newfoundland remains a profoundly seasonal employment. If we add it up, it means that more people are working for shorter periods of time during the year and becoming increasingly more dependent on the UI program. In 1990, 66 percent of all fish plant workers who qualified for UI did so on the basis of between 10 and 19 weeks of employment.[58]

Underlying all this overcapacity is the fear that what must be done may mean encouraging perhaps half the workforce to find other work as possibly as many as half the processing plants have to close. The Harris panel broadly addresses this question in the conclusions of a long report. They put the "open question" in these terms: Whether the fishery should become the preserve of professional fishers and plant workers, all of whom can earn from it an adequate living; or whether it should continue as at present a social relief mechanism, offering some measure of gainful employment and hence of dignity to a large number of participants most of whom will continue to require income supplementation.[59] No one would envy those making such a choice. What remains to consider is the structure through which such decisions might be made.

FEDERAL-PROVINCIAL CONFLICT

The figures for numbers of processing plants and numbers of fishers given above are interesting in themselves, but they are cited to introduce the issue of federal-provincial divided jurisdiction in the fishery. We understand something now of the various responsibilities of each order of government. In addition to the regulation of vessels, the gear carried, and the quantity and species of fish caught, the federal government licenses commercial fishers by means of a personal registration. To this day access is relatively open. An individual may be similarly qualified for a species licence if one is available.[60] For the future, the question still to be settled is whether access remains open, or becomes restricted to a "professional" group capable of earning a reasonable income.

But individuals who fish must have somewhere to sell their fish, somewhere to have it processed. The character of the fishery is affected by this issue and the licensing of fish processing plants and the labour relations in those plants is the responsibility of the provincial governments. The provinces also have a critical role in the acquisition by fishers of vessels and gear. The Harris panel has pointed out that there is an obvious relationship between all these factors of production and the health of the resource itself. The record of *ad hoc* federal-provincial cooperation on fisheries questions is not encouraging. Two instances are cited to illustrate this point.

First we have some rather pointed data from the Kirby Report. It notes that in the era of plant expansion between 1977 and 1979 the Department of Regional Economic Expansion, with the support of the Department of Fisheries and Oceans, financed a number of "reasonable" cases. However, "in the province of Newfoundland and Labrador, of 34 applications for assistance turned down by federal authorities, 22 plants were nevertheless built with provincial or bank support."[61]

In the second instance, it is the private sector, possibly in league with the provincial government, that rendered federal effort ineffective.[62] In 1979 a subsidiary of H. B. Nickerson and Sons of Nova Scotia applied to DREE for financial aid to build a fish processing plant in Jackson's Arm, Newfoundland. DFO recommended against the application on the grounds that the community already had a plant and the fish resource in White Bay was insufficient to warrant additional processing capacity. DREE accepted the DFO recommendation and rejected the application. Nevertheless the plant was built (reportedly at a cost of $9 million) with a loan from the Royal Bank. After being used only at 12-percent capacity in 1980 and 28 percent in 1981, the plant closed in October 1981.[63] The second Jackson's Arm plant made no economic sense. It is equally clear, however, that DFO was outflanked by the Royal Bank with the help of the province of Newfoundland which, after all, had to license the new plant.

Left to its individual devices, each government pursues conflicting goals. While one jurisdiction seeks to maximize employment, the other may be stressing conservation; while one seeks to decentralize processing to small plants supplied by inshore fishers, the other can promote the interests of large vertically integrated corporations. This conflict matters more in Newfoundland because the fishery matters more than in any other province. About 16 percent of the province's employed population is in the fishery, compared to about 6 percent in Nova Scotia.[64] Such numbers do not convey the extent of the tie between the whole society and the fishery. The Cashin Report calls the dependency "staggering." The report notes that in Newfoundland there are three pulp and paper towns; one mining town and one town based on hydro-electricity. There are a handful of small farming communities and the administrative centres of St. John's and Gander. But "almost all of the other 700 communities in the province depend directly on the fishery. Indirectly, other communities and businesses exist in large measure to provide services to the fishery-dependent communities."[65]

Although the question of the joint federal-provincial management of the fishery was discussed historically[66] it reached a new level of discord in the late 1970s and early 1980s when Premier Peckford of Newfoundland engaged the federal government in the so-called "cod wars."[67] The issue then was the division of the catch between the inshore (Newfoundland) fishery and the offshore fleets that might be licensed from Nova Scotia to fish in "Newfoundland waters."[68] Peckford's administration also tried for and failed to achieve a constitutional transfer of powers. There was little support in Ottawa or in other provincial capitals for such a transfer.[69] The provincial government was more successful in having its preferences met for the inshore fishery. From 1980 onwards, "the inshore fishery was allowed to catch essentially as much as it could, within its seasonal and technological constraints."[70]

Premier Clyde Wells, Peckford's successor, holds the position that joint management does not require constitutional change. Coyne contends that former Prime Minister Brian Mulroney made an offer of joint federal-provincial management during the Meech Lake process, but Wells refused the offer based on his principles and interpretation of the joint management issue.[71] Today the province's view is that there is an already existing model upon which a new form of intergovernmental collaboration can be built. The model is the Canada/Newfoundland Offshore Petroleum Board established in 1985.[72]

There is mounting pressure for some sort of formal federal-provincial management regime. In addition to the model proposed by the provincial government is the recommendation, rather more unclear in detail, coming from the Harris panel. This report too calls for the establishment of a "permanent Federal-Provincial board or commission in the context of which information can be shared, management objectives clarified and coordinated, policy directions, and strategies developed."[73] In the context of these calls for action, the federal government has taken some important, if incomplete measures to reform fisheries management.

MANAGEMENT REFORM

Five months after being appointed minister of fisheries, John C. Crosbie addressed the Fisheries Council of Canada and explained some of the facts about his job.[74] The Annual Groundfish Management Plan involved over 400 allocations among scores of applicants who "seek to bend every rule to harvest everything except what was offered..." All these decisions are required by law to be made by the minister. In a second category of detailed adjudication which had to be done at the ministerial level, were in 1990 the 128 licence appeals coming forward from the Atlantic Licensing Appeal Board, which in turn dealt with decisions by 13 area licensing appeal tribunals. Third, Crosbie listed the "enormous edifice" of 108 advisory committees that had been instituted.

This amazingly frank detail on some of what goes on in the "black box" of fisheries management went on to note that the volume of detail did not include decisions regarding the 200 page *Atlantic Fisheries Regulations*. Obscured from public view was a vast "latticework" of terms and conditions attached to individual fishing licences. These terms and conditions were driven in Crosbie's view, by an *ad hockery* (sic) comprehensible only by looking at the pressures that existed on the day when each individual decision was made. Many of these decisions were dealt with at the regional level. But many, too many, went to headquarters. In Crosbie's view too many senior officials had to commit the time, energy, and effort to prepare individual cases for the minister. The result was that the professional, diligent "leading minds" in the department spent most of their time in a "politically charged swamp" rather that concentrating on broad policies to deal with the industry.

What was needed was to simplify the rules, and to establish an arm's length and accountable regulatory agency. The aim was to have direct contact between those affected and those who make the decisions. A division of functions was required. Five months later the minister published a document, "Fisheries Management, A Proposal for Reforming Licensing, Allocation and Sanctions

Systems" which was the result of consultations between departmental officials, provincial and territorial governments, and industry working groups formed on the Atlantic and Pacific coasts. Three days later the minister introduced legislation in the House of Commons, designed to establish two new arm's length regulatory bodies; one for conservation, and a second for licensing and allocation.[75]

As it turned out, only the first of these bodies, the Fisheries Resource Conservation Council (FRCC), was set up. With members drawn from industry and science the Council was authorized to make formal public recommendations to the minister on TACs and conservation measures for the Atlantic fishery. It was also to serve as the minister's advisor on scientific research and assessment priorities. The chairman is a former executive of Fishery Products International (the largest fish processing company in Newfoundland) and a former clerk of the executive council and secretary to the Cabinet in the Government of Newfoundland. In its first year the Council held extensive public hearings throughout the region before presenting to the minister, in November 1993, its recommendations on TACs and other conservation measures for the coming fisheries year.

The second set of boards (one for the Atlantic and one for the Pacific), which would also operate at arm's length from the minister, were to assume responsibility for licensing, allocation, and sanctions in marine commercial fisheries. These are, of course, the issues at the heart of policy. To take resource conservation "out of politics" is one thing; to achieve the same thing for economic and social policy considerations is quite another. As envisioned by the legislation, the Atlantic board would have consisted of seven members, authorized to establish panels, the latter to be organized along the lines of DFO regions in the Atlantic and by fish species on the Pacific coast. The recommended allocations would be made public before going to the board executive for a final decision.

These proposals came to naught because to the Newfoundland government it meant that at the board level, with each of the five Atlantic provinces represented by one member, Newfoundland could be consistently outvoted. Other provinces eyeing the depleted stocks in the Gulf, could gang up on Newfoundland's prime concern, the northern cod. If there could be no bilateral agreement with Ottawa, there would be no agreement.

The latest proposal for structural change comes from the Cashin Task Force which calls for "Fishing Industry Renewal Boards," operating at arms length from both government and industry. These independent bodies, "composed of experienced, knowledgeable persons" would have as their primary task the long-term renewal in the fishery.[76] "Renewal" in this context means reduction in capacity. Cashin is blunt. "In the long term, the reality is that perhaps half the plant workers, fishermen and crew members will never work in the fishery again."[77]

What evidence we have, however, suggests that few will choose to leave the fishery with even very modest pushing by government. The 1993 "Report of the Auditor General of Canada" points to the reluctance of those in the fishery to train for employment elsewhere. The NCARP participants were required to select one of five program options: training within the fishery, approved fisheries-related work, training outside the fishery, early retirement for those over 55, and minimum payments (by choosing none of the above). The Department of Fisheries and Oceans expected that, of the 19,000 program participants, 33 percent of the fishers (3,000) and 50 percent of the plant workers (5,000) would leave the fishery. As of August 1993, of the 26,338 actual program participants, only 20 percent of the fishers and 30 percent of the plant workers were enroleed in components leading to a possible exit from the fishery. Moreover anyone who enroleed in a program leading to an exit from the fishery was under no obligation to do so.[78]

Having laid out the reluctance of Newfoundlanders attached to the fishery to either train to exit or retire, the Auditor-General's Report goes on to acknowledge an obvious point. "There are limits to what the federal department can be expected to achieve." The majority of NCARP recipients are plant workers, an area of little direct influence by federal authorities. "Any attempt to influence directly the number of plants, the employment practices of plant owners, or the future decisions of individuals to work in a fish plant would intrude directly into provincial jurisdiction."[79]

Parenthetically, one could add that the DFO has faced another limitation, this time within its own government. Until the joint announcement of the new income support program by both the minister of fisheries and the minister responsible for human resource development, the Unemployment Insurance program was not linked to DFO's plans. For perhaps the last 30 years DFO has known what should be done: reduce the numbers attached to the fishery. But unemployment insurance introduced in 1957, has in recent years come to mean income supplementation, not unemployment insurance. Twelve to fourteen weeks of work in any sector of the industry means income for nine or ten months. While fisheries policy might argue for a gradual downsizing, UI regulations continue to attract individuals into the industry.

CONCLUSIONS

The fisheries policy community has regularly had to deal with a variety of crises over the years. In official report after official report, from both federal and provincial governments, recommendations have centred on the need to cut subsidies and reduce the number of families and communities dependent on the industry. But as has been pointed out above, politicians and local fisheries managers have deflected long-term policy goals in order to maintain employment and improve the incomes of fishers. The moratorium when it came, entailed the largest lay-off in Canadian history and the impact was concentrated on the east coast of Newfoundland and Labrador and the lower north shore of Quebec. For some 400 remote rural communities, survival depends on either the fishery or government transfer payments. The choices are that stark.

The crisis of the 1990s will not be solved, however, by continued payments to those affected and hoping for the return of the fish to their previous levels. We, as Canadians, have presided over the depletion of one of the world's great fisheries. Domestic mismanagement has been more than matched by offshore foreign effort. This heavy overfishing, unregulated by any international organization, remains a threat to the stock itself and to that sector of the fishery in Newfoundland that depends on the migration of these same stocks from deep waters offshore to the inshore grounds. For too long Canada's diplomatic efforts remained unfocused and protracted. But as we have already pointed out, Canadian domestic policy has been equally unfocused and uncoordinated. On the one hand, the government recommends capacity reduction; on the other, the total expenditures in transfers and subsidies to the Newfoundland fishery, from both federal and provincial governments, nearly doubled between 1981 and 1990.[80]

Opportunities to follow a new course have been missed. The scientific community has a lot to answer for. Their's is a difficult job — counting fish one cannot see is not easy — and maybe it is their lot in life to be mistrusted. But maybe too they were overconfident, insufficiently cautious, or lacked the humility to recognize that others also knew something worth knowing. Fishers — the good ones, the "highliner" skippers — know their business, even if they lack a formal education. Between about 1986 and 1992, they and their representatives argued long and hard that the resource was in serious trouble. They were largely ignored. It seems a shame that these two bodies of knowledge could not have been integrated long before the current efforts. There does seem to be some improved temper between fishers and scientists today due to the new Fisheries Resources Conservation Council. The scientists make their recommendations public, the Council hears the opinions of those in the industry throughout the region, and in turn, makes its recommendations, in public, to the minister. It seems to be working.

What is not working is the effort to deal with the issue of divided jurisdiction. It has not proved possible to set in place the fisheries equivalent of the Canadian Radio-Television Commission. Crosbie has given us a vivid portrait of the politics surrounding decisionmaking in the Department of Fisheries and Oceans. Undoubtedly, it serves the interests of many of the players in the policy community to retain these processes. But an opportunity has been missed not once but twice to set new structures in place. Undoubtedly, Newfoundland has a special interest in seeing that its vital social and economic concerns are not sacrificed to mere majority voting. But equally, the other Maritime provinces will never agree to any sort of bilateral Newfoundland-Canada management board. In the Gulf of St. Lawrence there has to be regional management.

And we are not talking about a dead issue. There is still fishing in Atlantic Canada. A recent report states that in spite of a cod catch that has fallen by 85 percent, the overall value of the fishery, finfish and shellfish, was worth 25 percent more to the region in 1993 than a decade earlier, even after adjusting for inflation.[81]

None of this, however, deals with the future concerns of the men and women hit by the moratorium. To them the federal government is responsible for what has happened to the northern cod and for the depletion of other stocks of fish throughout the region. In 1977 the Department of Fisheries and Oceans said they could manage the resource. It failed. Therefore, NCARP payments are viewed as *compensation*, something to which the recipients are entitled for the loss of a way of life. The $1.9 billion over the next five years to be spent on income support is not, in fact, seen as transitional aid from the state, as a means to become "job ready" for other employment. In truth, short of some draconian measure unpalatable in a democratic state, the only way to induce individuals out of the fishery is with alternative employment, and that is not going to be easy to provide. In the current circumstances, income support payments have bought time.

But the next step is proving difficult to take. No one would envy governments that must make decisions. But plant workers cannot be left hanging onto the illusion that their fish plant will reopen rather than the plant in the next community. Fishers cannot be led to believe that their gear sector will have enough fish because it will be taken away from another gear sector. If such empty promises are made, then a great many people will simply wait where they are. Like death, the decision to permanently shut a plant would be painful, but it would at least bring closure to the issue. Leaving it to the market place or happenstance, would only serve to further alienate citizens from their governments. Much of the workforce is young, educational and training options are available, and there are community development components in the current income support programs. The provincial government has enunciated a strategic economic recovery program. All of which, taken together, might give people the tools and the opportunity to get on with their lives, to build a future in the new reality, to shape their lives as they have done throughout Newfoundland's extraordinary past. But no one literally and emotionally "attached" to the fishery will make these choices until governments first make theirs.

NOTES

1. The Task Force on Incomes and Adjustment in the Atlantic Fishery, *Charting a New Course: Towards the Fishery of the Future,* Table 15, reports total employment in the entire Atlantic fishery for 1990 as 104,790. The number of individuals receiving compensation for the failure of the northern cod, however, is approximately 35,000 persons. Hence our number for a 50-percent reduction is as stated, based on a nothern cod fishery employing 35,000.

2. Rosemary Ommer, "One Hundred Years of Fishery Crises in Newfoundland," *Acadiensis* (Spring 1994), pp. 5-20.

3. Gordon R. Munro, *A Promise of Abundance: Extended Fisheries Jurisdiction and the Newfoundland Economy,* a Study prepared for the Economic Council of Canada (Ottawa: Minister of Supply and Services, 1980), p. 17, Table 3-1.

4. Ibid., p. 19, Table 3-3.

5. Ibid., p. 19.

6. Edward G. Clarke and Annette M. White, "Identification of the Causes of the Northern Cod Moratorium and the Immediate Effects on the Department of Fisheries and Oceans" unpublished paper, Centre for Newfoundland Studies, Memorial University, August 1993, p. 8.

7. In 1950 the international regulatory agency, the International Commission for Northwest Atlantic Fisheries (ICNAF) divided the waters of Atlantic Canada into various letter and numbered zones. The "northern cod" are the fish stocks in sub-areas 2J3KL. The Grand Banks to the south of Newfoundland are in sub-area 3NO.

8. "Environment versus Fishing," *Fisheries News,* April 1994.

9. Independent Review of the State of the Northern Cod Stock, *Final Report,* submitted by Dr. Leslie Harris, February 1990. Department of Fisheries and Oceans (Ottawa: Minister of Supply and Services, 1990).

10. Ibid., p. 9.

11. Ibid., p. 41

12. Ibid., p. 118.

13. Ibid., p. 46.

14. Ibid., p. 48.

15. D. H. Steele, R. Andersen and J. M. Green, "The Managed Commercial annihilation of Northern Cod," *Newfoundland Studies* 8, 1 (1992): 34-68.

16. Ibid., p. 56.

17. Ibid., p. 63.

18. Harris Report, p. 93.

19. Northern Cod Science Program, *Annual Report 1991/1992,* DFO (Ottawa: Supply and Services, 1993), p. 1.

20. D. L. Alverson, "The Management Challenge," in *The Newfoundland Groundfisheries: Defining the Reality,* Conference Proceedings, Institute of Social and Economic Research, Memorial University, July 1993, pp. 87-88.

21. A. Paul Pross and Susan McCorquodale, *Economic Resurgence and the Constitutional Agenda: The Case of the East Coast Fisheries,* (Kingston: Institute of Intergovernmental Relations, Queen's University, 1987), p. 41.

22. Harris Report, p. 9.

23. Ibid., p. 7.

24. Ibid., p. 8.

25. News Release, Department of Fisheries and Oceans, 2 April 1992.

26. Clarke and White, "Identification of the Causes of the Northern Cod Moratorium," p. 15.

27. Notes for a Statement by the Hon. John C. Crosbie to the Fisheries Council of Canada, Charlottetown, P.E.I., 8 October 1992.

28. Jeffrey Simpson, "Crosbie Hooks the European Community and Lands a Good Fish Deal," *The Globe and Mail,* 22 December 1992.

29. Kevin Cox and Graham Fraser, "EC Gives Promise to Cut Fishing," *The Globe and Mail,* 22 December 1992.

30. Craig Jackson, "'Fed Up' With Fishery Critics, Angry Crosbie Rejects Blame," *Evening Telegram,* St. John's, 21 March 1992.

31. News Release, Government of Canada, 16 April 1993.

32. News Release, Department of Fisheries and Oceans, 10 February 1994.

33. Giles Gherson, "What Price Will Canada Pay for Nabbing Foreign Boats on the High Seas?" *The Globe and Mail,* 5 April 1994.

34. The Globe and Mail, 29 June 1994.

35. Populations and population biomass are two different things. Population refers simply to the number of fish; population biomass means the aggregated weight of fish. A population of 1,000 fish weighing 2 kilograms each would constitute a population biomass of 2,000 kilograms. That same biomass would exist if we had only 100 fish weighing on average 20 kilograms each. (Explanation courtesy of the Harris Report, p. 63)

36. L. W. Coady, "The Groundfish Resource Crisis: Ecological and Other Perspectives on the Newfoundland Fishery," in *The Newfoundland Groundfish Fisheries: Defining The Reality,* Conference Proceedings, Institute of Social and Economic Research, Memorial University, July 1993, pp. 56-93, p. 72.

37. "Environment versus Fishing," *Fisheries News,* April 1994.

38. Task Force on Atlantic Fisheries, *Navigating Troubled Waters: A New Policy for the Atlantic Fisheries,* Michael J.L. Kirby, Chairman (Ottawa: Minister of Supply and Services, 1983), Table 4.2, p. 24. (Hereafter referred to as the Kirby Report.)

39. These links between fishers and federal scientists continue, this time in Nova Scotia. See "Casting a Net of Co-operation," *The Globe and Mail,* 10 August 1994.

40. Northern Cod Science Program, *Annual Report 1991/1992,* pp. 9-21.

41. Harris Report, p. 76.

42. Harris Report, p. 76, quoting J.A. Gulland, *Seals and Fisheries: A Case for Predator Control,* 1971.

43. Ibid., p. 5.

44. Alverson, "The Management Challenge," p. 89.

45. Kirby Report, pp. 19-20.

46. Harris Report, p. 107.

47. Peter R. Sinclair, *The Fisheries Crisis of 1990*, Economic Recovery Commission Discussion Paper no. 1 (St. John's: Government of Newfoundland and Labrador, 1990), p. 10.

48. Kirby Report, p. 67.

49. *Canadian Fisheries Annual Statistical Review 1982*, Table 79. (These figures are quoted by Sinclair, *The Fisheries Crisis of 1990*, p. 12).

50. R.G. Kingsley, "Overview of the Newfoundland and Labrador Groundfish Processing Industry," *The Newfoundland Groundfisheries*, pp. 125-131.

51. Ibid., p. 128.

52. Beverley A. Carter, "Employment in the Newfoundland and Labrador Fishery," in *The Newfoundland Groundfisheries,* pp. 132-165.

53. In 1966, fishery employment accounted for 22.5 percent of total employment in the goods producing industries of Newfoundland; by 1986 it accounted for over 45 percent. These figures reflect employment declines in the mining and forest industries due to changing technology and downsizing in these two industries. Labour flowed to the fishery as it was pushed out of other industries and as government policy pulled employment in one direction, ibid., p. 137.

54. The Task Force on Incomes and Adjustment in the Atlantic Fishery, *Report,* Richard Cashin, Chairman (Ottawa: Minister of Supply and Services, 1993), the Cashin Report. The Task Force adds that about 27 percent of fishermen in the region are 45 years of age or older, p. 8.

55. Carter, in "Employment in the Newfoundland and Labrador Fishery," p. 142.

56. The Cashin Report also draws attention to the lack of "basic Literacy and numeracy skills," in the fishing industry and recommends community-based adult education as the first step in "training for new opportunities," p. 43.

57. Ibid., p. 145.

58. Ibid., p. 162.

59. Harris Report, p. 180.

60. Cashin Report, p. 61.

61. Kirby Report, p. 31.

62. What follows is based on a paper, "Extended Fisheries Jurisdiction and the Current Crisis in Atlantic Canada's Fisheries," by William E. Schrank, Department of Economics, Memorial University, a paper prepared for the annual meetings of the Canadian Economics Association, Calgary, Alberta, June 1994.

63. Ibid., p. 28.

64. Cashin Report, p. 8.

65. Ibid., p. 90.

66. Canada, Royal Commission on Dominion-Provincial Relations, *The Rowell-Sirois Report*, vol. I (Ottawa, 1940), p. 255.

67. Susan McCorquodale, "The Management of a Common Property Resource: Fisheries policy in Atlantic Canada," in Michael M. Atkinson and Marsha A. Chandler (eds.), *The Politics of Canadian Public Policy* (Toronto: University of Toronto Press, 1983), pp. 151-171, p. 124.

68. Douglas M. Brown, "Sea-Change in Newfoundland: From Peckford to Wells," in Ronald L. Watts and Douglas M. Brown (eds.), *Canada: The State of the Federation 1990* (Kingston: Institute of Intergovernmental Relations, Queen's University, 1990), pp. 207-210.

69. Pross and McCorquodale, *Economic Resurgence and the Constitutional Agenda.*

70. Brown, "Sea-Change in Newfoundland," p. 209.

71. Deborah Coyne, *Roll of the Dice* (Toronto: James Lorimar and Company, 1992), p. 128.

72. See David A. Vardy, (until recently the deputy minister, Department of Fisheries, Government of Newfoundland and Labrador.) *Joint Management of the Newfoundland Fishery*, Research and Policy Papers no. 19 (St. John's: Institute for Social and Economic Research, Memorial University, 1994).

73. Harris Report, p. 108.

74. John C. Crosbie, Notes For An Address to the Fisheries Council of Canada, Ottawa, 3 October 1991.

75. 13 May 1993, Bill C-129, an Act to establish the Atlantic Fisheries Board and the Pacific Fisheries Board.

76. Cashin Report, p. 38.

77. Ibid., p. 22.

78. "Report of the Auditor General of Canada, 1993," chap. 15, p. 409, para. 87.

79. Ibid., para. 15.98.

80. Schrank, "Extended Fisheries Jurisdiction," p. 14

81. "Report on the Atlantic Provinces," *The Globe and Mail,* 5 July 1994, p. B15.

6

Post-Modern Ontario and the Laurentian Thesis

David R. Cameron

Pendant les années quatre-vingts et quatre-vingt-dix, l'Ontario est devenu plus distinctif et plus assuré au sein de la fédération qu'il ne l'a été depuis plusieurs générations. Le gouvernement néo-démocratique a mis de l'avant une théorie, centrée sur l'Ontario, d'un «fédéralisme à parts équitables», théorie qui n'est pas représentative du comportement ontarien depuis l'après-guerre. Ce chapitre pose la question quant à savoir si ce changement reflète des changements an plan de la position sociale, économique et politique de la province, ou s'il est simplement le résultat de tendances cycliques et d'un gouvernement fédéral déterminé à ignorer les problèmes de l'Ontario? L'Ontario deviendrait-il une province régionalisée comme les autres?

L'auteur examine trois enjeux en répondant à ces questions : l'effet de l'immigration sur la communauté ontarienne, la nature du développement des partenaires de l'Ontario au sein de la confédération et l'évolution «géo-économique» de la situation ontarienne. Il suggère que la province a été plongé dans un processus complexe de changement structurel depuis la Seconde guerre mondiale, quoique le développement général de la province s'est orienté dans plusieurs directions en même temps. L'attachement politique et sentimental à l'égard du Canada est toujours fort, quoique pas aussi fort qu'il l'a déjà été. La remarquable transformation socio-économique de la région du grand Toronto, éperonnée par l'immigration, contribue probablement à détacher les amarres qui reliaient le Sud de l'Ontario au reste du pays; elle transforme certainement l'image qu'a le Sud de l'Ontario du pays. Avec le Pacte de lauto et le démantèlement des barrières commerciales entre le Canada et les États-Unis, une partie vitale de l'économie ontarienne s'intègre dans une version post-moderne de l'empire laurentien. De nos jours, le siège de l'empire n'est pas à Montréal ou à Toronto, mais dans les banlieues de Détroit, Cleveland et Pittsburgh.

THE PART OF CANADA THAT DARE NOT SPEAK ITS NAME

"The part of Canada that dare not speak its name." Premier Bob Rae described Ontario in these terms in a speech delivered 8 November 1993.[1] He declared that the country seems to have been "based on the premise that everyone else could speak ill of Ontario, and at the same time this inherently wealthy place would continue to bankroll Canada."

The premier argued that the traditional formula for Ontario prosperity of high tariffs and ample resources began to be shaken with the oil and energy shocks of the 1970s. The province's dramatic economic recovery of the 1980s created a false complacency which was rudely shattered at the end of the decade when "the bottom began falling out." The premier identified several of the forces that he perceived to be at work:

- The Free Trade Agreement with the United States demonstrated that Ontario could no longer assume its place in Canada or the world.
- The federal government changed the rules on cost-sharing to the disadvantage of Ontario.
- Ottawa also imposed a high-interest rate policy and introduced cutbacks just at the moment of the province's greatest vulnerability.

Ontario, he contended, had to face this crisis in the absence of the traditional partnership with Ottawa that helped Premier Bill Davis fight off the recessions of the 1970s and 1980s; Mitch Hepburn got more help from Ottawa and fewer burdens than has the NDP government of Ontario.

So convinced was Bob Rae that this abandonment was structural that he asked the consulting firm, Informetrica, to take a hard look at the situation.[2] With this step, Ontario embarked with a vengeance on the cost-benefit analysis of Confederation which has become an increasingly noticeable feature of our federation in the last several decades. In Ontario it is known as the "fair-shares" argument. Other parts of the country have engaged lustily in actuarial federalism for years; now Ontario is doing it too.

Is this just the understandable carping of a government that has found itself in office during the biggest economic slump the province has known in more than half a century? Or is Bob Rae's hunch right? Is a structural shift in Ontario's circumstances and place in Confederation underway? The very fact that the premier of Ontario finds it politically desirable to promote an explicitly Ontario-centred approach to intergovernmental relations is itself an indication that something is going on that is worthy of attention. While some of his postwar predecessors were no slouches when it came to representing Ontario's interests, their chief focus was on integrating provincial needs smoothly into the national interest, or "Ontarianizing" the national interest, rather than loudly asserting the claim that Ontario is one of Confederation's losers. Are the people of Ontario beginning to think of themselves more as Ontarians and somewhat less as Canadians? Is Ontario becoming a region? As a result of the sentiment of adversity, the workings of the national and international economy, the recurring threats of separation emanating from Quebec, the alteration in the province's demographic makeup, or for some other reason, are Ontarians becoming members of a more self-conscious regional community?

If the consciousness of a distinct identity is a necessary component of any self-respecting region or subnational community in Canada, then one might think that the fact that the government of the part of the country that dare not speak its name is daring to speak its name means that Arthur Lower's provocative question, *Does Ontario exist?* is being answered in the affirmative 26 years later. Lower's 1968 article, "Does Ontario Exist?" makes curious reading today, with its talk of "sturdy yeoman," "a peasantry of not very elevated status," and the "poor-white areas" of the province (honestly!).[3] He makes, however, an important point: contrasting Ontario with Nova Scotia, Lower argues that a region with no evident "collective will" is difficult to regard as a unit in any significant sense. In the New Democratic Government of Ontario we certainly have today political leadership that is prepared to act on behalf of the "collective will" of a region; the jury is still out, however, on whether there exists a regional community in Lower's sense for the political leadership to represent.

Understanding the distinctive character — even the existence — of this part of Canada has bedevilled students of Ontario for years. For people living in other parts of Canada it has never seemed that difficult; Ontario is the eternal "other" — the cause of your problems, the imperial and imperious centre, the place where people live high off of someone else's hog, the tilt in Confederation's pin-ball machine, the soulless place where your kids have to go to get work. Nevertheless, what then Ontario Premier John Robarts was fond of calling the "golden hinge" of Confederation and Northrop Frye surmised was "surely one of the most inarticulate communities in human culture"[4] is a difficult place to get to know — unless you happen to live somewhere else.

The Ontario historian, Peter Oliver, wrote an essay in 1975, entitled "On Being an Ontarian," in which he made the following plaintive comment:

> The extent of internal regional diversification, an undeniable lack of social and cultural definition and the pallid picture which exists in literature surely seem reason enough to account for the underdeveloped state of Ontario historiography. Why should anyone attempt to write the history of a region which isn't? Why should historians labour to define regional characteristics of a society so elusive or so bland as to defy definition? The answer of course is that they should not; and the result is that they have not.... Put simply, there seems to have been a tacit, almost unthinking, assumption that a regional approach to Ontario History is neither necessary nor appropriate.[5]

The prefatory comment which the editors and the Board of Trustees of the Ontario Historical Studies Series place before their publications, identifying the emergence and consolidation of the Canadian nation as the principal theme of English-Canadian historiography, notes that:

this theme has been developed in uneasy awareness of the persistence and importance of regional interests and identities, but because of the central role of Ontario in the growth of Canada, Ontario has not been seen as a region. Almost unconsciously, historians have equated the history of the province with that of the nation and have often depicted the interests of other regions as obstacles to the unity and welfare of Canada.[6]

That something significant is going on in Ontario, despite these embarrassed ruminations, will, I hope, be made evident in what follows.[7] The question for us in this chapter is: What does it all amount to? Are we witness to an historic structural shift in the life and fortunes of the Canadians living in this part of the country? Or are we simply observing the cyclical changes that come and go in the life of any community?

Until recently there has been a pronounced reluctance on the part of Ontario politicians to attempt to fashion the ten million Canadians who live in the province into a regional community, abetted by the apparently equally pronounced reluctance of Ontarians to be so fashioned. Province-building has not been the Ontario way. The same reluctance has not been exhibited by analysts and observers who have shown themselves quite willing to enunciate Ontario's position and role in Confederation and to explain provincial policy and the provincial conduct of intergovernmental relations as the logical manifestations of the pursuit of Ontario's interests.

I THINK I'VE HEARD THAT SONG BEFORE: THE CONVENTIONAL UNDERSTANDING OF ONTARIO

Ian Scott was Attorney General of the Province of Ontario during the dying days of the Meech Lake Accord. Contemplating the likely reaction of Québécois to the demise of Meech, he joked that Ontario should say to Quebec: "If you're leaving, we're going with you."

With this zany comment, which helps to explain why so many civil servants delighted to work with him, Scott in fact points to a profound and important reality. The two communities that inhabit what are now the provinces of Ontario and Quebec have a shared historical experience which goes back at least to 1791 when the *Constitutional Act* divided the Province of Quebec into Upper and Lower Canada. As much as anything else, it was the political difficulties these two communities were experiencing in the United Province of Canada that precipitated the Confederation settlement in 1867. A central part of any account of the emergence of modern Canada is the manner in which these two communities, sharing the St. Lawrence River system, sought to advance their interests and prosperity as the country grew.

Indeed, the concept of the commercial empire of the St. Lawrence, rooted in an understanding of the ambitions of central Canada, has been widely employed as a way of explaining the development of British North America and certain of the chief ends that Confederation was meant to serve. The "Laurentian" thesis has helped to account for the privileged positions of Quebec and Ontario, particularly Montreal in the early years, as well as the tensions between "outer" and central Canada which have been such an important feature of Canadian life. The congeries of purposes and aspirations which shaped the ideology underpinning the Laurentian commercial empire was given public policy shape by Macdonald's National Policy.

Macdonald defeated Mackenzie's Liberal government and was restored to power in 1878. He had campaigned on the need for a new economic strategy consisting of three interrelated components. First, the railway to British Columbia would be rapidly completed. Second, tariffs would be raised, increasing the revenues of the central government and affording protection to the infant domestic manufacturing sector. Third, the government would encourage immigration to settle the western agricultural land made accessible by the construction of the railroad, thereby increasing Canadian agricultural production and exports and providing a captive market for eastern manufacturing.[8] While the achievement of the goals that the National Policy sought had to await the world economic recovery at the end of the century, the policy paradigm constructed by Macdonald remained in place for years and in time "the National Policy" imprinted itself on the Canadian imagination as a powerful explanation of why things in Canada are the way they are.

It is my impression that the brooding images of the commercial empire of the St. Lawrence and the National Policy lie behind the views that a great many Canadians outside central Canada (and many within) have of Ontario and Quebec. Prior to the Quiet Revolution in Quebec and prior to the decline of Montreal as the Canadian centre of commerce and finance, it was possible for westerners to speak generically of central Canada. It was not just the "goddamned" CPR that was castigated, it was the financiers and bloated capitalists on St. James Street and Bay Street. St. James Street is now called Rue St. Jacques and has disappeared from the lexicon of occidental infamy, and Montreal has ceded its place of preeminence in national commerce and finance to Bay Street and to Toronto. This complicates the demonizing of central Canada to some extent, but where there's a will there's a way. Quebec's alleged place of privilege is now seen to be the product of an assertive nationalism that can command attention and sympathetic national policies by threats and alarums. This is a view that many Ontarians now share with other parts of English-speaking Canada. Ontario itself, in the eyes of the rest of English-speaking Canada, has had to take the heat pretty much on its own for the bad reputation of the National Policy. It is now regarded as the main beneficiary of Confederation and of the national economic development strategy which has supported it since the nineteenth century.

The conventional understanding of Ontario and its place in Confederation has, or has had, a good deal to recommend it. Regarded by others as the place that has done best out of the country, the province seems to be viewed in the same fashion by its own residents. Again and again, opinion surveys show Ontarians as the least alienated of Canadians and the most likely to believe that their part of the country has not been disadvantaged by its membership in Confederation. Tom Courchene has listed some of the elements of the reality that underlies this conventional understanding of Ontario.[9] He calls them "stylized facts" (only economists can get away with stylizing facts):

- Ontario's size and dominant position have meant that national policy has typically been cast in a pro-Ontario light.
- Ontario has been and is in favour of a strong central government.
- The political activities and loyalties of Ontarians are directed more towards the federal than to the provincial government.
- Management of the big levers of economic stabilization have always been carried out with the Ontario economy in mind.
- Ontarians and their government would much rather block federal or sister-province initiatives contrary to Ontario's interests than acquire greater provincial powers to pursue their interests autonomously.
- Ontario traditionally has supported the erection and maintenance of barriers to international trade and the elimination of barriers to domestic trade.
- Ontario was never, until the 1980s, an innovator in social policy.

Ontario's performance was classically in accordance with this conventional understanding during the 1980-82 period. Its economic, constitutional and intergovernmental policies fitted the traditional paradigm to a "T" as Prime Minister Trudeau in his last administration took the country on a merry ride. Bill Davis backed the central government to the hilt in its unprecedented battle with the other provinces for hegemony and for the loyalty of Canadians. The National Energy Program, FIRA, and the federal constitutional initiative received the active support of the Conservative government of Ontario — as far as one can tell, with the approval of the Ontario population at large. There appears to have been an acceptance both of the reassertion of federal power and of the economic and constitutional policies by which this reassertion was expressed.[10]

WE THOUGHT WE KNEW YOU: OFF-SIDE IN THE EIGHTIES

If a far-reaching realignment of forces within Ontario is underway and if the province's position within Canada is being redefined, the 1980s will surely count as a crucial decade in that process. The liberation of international capital, abetted by the dominant right-wing ideology, was reshuffling the deck for many countries and subnational jurisdictions during this period, but the province, experiencing forces relatively unknown elsewhere in the country, began to march to its own drummer, and in several fields the Government of Ontario began to behave in uncharacteristically un-Ontarian ways.[11]

SOCIAL AND ECONOMIC FACTORS

The provincial economy, which had lagged behind that of the rest of the country during the 1970s, roared back to life after the 1981-82 recession. Real annual growth averaged 5.9 percent between 1983-89, not just out-pacing the rest of the country, but most of the industrialized world as well. Almost 900,000 new jobs were added during the 1980s, 47 percent of all the new jobs created in Canada.

The booming economy acted as a magnet for internal migration and immigration, and most of the new arrivals came to the Greater Toronto Area. Ontario's share of immigration rose to over 50 percent, and despite the influx unemployment fell to 5 percent by 1988, almost three points below the national average. Toronto, which for three decades has received more than twice its share of immigrants, continued to display the most rapid increase in ethnic diversity in the country.

The robust economy generated some other forces in Ontario's society. It produced buoyant provincial government revenues at a time when most other jurisdictions were feeling the pinch. Combined with the rapid and concentrated population growth, economic development strained southern Ontario's infrastructure and many of its social services. Towards the end of the decade, an over-heated economy created localized inflationary pressures which shaped national monetary policy. In 1988, for example, annual consumer price index increases were close to 7 percent, while the national figure was well under 5 percent.[12]

One of the national trends observed in the 1980s received powerful expression in Ontario. Michael Adams and Mary Jane Lennon wrote in the 1990 edition of *Canada: The State of the Federation* of the increasingly centrifugal nature of Canadian attitudes.[13] In examining FOCUS CANADA data they found that there was a decline in the importance Canadians attach to certain symbols of Canadian identity, such as the national anthem, the prime minister's office, multiculturalism, bilingualism, the Governor General — even hockey.[14] They also reported significant increases in regional identification. Between 1980 and 1990 there was a 13-percent drop nationally in the proportion of respondents who said they identify more with Canada than with their province. All regions recorded a decline. Predictably, a higher proportion of Ontarians identified with the country as a whole than was the case anywhere else, both in 1980 and 1990, but what is of particular interest to our review is the fact that the fall-off was greater in Ontario than anywhere else — a 17-percent drop, five points greater than the next largest which was in the west, including British Columbia.[15]

POLITICS

Much to the puzzlement of the rest of the country, Ontario's politics were sharply distinct from those elsewhere during this period. In the middle years of the decade, while much of Canada and most of the Western world was moving sharply right, Ontario was moving left.[16] The international wave of neo-conservatism washed over Ottawa and many other parts of the country, but it found only a faint echo in Ontario. In 1985 David Peterson's Liberal Party, with the help of a formal accord with the NDP, replaced the 42-year old Conservative dynasty which had held office continuously for longer than any other administration in modern Canadian history. The 1985 election was a very close run thing, with Frank Miller's Conservatives getting 52 seats to the Liberals 48 and the NDP's 25, and the Liberals in fact beating the Tories by one point in the popular vote. Two years later, the Liberals were returned to office with a thumping majority.

The Ontario Liberals, in office until 1990, were consistently at odds with the Mulroney Conservatives who swept into power in 1984 with an unstable coalition of forces heavily dependent on western Canada and Quebec, and much inclined to view Ontario as the over-privileged child of Confederation. Partly as a consequence of this configuration of national political forces, the federal government became less attentive to the needs of Ontario and in fact was not above drawing political benefit elsewhere from policies that disadvantaged the province.[17]

As a party espousing positive, activist government in a period of rapid provincial growth, the Liberals were in clear ideological conflict with a federal Conservative Party hostile to big government and civil servants, and to the social policy and the public-private mix of enterprise Canada had known for years. The Meech Lake Accord aside, on which they agreed, the two governments appeared to be in disagreement on most public policy issues in which they were both involved, although the Peterson government's resistance to several federal initiatives seemed to be half-hearted.[18]

POLICIES

The pounding economic engine of southern Ontario drove metropolitan Toronto and the area around it forward, spawning a wide range of public policy pressures. As people poured into the region from all over, housing was increasingly expensive and in short supply; massive construction sites around Toronto were transformed into new communities; sewers, roads, public transportation, schools, hospitals were old, in the wrong place, or simply inadequate to meet the demand. Immigration altered the racial character of the city, creating problems of adjustment. Writing at the end of the decade, H.V. Nelles describes what faced the Government of Ontario during this period:

> The political challenge in Ontario is, first, to service growth with schools, hospitals, roads, subdivisions; second, to mediate social conflict with equity, welfare, and distributional social policies that integrate disparate groups; and third, to direct change in a way so as not to alienate the vested majority. And all of this must be done with taxes raised at home.[19]

Ontario, under David Peterson, worked closely with Quebec, Ottawa, and other provinces on the Meech Lake Accord and put substantial effort into bilateral cooperation with Quebec to try to ensure that the links between the country's two largest provinces would be strong and amicable. In keeping with the spirit of the times, it became very active on the international front, among other things becoming the North American member of the "Four Motors of Europe," a kind of international summit of subnational, hi-tech regions located in Germany, France, Spain, and Italy. The Peterson government criticized the Bank of Canada for what it saw as its obsession with fighting inflation, although here it was following the traditional pattern of its predecessors and of most of the other provincial governments of the era. More distinctively, it also fought the Government of Canada on the question of the Free Trade Agreement (FTA) with the United States.

Its FTA position, which occasioned a rift between Queen's Park and Bay Street, recreated the curious alliance between the largest and the smallest provinces in Confederation that was a feature of the patriation battle in 1980-82. Although this time Prince Edward Island and Ontario stood alone against all other jurisdictions, including the federal government. The anti-FTA position of the province was greeted with contradictory reactions, suggesting perhaps the degree to which the old categories of understanding were being corroded. Some people, especially in Quebec, reacted with amazement, contending that it was almost unbelievable that the Peterson government could act in a way that was directly and manifestly contrary to the interests and requirements of the province. Others saw in this action yet another coarse demonstration of central Canadian self-interest as Ontario moved to protect its privileged position in the old federal system, whatever the cost to other members might be. Was Peterson flouting or advancing Ontario's interests? His critics could not seem to agree, and his supporters were not too sure either.

"I WANTED TO BE PREMIER IN THE WORST WAY:"
THE NDP IN THE NINETIES

While the election of the New Democratic Party on 6 September 1990 was one of the most "efficient" victories on record — the NDP won a majority with only 37 percent of the popular vote — the important thing about it from the point of view of our story is that the left-leaning inclinations of the provincial electorate continued. Votes for the NDP rose by 12 percent, votes for the Liberals fell by 15 percent, and support for the Tories remained virtually unchanged at just under a quarter of the popular vote. The Government of Ontario's distinctive and unconventional behaviour also continued, albeit under an NDP mantle and in the midst of a severe economic downturn.

Bob Rae has joked that he wanted to be premier in the worst possible way — and he got his wish. Certainly he and his party had the misfortune to assume office on the cusp of the most severe recession in decades. Having flown so near the sun in the 1980s, Ontario's descent was the more precipitous when it came. There has been in recent years a burst of economic pessimism about the "de-industrialization of Ontario" reminiscent of the identification of a permanent westward shift in "the terms of trade" much bruited about after the run-up of energy prices in 1979. In an as yet unpublished paper, H.V. Nelles has challenged the gloomy talk about the decline of Ontario. Examining Statistics Canada data for the period from 1983-92 he finds that Ontario has become more dominant in the national economy and its residents richer relative to the rest of the country. In addition, he notes that Quebec's economy is slightly more than half the size of Ontario's, and getting smaller, arguing that it is the Quebec economy, not Ontario's, that is in relative decline in central Canada.[20]

The Statistics Canada data cited by Nelles, however, obscure the fact that, while the descent began at a higher point, the Ontario economy fell further faster than most other parts of the country. Between 1989 and 1992 unemployment in the province went from 5.8 percent to 11.3 percent, as a rash of plants closed and lay-offs occurred. Individual unemployment insurance claimants rose to over 1.2 million in 1992, and 10 percent of the province was on social assistance in 1993.[21] Toronto's unemployment rate, now equivalent to that of Montreal, has been above the national average during the recession.

After a controversial first budget, more in tune with the booming eighties than the depressed nineties, the NDP government reined in its expenditures and attempted to control the growth in the deficit as the provincial economy fell in. The inexorable logic of expanding public sector debt bleached most conventional social democratic ideology out of provincial fiscal policy. The social-contract process for securing significant restraint in the larger public sector was a valiant attempt to find a way to cut back as if social democracy mattered.

Federal policy exacerbated an already worsening situation, as can be seen most clearly in the field of social assistance.

While a series of alterations by Ottawa to unemployment insurance, training, housing and refugee programs all increased the burden on provincial social assistance programs, the big ticket item was the unilateral 1990 decision of the federal government to put the lid on growth in Canada Assistance Plan transfers to the provinces not receiving equalization (Ontario, Alberta, and British Columbia). This was a frontal assault on those provinces, particularly on Ontario where the recession was fiercest and the growth in the social assistance bill highest. CAP-eligible expenditures in Ontario rose from just over $3 billion in 1988-89 to close to $8 billion in 1992-93; by the end of 1994-95 the federal government's decision will have cost the province of Ontario about $7 billion. And, so far, despite the fact that the policy is supported by no defensible principle or rationale, the Liberal government, which inherited the arrangement from the Tories, is not budging on Ontario's demands to restore its full share of CAP funding.[22] The Province of Quebec is now receiving 10 percent more federal funds than Ontario under this program with 43 percent fewer beneficiaries.[23]

More than any other single thing, the federal initiative to "cap the CAP" provoked a reconsideration within the Government of Ontario of the costs and benefits of federalism. Faced with a recession-driven explosion in social assistance expenditures, the federal decision was a formative event in shaping the attitude and outlook of the new NDP government.[24] It highlighted an apparent bias in federal policymaking; in reaction, the premier and his Cabinet colleagues elaborated a "fair-shares" theory of federalism and began to introduce it into public debate. The ten studies prepared by the Ottawa consulting firm, Informetrica, analyze in exhaustive detail the full range of major intergovernmental fiscal and program arrangements as they relate to Ontario, thereby providing the intellectual underpinnings for this theory, which has been complicated, but by no means nullified by the accession to government of the federal Liberals, with all but one of Ontario's seats in Parliament.[25]

Grounded in what is in recent memory the unfamiliar contention that Ontario has not been treated fairly by the federal government in the allocation of the benefits and burdens of Confederation, the critique is in some respects a throw-back to earlier periods in Ontario's political history. For example, Oliver Mowat, Premier of Ontario from 1872 to 1896 and the real father of the provincial rights school, took on John A. Macdonald in a battle for provincial control over provincial resources, and Mitch Hepburn fought the Mackenzie King government's desire to secure greater fiscal dominance in the federation.

As the national and international ground shifts beneath Ontario's feet, there is a growing realization at Queen's Park, less so in the province at large, that the postwar verities that have defined Ontario's place in Confederation no

longer hold true. In an article published several years ago, H.V. Nelles speculated that Ontario might become the Quebec of the 1990s. He argued that:

> Ontario will likely become much more assertive and determined to pursue its own
> agenda in national and international councils. In the process, Ontario's self-
> conscious identity as a distinct society, with imperatives separate from those of
> other provinces in the federation, will grow.[26]

How right, so far, he seems to have been.

Ontario has displayed a determination to set its own course in other fields as
well. One of the first of the initiatives of the new government in 1990 was to
recognize the inherent right of self-government of Aboriginal peoples in the
province. "The Statement of Political Relationship," signed on Mount Mackay
on 6 August 1991, confirmed a commitment the premier had made in a speech
the previous October, just weeks after being elected, making Ontario the first
Canadian government to formally recognize the inherent right. This step and
the policy and program activism that followed it, reflect the strong personal
commitment of the premier and senior colleagues such as Bud Wildman,
Minister Responsible for Native Affairs, to address the aboriginal question. The
province showed a determination to move its agenda forward, even in the face
of flagging interest on the part of the Conservative government in Ottawa, and
it was at Ontario's insistence that the four aboriginal organizations were fully
included in the Charlottetown round of constitutional negotiations.

The Charlottetown Accord itself was another field in which a new Ontario
approach could be discerned. In previous rounds of constitutional discussion
Ontario could be expected to play the role of honest broker, not advancing
specific priorities of its own, but seeking to throw its weight behind the forces
of compromise and broadly acceptable change. Sometimes, as in the case of the
Confederation for Tomorrow Conference in 1967, that meant crossing the
federal government and offering some carefully designed interprovincial leadership; sometimes, as in the 1982 patriation round, that meant backing Ottawa
and a package of measures that had broad popularity but which was resisted by
most of the provinces.

In these and other rounds, prior to Charlottetown, it seems fair to say that
Ontario did not fundamentally *care* about constitutional change; it had no
constitutional aspirations of its own, except to ensure that all of the actors came
away from the table reasonably satisfied with arrangements that kept the
country ticking over. Ontario's interests were in the preservation and the smooth
functioning of the system itself. Peterson played that role classically in the
Meech period, carrying system loyalty at the price of provincial abnegation so
far during June 1990, when he offered up six Ontario Senate seats, that his
actions became a factor in his defeat in the provincial election that followed
shortly thereafter. Certainly, senior officials with the incoming NDP were in no

doubt that Premier Peterson's preoccupation with constitutional issues and national unity played a large role in his defeat.

During the Canada round the situation was quite different. Ontario had precise objectives both with respect to the *process* by which constitutional discussion should proceed and with respect to the *substance* of eventual constitutional change, and the province pushed these aggressively throughout. Fearing that Ottawa and Quebec would manufacture a take-it-or-leave-it proposition for the rest of the country as the count-down to Quebec's threatened referendum on sovereignty approached, Ontario rallied other provinces and put heavy (and successful) pressure on Ottawa to agree to a multilateral process; as noted above, it also was able to bring aboriginal representatives fully in to the negotiations.

As for the substance or the agenda of constitutional discussion, Ontario, acting true to traditional form, wanted to ensure that proposals acceptable to Quebec were contained in whatever emerged from the discussions, even though Quebec itself was not at the table to defend its own interests. It had, however, quite uncharacteristically, several clearly developed priorities of its own. First, it sought to have the inherent right of aboriginal self-government entrenched in the constitution. Second, it wanted to have a social charter inserted in the constitution as a way of confirming the commitment of Canadians and their governments to the social infrastructure which increasing numbers of people identified with their citizenship.[27] Third, it made the formal argument that there should be constitutional expression of a stronger Canadian economic union, a priority that became somewhat frayed towards the end of the process as concerns about limiting provincial capacity to pass progressive legislation grew.[28] Finally, Ontario resisted as best it could the demands of "outer Canada" for a full-scale Triple-E Senate, both for its own sake and because it felt certain that Quebec, absent from the talks, would be unable to accept this proposal either. Against a powerful Triple-E Senate, it argued in favour of the democratic principle of representation by population.

I think it is fair to say that Ontario has never had a constitutional agenda as explicit, as distinctive, and as well developed as it had during the Charlottetown round. Despite that fact, it would be possible to argue that Ontario's concerns, while identified and advanced with unusual self-consciousness and energy, were nevertheless concerns about how the country might be made to run better, rather than bids for more power or position for Ontario itself, and, in that sense, in the traditional mould. That would be generally true, although the province's resistance to Triple-E has about it the strong flavour of protecting Ontario's interest. Having said that, the province's behaviour in the last round of constitutional discussions remains out of the ordinary. It is possible that some of the reasons for this were circumstantial:

- The existence of a federal government aggressively assaulting the transfer system and showing no serious interest in significant social policy reform.

- A federal government as well which was opposed to the multilateral process until forced to enter it, and which was divided and ambivalent about it thereafter.

- The absence of Quebec from most of the negotiations.

- The personal commitment of the political leadership in Ontario to the aboriginal issue.

- A party/ideological interest in embedding social rights in the constitution.

Nevertheless, the pattern on the constitution does fit comfortably into the role played by the generally more assertive province that Ontario has become in recent years. How does it link up with fair-shares federalism? That is not altogether clear. However, it is possible to reconcile fair-shares federalism and Ontario's Charlottetown agenda by contending that the former could lead logically to the more balanced, equitable, and stable approach envisaged in the social charter, and that it does no one any good to have the province making the largest net contribution to Confederation increasingly sullen and discontent with its role. The Government of Ontario has not set its face against the redistribution system embedded in the formal equalization arrangements. What it has objected to is the kind of implicit double equalization reflected in the cap on CAP and in other federal-provincial programs. If left unaddressed for too long, however, the concern with fair shares could encourage a growing withdrawal of Ontario from the affairs of the federation and an attempt to wrest greater fiscal and policy control from Ottawa so that Queen's Park can act autonomously on its own behalf.[29]

THE TRANSFORMATION OF ONTARIO

Let us, in the light of all that has been said above, return to the basic question we asked at the beginning of this chapter. It seems clear that politically, economically, and demographically, much has been going on in Ontario over the past decade that distinguishes this period of Ontario history from its recent past and that has set it apart from much that has been happening elsewhere in the country. How are we to understand this phenomenon? How are we to make sense of it?

There is a tendency, when confronted with these situations, to reach for a single, clear, and simple explanation for what is going on, but this is probably not the course of wisdom. A society of ten million people is nurtured by many streams and sources, sustained by many activities and institutions, and altered by many impacts and influences. Many phenomena point in more than one direction at once, and their full implications are unclear. It seems likely that the energy that has been put into improving Ontario's relations with its Aboriginal Peoples has its source in the strong personal commitment of Bob Rae — yet a review of the last three decades reveals a steadily accelerating tempo of activity in this field, spanning three different governments. The fact that Ontario moved left while the world moved right may be just one of those things that happens occasionally — yet the demographic and commercial expansion of southern Ontario in the 1980s and the pressures it created made the election of a series of activist governments with a social conscience perfectly reasonable. The apparent decline of national sentiment in Ontario may just be part of the ebb and flow of feelings of identification characteristic of many decentralized regimes — yet the decline is evident everywhere in Canada and the drop is greatest, as we have seen, in Ontario. The conflict between Queen's Park and Ottawa during the past decade may be accounted for simply by the play of partisan politics — yet the cap on CAP has been sustained by the Liberals, notwithstanding their massive representation from Ontario. The uncharacteristically aggressive role played by Ontario in the Charlottetown constitutional talks may be explained simply by the unusual circumstances that prevailed after the demise of Meech — yet it might also herald the emergence of what Nelles calls "Ontario's self-conscious identity as a distinct society."

If Ontario is being transformed in ways that are deeper, more permanent, and more fateful than the incremental adjustment of the simple onward march of events would indicate, there are, I would suggest, three areas where one might look for evidence of this fact: the impact of immigration on the Ontario community; the nature of the development of Ontario's partners in Confederation; and Ontario's "geo-economic" situation.

IMMIGRATION

Immigration is now overwhelmingly an urban phenomenon and it is primarily a story of three provinces — British Columbia, Quebec, and Ontario. Indeed, it is largely a story of Canada's three metropolitan centres: the Lower Mainland of Vancouver, Montreal Island, and the Greater Toronto Area. The concentration of immigration in a few large urban centres places them on a development trajectory markedly different from that of the rest of the country. The civilizations in creation in these large metropolitan regions have less and less to do with the life led in the rest of the country, but their magnetism and power have the capacity to transform the rest of the country nevertheless. That their influence has not already been greater is probably explained in part by the fact that they are constitutionally the creatures of the provinces whose seams they are bursting and by the fact that their collective energies are blunted by political division into a multiplicity of municipalities and a relatively weak metropolitan government structure.

Toronto has moved down this late twentieth century development path more rapidly than any other part of the country. For more than three decades Toronto has received nearly twice its share of immigrants; as a consequence it has grown more rapidly than the rest of the country and has demonstrated the most rapid increase in ethnic diversity. The Canadian reality as it is experienced in metropolitan Toronto is a polyethnic, multiracial, pluralistic, urban society, further accentuating the existing regional differentiation that exists within the province. It is difficult to believe that the aspirations and preferences of this society, which contains the largest concentration of population and the most powerful economy in the country, will not make its presence powerfully felt in national affairs. That is already starting to happen. Its priorities will be focused on making this kind of community function effectively, on working out what is required for sane race relations, equity, economic development, welfare, health, education, and social services. The willingness of a community such as this to accede to an image of the nation that turns on the historic relationship between French-speaking and English-speaking people is likely to decline over time. It is possible that its willingness to support a set of redistributional policies based on an increasingly tattered Confederation settlement will decline over time as well. The Canadian Charter of Rights and Freedoms speaks to a community such as this with an authority that historical narratives having to do with the accommodation of two great language communities in British North America cannot rival.

A highly pluralistic society is likely to espouse the values of freedom, equality, equity, and open access in a system serving all; to the extent that collective identities are in play, they will not be defined by region or biculturalism. What will this society have in common with Chicoutimi, 90 percent of whose residents are French in origin, or with St. John's, 93 percent of whose population is British? Never in their wildest dreams did the Fathers of Confederation contemplate such a state of affairs; it is small wonder that the constitutional structure which they fashioned will have to struggle mightily to contain these demographic forces in the twenty-first century.

ONTARIO'S CONFEDERATION PARTNERS

Ontario's evolution obviously does not take place in a vacuum. The country as a whole has been changing at a steady clip, pushed by international forces and by development impulses in many regions of Canada. We have witnessed (and been changed by) Quebec's remarkable transformation during the last 30 years, a bubbling energy that has imposed major stress on the federation. Alberta's economic circumstances have waxed and waned radically with the international and domestic politics of oil and gas. New Brunswick is seeking to forge a path to much greater self-reliance, in the belief that the old ways will not hold for much longer. British Columbia is redefining its identity and shaping its future as a Pacific Rim society. All parts of the country are looking outward to secure or establish their economic prospects.

Each set of provincial and local circumstances feeds into all the others and all contribute to the shaping of our national politics. There is an uneasiness and an incipient attitude of *sauve qui peut* in our politics just now and in the behaviour of the various regions of the country, and a disengagement from national affairs that can be felt in many Canadian communities. The end of the Cold War made the Western Alliance obsolescent and radically trimmed the security function of Western states. The expansion of free trade — whether in the guise of GATT, the FTA, or NAFTA — corroded the link between patriotism and economic enterprise, creating zones of legitimate economic interest that transcend the borders of nation-states. When Northern Telecom, for example, decides to relocate its 650-job telephone switching equipment unit from Aylmer, Quebec, to Georgia, it is difficult in the present environment to charge the firm with being un-Canadian; if it makes good business sense, who can reasonably stand against it? Canadians, who used to acknowledge the competence of the federal government, whatever they may have thought of the substance of federal policy, now are more inclined to regard Ottawa as a debt-ridden burden on the nation, frequently impeding growth, rather than stimulating it. As a consequence of these and other factors, the sense that we are all in it together has faded: Who are we and what is it?

ONTARIO'S CHANGING GEO-ECONOMIC SITUATION

Much has been said and written about Ontario's place in the domestic and international economy; the variety of the comments suggest the complexity of the reality. Let us begin by noting some features of Ontario's economic situation which a review of the data reveals.

- Ontario has become less reliant on the Canadian market and more reliant on the U.S. market in its output of primary and manufactured goods. Between 1979 and 1986, sales to the rest of Canada dropped from 22.6 percent to 15.9 percent of total sales while exports to the United States increased from 24.6 percent to 31.9 percent.[30] All of Ontario's foreign export growth during this period was accounted for by auto and auto parts sales to the United States. It is presumably such data as these that led H.V. Nelles to state flatly that "Ontario is the least reliant of all the provinces upon the national market."[31] The trend may have ended in the late 1980s; data indicating destination of supply in

1989 show sales to the rest of Canada increasing to 18.8 percent of the total, with a corresponding decrease in international exports.[32]

- With respect to the export of services, Ontario, with 13.3 percent of its total supply being exported interprovincially, stands in seventh place, after Manitoba, P.E.I., Alberta, Nova Scotia, Saskatchewan, and New Brunswick. The concentration in Ontario of national commercial and financial services (banking, insurance, investment, communications, transportation) is not evident from this indicator. As for international exports, Ontario comes fifth, after Saskatchewan, B.C., New Brunswick, and P.E.I.[33]

- In terms of total supply (primary and manufactured goods plus services), among the three largest provinces, Ontario during the 1980s was less dependent on the rest of Canada as a market than was Quebec, but substantially more reliant on the national market than B.C.[34] Whatever one might say about Newfoundland's dependence on fiscal transfers derived from other more prosperous parts of the country, in 1989 it was the least reliant of all provinces on the national market for the sale of its goods and services.

- Ontario's reliance on imports from the rest of Canada is low and was declining during much of the 1980s, from a figure of 11.1 percent in 1984 to 8.8 percent in 1989.[35] In the latter year, it was the least reliant of the provinces on interprovincial imports, and depended more heavily than other provinces on international imports.[36]

- Ontario and Quebec were the only two provinces to register an interprovincial trade surplus in total goods and services in 1989, although Ontario's, at $21.9 billion, was 12 times larger. Both had substantial international trade deficits. Ontario and Alberta were the only two provinces to record a positive total trade balance in 1989 ($12.7 billion for Ontario).[37]

- Finally, one of the Informetrica studies commissioned by the Government of Ontario examines the system of redistribution of resources among the provinces. Using Statistics Canada Provincial Economic Accounts data, it found that in 1991 residents of Ontario contributed almost $15.5 billion or 5.5 percent of Ontario's Gross Domestic Product to the federal government for redistribution to other parts of the country. The other two provinces making positive contributions in 1991 were British Columbia ($3.8 billion, 4.6 percent of GDP) and Alberta ($2.8 billion, 3.9 percent of GDP). On a per capita basis, this amounts to $1,506 per Ontario resident, as compared to per capita amounts of $1,200 for B.C. and $1,106 for Alberta.

What do these data suggest about the economy of Ontario and its prospects? They do not, it seems to me, speak with a single voice or point to an easily understandable linear direction of development. Taken together, they do appear to suggest that the two provinces least reliant on the rest of Canada are the two provinces making the largest fiscal contribution to the rest of the country, namely, Ontario and British Columbia. Both make net contributions to the federation and both display a relatively high level of international activity, B.C. being more diversified in its international trading patterns than Ontario. Ontario's manufacturing sector is shaped more by its extensive integration into the North American auto industry than by any other single factor. The state of Michigan is Ontario's biggest trading partner by far. So intimate and seamless are the operations of this industry, constructed on the basis of the 1965 Canada-U.S. Auto Pact, that it seems almost to be a misnomer to describe the exchanges that occur under this umbrella as "international trade." Ontario's economic fortunes are radically dependent on the health of this North American industry; all other international trade of the province pales in significance by comparison.

Services compose as large a part of the national economy and of the economy of each province as do primary and manufactured goods, but the trading of services is much more heavily concentrated within the given province, reflecting in part the fact that such services as retail trade and a wide range of personal services are naturally consumed within the province. [38] Ontario's domestic consumption figure of 79.1 percent in 1989 is not out of line with that of other provinces, nor is its interprovincial and international trading pattern.

The integration of Ontario's manufacturing sector into the United States' economy, a process that has been going on for three decades in the automobile industry, seems almost certain to affect public attitudes and politics in the long run, particularly when it is fostered and legitimized by a series of high-profile trade agreements, such as GATT, the FTA, and NAFTA. It is possible that the decline in the national sentiment of Ontarians and the fair-shares federalism rhetoric of its government are rooted in part in this profound economic phenomenon. Yet it is clear that the Ontario economy is made up of much more than the manufacturing sector, and that much of the rest of the province's economic activity is of quite a different character. In addition, economics is by no means the sole factor shaping public attitudes and politics.

THE LAURENTIAN THESIS REVISITED

Let us return now to the Laurentian thesis and Ontario's position in the country. Ralph Heintzman has pointed to the ambiguity that lies at the heart of the concept of the commercial empire of the St. Lawrence:

> the St. Lawrence river system always pointed into the heart of the continent just as much as it did toward the Canadian west, perhaps rather more so. It was

political, military and cultural factors, not economic ones, that cut off the river
system from its "natural" hinterland below the Great Lakes, and they always
retained the power to knit up the old breach.[39]

Donald Creighton in fact acknowledged this ambiguity in a passage that is
worth quoting at length:

> This Laurentian theme has its basis in the fact that the St. Lawrence is one of the
> great river systems that leads from the Atlantic seaboard to the heart of the
> continent of North America. Its owners, the Canadians, have held in it a unique
> possession; and the realization of its potentialities has been one of the most
> persistent and compelling aims of their existence as a people. The river has
> inspired generations of Canadians to build a great territorial empire, both com-
> mercial and political, in the western interior of the continent. The prime feature
> of this imperial drive is therefore western expansion — expansion across the
> continent to the Pacific Ocean. At first, during the French regime and the early
> days of British rule, the undivided west was sought as a whole; but after the Treaty
> of 1783 had drawn an unnatural and unhistorical boundary line across the middle
> of the continent, the Canadians were faced with a choice between two alternatives
> and two quite different kinds of western expansion. They could seek to gain either
> an international commercial empire on both sides of the new boundary or a
> commercial and political empire to the north of it.[40]

The latter was the course the British North Americans were driven to choose
and Confederation provided the institutional architecture for the accomplish-
ment of that ambition. For generations Ontario was the junior partner in this
enterprise, but with the development of the North American economy after the
Second World War, the centre of Canadian commerce and finance shifted
decisively from Montreal to Toronto[41] and Ontario assumed preeminence. With
the Quiet Revolution Quebec disengaged from its fading national economic
mandate and the mantle fell more heavily on the shoulders of Ontario.

The times, however, were changing. Postwar North American economic
integration contributed to the step-by-step scrapping of the residual economic
elements of the old National Policy and the dismantling of the policy paradigm.[42] A recent Statistics Canada study of structural change in the manufacturing sector from 1970 to 1990 concludes:

> Structural change has taken place continuously in Canada throughout the post-war
> period as successive tariff reductions have reduced the protection enjoyed by
> Canadian industries. GATT rounds of tariff reductions, the US-Canada free trade
> pact, and the North American Free Trade Pact have led to successive reductions
> in tariffs that have increased export opportunities for some industries and in-
> creased competition from imports for others.[43]

The liberalization of trade effectively reduces the significance of the political
border upon which Canada was built and alters the logic of Ontario's geopoliti-
cal situation. Geography and economics begin to prevail over politics, and the

earlier potentiality of the commercial empire of the St. Lawrence to which Creighton alludes begins to reassert itself — in reverse — in post-modern garb. The builders of economic empires in the heart of the North American continent no longer inhabit the shores of the St. Lawrence, and have not for a long time, but live in the suburbs of Detroit, Cleveland, and Pittsburgh.

> The shadow of the old southern empire has fallen across the northern empire from the start: it has never ceased to beckon the St. Lawrence back to its earliest vocation as an avenue of commerce for the whole continent. Today, as at every other moment in its history, this tension or ambiguity lies at the heart of the Laurentian system.[44]

What continuous structural change in its material conditions has meant for Ontario is the inexorable realignment of vital parts of its economy away from the rest of Canada and towards the United States. Ontarians as citizens and patriots may still look east and west; as workers and managers — as economic actors — many now look south. Has Ontario been going through structural change? Yes, for years. Perhaps the adjective is neither necessary nor helpful. If politics and culture follow economics, then Ontario may have embarked on a journey whose ultimate destination point seems clear. If, however, as I believe, economics, politics and culture are siblings and rivals, not links in a causal chain, then Ontario's future remains to be constructed rather than deconstructed — and that is much more interesting.

NOTES

1. Bob Rae, "Join Us to Make Canada Work Again," speech to the Provincial Renewal Conference, Toronto, 8 November 1993.

2. The papers, while clearly commissioned to serve a political purpose, contain masses of data and useful information for the student of Ontario government and politics. Six were released on 8 November 1993:

   • The Distribution of Federal Spending and Revenue: Implications for Ontario and Other Provinces.
   • Review of the Established Programs Financing System.
   • Ontario and the Canada Assistance Plan.
   • The Consequences of Deficit Shifting for Ontario.
   • Labour Market Development and Training.
   • Recent Canadian Monetary Policy: National and Regional Implications.

   The last four of the series were released in August 1994:

   • Immigration Settlement in Canada and Ontario.
   • Social Housing.
   • Ontario and the Unemployment Insurance System.
   • Regional and Industrial Development Assistance.

3. A.R.M. Lower, "Does Ontario Exist?" *Ontario History* 60 (June 1968): 64-69. The quotations are from p. 64.

4. Northrop Frye, *The Bush Garden: Essays in the Canadian Imagination* (Toronto: Anansi, 1971), pp. 7-8.

5. Peter Oliver, *Public and Private Persons: The Ontario Political Culture 1914-1934* (Toronto: Clarke, Irwin and Company, 1975), pp. 7-8.

6. See, for example, *Sir Oliver Mowat* by A. Margaret Evans (Toronto: University of Toronto Press, 1992), p. ix.

7. The work of Tom Courchene, H.V. Nelles, Richard Simeon and Don Stevenson, referred to elsewhere in this article, have made notable contributions to our understanding of contemporary Ontario. Rodney Haddow has just published an informative essay on Ontario in *Canadian Politics*, 2d ed., James Bickerton and Alain-G. Gagnon (Peterborough: Broadview Press, 1994).

8. See the discussion in Richard Simeon and Ian Robinson, *State, Society and the Development of Canadian Federalism* (Toronto: University of Toronto Press, 1990), p. 33 passim.

9. *What Does Ontario Want?* The 1989 Robarts Lecture, (Toronto: York University, 1989), pp. 21-24. Richard Simeon writes of a number of these characteristics as well in "Ontario in Confederation," *The Government and Politics of Ontario*, 4th ed., ed. Graham White (Toronto: Nelson Canada, 1990), pp. 173-83. Don Stevenson offers an assessment of Courchene's arguments in "Ontario and Confederation: A Reassessment," in Ronald L. Watts and Douglas Brown (eds.), *Canada: The State of the Federation 1989* (Kingston: Institute of Intergovernmental Relations, Queen's University, 1989), pp. 53-74.

10. Don Stevenson has argued that one element in Ontario's traditional pattern of behaviour was suspended during the 1980-82 period, namely its mediating role among other governments and regions of Canada. That pattern reappeared in the latter part of the 1980s with David Peterson's strong support of Meech. ("Ontario and Confederation," pp. 64-65.)

11. The behaviour may in fact be a throwback in some ways to earlier periods of Ontario history, but it stands apart from most postwar Ontario conduct.

12. See Don Stevenson, "Ontario and Confederation," p. 55; H.V. Nelles, "'Red Tied': Fin de Siècle Politics in Ontario," in Michael Whittington and Glen Williams (eds.), *Canadian Politics in the 1990s*, 3d ed., (Toronto: Nelson Canada, 1990), p. 77. Nelles' article provides an excellent account of the forces at work in Ontario in the 1980s.

13. Michael Adams and Mary Jane Lennon, "The Public's View of the Canadian Federation," in R.L. Watts and D.M. Brown (eds.), *Canada: The State of The Federation 1990* (Kingston: Institute of Intergovernmental Relations, Queen's University, 1990), pp. 97-108.

14. Ibid., p. 100.

15. Ibid., see Figure 5.2, p. 105.

16. Rodney Haddow draws attention to another significant shift in the politics of Ontario during this period, namely, the marked increase in the instability of the

party system. See "Ontario Politics: Plus Ça Change...?" in James Bickerton and Alain-G Gagon (eds.), *Canadian Politics*, 2d ed., (Peterborough: Broadview Press, 1994), pp. 471-72, 479-80.

17. The federal designation of Montreal and Vancouver, but not Toronto, as international banking centres was a decision of high symbolism; the location of the Space Agency in Montreal showed many Ontarians what a powerful political ally of the federal Tories could accomplish; and the ceiling on the rate of growth of federal CAP transfers was designed to hit the three equalization-contributing provinces, Ontario the hardest. The Informetrica studies tell the story in great detail.

18. For example, the effort Ontario put in to the squabble about the location of the federal space agency was tepid by comparison to that of the Quebec government, which launched a full-court press involving the direct intervention of Premier Bourassa when it feared it might lose the agency. It was ultimately located in the greater Montreal area.

19. Nelles, "Red Tied," p. 83. Rodney Haddow describes a number of the key initiatives undertaken during the Peterson era. See "Ontario Politics," pp. 480-81.

20. Nelles, "Ontario: A Declining Centre?" paper presented at the York University's Robarts Centre Conference, "The Rest of the Country: Canada Outside Quebec," 29 April – 1 May 1994.

21. Informetrica Study no. 3, *Ontario and the Canada Assistance Plan*, November 1993.

22. As a result of this restraint, the federal share of what used to be a 50:50 cost-sharing program had dropped to 28 percent in 1993.

23. See the Informetrica study, *Ontario and the Canada Assistance Plan*.

24. For example, Ontario's drive, supported by B.C. and Alberta, to make provision for constitutionally binding intergovernmental agreements in the Charlottetown Accord was a direct outcome of the bitter experience with CAP.

25. Study no. 9 examines the national and regional implications of federal monetary policy.

26. Nelles"'Red Tied': Fin de Siècle Politics in Ontario," p. 95.

27. This was, in part, yet another consequence of the cap on CAP.

28. This had been a concern of the Davis government as well, as it entered the 1980-82 round of constitutional talks.

29. Another distinctive policy field, not directly germane to our story, is the system of international representation which the provinces have built up over the years. In the spring of 1993, Ontario announced a bold move: the closing down of all its international offices, including the office in the United Kingdom which had been established in 1861. All 17 would be shut to save money, to end unnecessary duplication of service with the federal government and to force the province to exploit the technologies and the ways of doing international business of the late twentieth and twenty-first centuries. This decision sent a tremor through other provincial governments and created some heartburn in Ottawa, now faced with the prospect of using its diminishing resources to respond to Ontario's demands for effective international trade representation. Ontario's move will be watched

closely in an attempt to determine whether it was a dramatic and successful innovation or whether it was a risky experiment that failed. The difficulty is that in a notoriously soft area such as this, it will be hard to tell.

30. *Ontario 1988: An Economic Perspective* (Office of the Economic Development Coordinator for Ontario, July 1988).

31. Nelles, "Red Tied," p. 78.

32. *The Daily*, 24 August 1993 (Statistics Canada: Catalogue No. 11-001E), Table 3, p. 7.

33. Ibid.

34. *Interprovincial and International Trade Flows, 1984-89* (Statistics Canada, Input-Output Division).

35. Ibid.

36. *The Daily*, 24 August 1993, Chart 3, p.3.

37. Ibid., Chart 1, p.2.

38. Services, as calculated by Statistics Canada, contributed $546 billion to total trade flows in 1989 as compared to $538 billion for primary and manufacturing goods. *The Daily*, 24 August 1994, Tables 6 and 7, pp. 8-9.

39. Ralph Heintzman, "Political Space and Economic Space: Quebec and the Empire of the St. Lawrence," unpublished paper, August 1991, p. 2. Forthcoming in the *Journal of Canadian Studies*.

40. Donald Creighton, *Towards the Discovery of Canada* (Toronto: Macmillan of Canada, 1972), pp. 160-61.

41. Jane Jacobs has an illuminating discussion of this interurban migration of economic power and its impact on the federation as a whole in *The Question of Separatism* (New York: Random House, 1980), chap. 2.

42. See Simeon and Robinson, *State, Society and the Development of Canadian Federalism*, chap.7, for a discussion of this period.

43. John Baldwin and M. Rafiquzzaman, *Structural Change in the Canadian Manufacturing Sector (1970-1990)*, (Ottawa: Analytical Studies Branch, Statistics Canada, 1994), p. 4.

44. Heintzman, "Political Space and Economic Space," p. 2.

Part III

7

Why *Should* Women Care About Federalism?

Jill Vickers

Ce chapitre fait, dans une perspective centrée sur les femmes, un tour d'horizon de plusieurs dimensions de la théorie et de la pratique du fédéralisme. En se concentrant sur les façons dont les femmes établissent un rapport à l'État différent de celui des hommes et en examinant la façon dont des femmes placées différemment font une expérience différente de l'activité étatique, l'auteur met en contexte les vues des femmes sur le fédéralisme et l'État fédéral. Alors que la plupart des femmes, particulièrement les Québécoises francophones, voient le fédéralisme comme un obstacle à la réalisation de leurs objectifs, certaines voient l'existence de nombreux points d'accès et de juridictions partagées comme stratégiquement utiles. Le chapitre conclut avec un examen des idées émergentes qu'ont les femmes quant à la façon dont le fédéralisme pourrait être reconceptualisé pour faciliter un genre de politique qui soit plus favorable aux femmes.

In this text I will argue that progressive Canadian women are, by and large, alienated from the discourse of federalism with its focus on territorially organized needs and interests. Certainly, the theory of federalism has not attracted any significant woman-centred analysis. Neither federalism's purported ability to limit the misuse of authority of governments by dividing their power, nor what some have assumed to be its superior record in safeguarding individual rights,[1] have recommended it to those considering Canadian politics from a woman-centred perspective.[2] Nonetheless, as women become more actively engaged in various forms of political activity, they bump up against the federal structures and processes of the Canadian state. They also encounter a range of assumptions about politics which come out of federal theory and practice but which square very badly with most women's experiences of politics. It is women's accounts of their experiences with federalism on which I will draw in this text.

The premises from which a woman-centred perspective begins are, first, that women are quite differently related to the Canadian state than men and, second, that women differently situated because of their majority/minority status (race, ethnicity, nation) or their personal status (sexual orientation, disability) may experience state policies, programs, and benefits differently. Such premises underlie the work of "femocrats"[3] in the government machinery for women (Status of Women Canada, Canadian Advisory Council on the Status of Women, etc), but they are little understood by most policy experts, academics or media commentators.

In the first part of this chapter, I will explore these underlying premises by examining several issues of particular concern to women over the past decade, especially family law and health. I will also examine women's analyses concerning the current "restructuring" of social support programs and of federal transfer payments which many women fear will result in a patchwork of programs and entitlements harmful to women and their children as well as lowered levels of support overall. By focusing on why some women feel threatened by such changes, while other women, especially francophone women in Quebec, welcome at least the decentralization that may be involved, I will demonstrate the issues federalism raises for differently located women and the way in which it is a barrier to more effective political solidarity among progressive women with the same policy goals. In general terms, then, I conclude that our form of federalism divides women's interests among levels of government in such a way that determining long-term strategies for women's movements is difficult and the levels of energy and resources required to achieve change are excessive.

WOMEN AND THE CANADIAN FEDERAL STATE

Women's relationships to the institutions of the Canadian state at all levels are different from men's because women's lives are significantly different than men's lives. As current Liberal Cabinet minister Anne McLellan argued in 1991, "Women are often in a weaker economic position than men; women are often at risk as the victims of sexual violence and physical abuse; women continue to be the primary care-givers in most families; women are excluded from full participation in many occupations and professions through systemic discrimination; and women continue to lack an effective political voice."[4] What difference do these realities of women's lives make in their relationships to the institutions of the Canadian state and to their experiences of federalism? How does the fact that women are more likely to be poor, abused, responsible for child- and elder-care, and virtually invisible in the powerful professions including politics affect these supposedly more abstract matters of political analysis?

A central result of women's current life opportunities is that they are *more dependent* on the state for socially-provided programs of support — everything from mother's "allowance" to health care and childcare. Indeed, as Carolyn

Andrew has argued, women played a crucial role in the creation of the Canadian welfare state as they responded to the needs of children and other women, especially by creating local agencies which were subsequently funded by the state and often ultimately absorbed into state institutions at the various levels.[5]

Helge Hernes has argued that the movement of "women's work" (childcare, nursing, elder-care, food preparation, etc.) out of the family and into the public realm has been a key force in the creation of the welfare state.[6] Consequently, women are not only more dependent on the state for programs and benefits, they are also more likely to be state employees, although not at decisionmaking levels. This means that women are more vulnerable to contractions of the welfare state. Both as consumers of state programs, benefits, and entitlements and as employees they are also more threatened in a federal state to changes in which level of government provides programs or performs services. The off-loading by governments of responsibility for social-protection services and programs ultimately affects them far more than men, as women are expected to resume responsibility for tasks such as childcare, elder-care, health care. Therefore, to the extent that women are still more state dependent than active as funders or decisionmakers, they are more negatively affected by contractions in state activity than are men.

Women's greater dependency on the state for social support extends beyond programs based on transfers to individuals. As I will argue in more detail below, women also experience a dependence in physical mobility which makes it far harder for them to move to where jobs are located. Consequently, women are more dependent on resource transfers to economically disadvantaged regions/provinces. This perhaps explains the significant presence of women in movements protesting or lobbying against threats to programs of regional adjustment. Similarly, women and their children are more dependent on publically provided and regulated transportation and communication rates (telephones) and are more threatened by changes in transfer payment arrangements as both the dominant consumers and workers in the affected sectors.

Women's greater dependency on the state is not an essential or inevitable relationship. Rather it reflects women's current unequal social, political, and economic situation. This dependency is shared by other people who are relatively powerless. But not all relatively powerless people turn to the state or see it as a potential ally in overcoming their inequality. Indeed some groups may be sufficiently distrustful of state institutions to see them as enemies rather than as potential sources of support. Throughout this century, however, most of the movements in Canada organized to improve women's status and condition have seen the state more as a source of support than as a potential danger to women. These movements have been led and dominated by women of the majority cultures (English and French in Quebec) who have anticipated enough potential benefit from influencing the state at all levels to focus on official politics. (I have described the operational code of the English-Canadian women's movement as *radical liberalism.*[7])

The final crucial way in which women are differently related to the state than men is in their overwhelming *lack of power* in the political and bureaucratic decisionmaking of the state at all levels. The flip side of this is men's *privilege* and dominance in these structures. Women, not men, required a section in the Charter to guarantee them equal treatment. Women are still a tiny fraction of most decisionmaking bodies. This is manifested in the inability of most decisionmaking bodies to undertake analysis that incorporates gender as a factor, even concerning social programs in which women and their children are the main recipients. Several recent examples will suffice. The $6 billion designated in 1994 by the federal government to fund infrastructure projects, for example, created jobs mainly in traditional male occupations at the same time that salary cuts and job losses in the federal government disproportionately hit women as the majority of the lowest-paid public servants. Similarly, the $1.9 billion Atlantic Groundfish Strategy assumed that women had no distinctive needs resulting from this resource catastrophe. Women were neither consulted nor were gender-specific needs (childcare, job counselling) included in the program.[8]

Most commentators on Canadian federalism agree that "federalism does tend to organize territorial issues into Canadian politics and to organize other issues out."[9] Yet this is generally deemed to be a rather minor problem since it is a general assumption of male-centred political analysis that politics is primarily about interests and needs that are captured within territory. As Diane Lamoureux has concluded about the differences in the representations of women: "nous sommes dispersées."[10] What this means is that the policy demands of women's movements "do not fit neatly into jurisdictional boxes"[11] in the current Canadian federal system. The 15 areas of concern[12] to women as named by the groups active in the 1981 constitutional debate (and therefore mainly from outside francophone Quebec) each required action at all three levels of government.[13] Federalism involves a division of jurisdiction and, hence, of authority to act, between two levels of government. It also weakens the local jurisdiction so critical for women's activism in unitary states. Yet as Trimble concludes "to be effective" women's groups seeking change "must lobby all three" levels of government.[14]

Before I examine some women's views about federalism in Canada, I will explore more fully the issue of *territory* in relation to women's goals, needs, and interests. This will also allow me to expand more fully on the insight that differently situated women may experience state policies, programs, and benefits differently *and* may have different views on such things as which level of government ought to perform which functions even when they agree on what should be done in terms of policy.

Women are generally less able than men to exercise independence concerning geographic mobility and relocation. In a political system that places value upon territorially organized needs and interests and which bases its political representation on territorial units, this is a fact of enormous importance. Until recently, married women were required by law to live where their husbands chose. This meant, historically, that women could be forced to move away from community support and employment opportunities, or that women could be prevented from moving *to* employment opportunities or better health and social services. In eras of limited mobility, this mattered less. When high geographic mobility is the norm, however, this has consequences for women's opportunities. Moreover, although the legal constraints on women's independence in mobility choices have ended, economic, cultural, and material factors make exercising legal autonomy difficult. Since women earn, on average, only about two-thirds of a man's wage and far more women are limited to part-time jobs without benefits, few families can choose to follow a woman's career opportunities. Given the shortage of public childcare, many must depend on family and trusted neighbourhood or community supports for childcare. Women's coping networks often depend on long-term family and neighbourhood relationships and these are especially important in times of economic and social dislocation.

The issues raised by women's constrained geographic mobility affect differently situated women quite differently despite common goals in terms of substantive policy issues. It was the issue of which jurisdiction should control divorce that, in the late 1970s and early 1980s, first revealed significant differences between francophone feminists in Quebec and most other feminists. As Ginette Busque notes "the Federation des femmes du Quebec ... was in favour of the transfer of powers [over marriage and divorce to the provinces] and ... saw this as an excellent opportunity to harmonize all of the provisions of the Civil Code affecting family law."[15] Moreover, she argues: "It is safe to assume this position was shared by the majority of Quebec women, because women's groups were already making their submissions to the provincial government ... and had included their views on divorce."[16]

By contrast, women's groups from outside Quebec and some non-francophone groups within Quebec opposed this transfer of jurisdiction over marriage and divorce to the provinces, fearing a resulting patchwork quilt with different grounds and waiting periods from province to province such as exists in the United States. In several provinces, women's groups feared that no divorce law would be passed. Francophone feminists in Quebec apparently did not fear the consequences of this variability, however, because most realize that they must accept the consequences of less mobility in order to live in French. In fact, since most accept that their lives will likely be lived primarily in Quebec, they wish to get the best possible system there and have confidence that they can. Other women, however, assumed they could be moved or choose to move from province to province if married and could be marooned in a province without a divorce law or with one not helpful to women. Women for whom life circumstances meant dependent and unpredictable relocations during their (and their daughters') lives were resistant to losing the legal stability provided by the federal control over something as basic as marriage and divorce. From the perspective of francophone women's groups in Quebec, the federal government's failure to return this jurisdiction to Quebec was more evidence that their feminist project was being hampered by federalism. This is an issue I will explore more below. (Ironically, prior to the Quiet Revolution, women in Quebec had been required to appeal to the federal Senate for permission to divorce.)

In the analysis that follows, it is important to keep in mind the full implications of the premises I have advanced to this point. Women's views of federalism reflect their recognition that they are, by and large, more likely to be dependent on the state than men for programs of support, legal protection of their rights, and employment. They are also well aware that the territorial organization of politics suppresses interests and needs which are not territorially contained. They also are increasingly aware that territorially organized systems of representation constrain their ability to hold political office (as the growing support among women for proportional representation in the electoral system illustrates). The same geographic constraints on women explored above also limit and shape their political participation. Federal and provincial legislatures alike are usually distant from home and women's mobility, as we have seen, is often constrained. Nonetheless, women's actual experiences of federalism vary quite considerably according to their situation. In both Quebec and the rest of Canada, racial and cultural minority women are often more dependent on state programs, but find that racism and other systemic biases make the programs less suitable to their needs and values, make it less likely that they will be state employees, and far less likely that they will be elected as legislators or selected as senior appointed decisionmakers.

SOME WOMEN-CENTRED VIEWS ABOUT FEDERALISM

Australian constitutional author Geoffrey Sawer has argued that "Believers in non-government are the only people likely to be positively attracted by the qualities of federalism.... To political activists, advocacy of federalism seems like an invitation to political frustration."[17] Most women involved in women's movements are activists in Sawer's sense of the word and are intensely frustrated by federalism. In this section, I will explore briefly the few views of federalism from a woman-centred perspective that have emerged thus far. I will also outline some of the strategic views about coping with federalism that have emerged out of women's frustrated experiences. Most activist women in Canada accept federalism as part of the political system with which they must engage. There is no sustained campaign to abolish federalism except among some francophone feminists in Quebec. While some research suggests that women outside Quebec (and perhaps also Alberta) may have weaker attachments to their regions or provinces than men,[18] feminists have focused their energies on reforming the electoral system so that non-territorially organized needs and interests can better be expressed through the electoral process. Not surprisingly, women put their scarce energies into gaining the equality sections in the Charter and defending the Charter against what many believe were threats embodied in the Meech Lake and Charlottetown constitutional proposals.[19]

As Canadian women become more familiar with the gains of women's movements elsewhere, it is increasingly apparent to them that federalism, as a state form, is one of the *structural barriers* they face in their efforts to gain equality. Like other political structures created by men in an era when women were legally or practically excluded from involvement, federalism now seems a brake on women's claims for just treatment and an obstacle to the development of needed programs such as childcare.[20] Certainly, Canadian women's movements have not conceptualized equality as meaning the same treatment as between men and women or as among women of different needs and circumstances. Instead Canadian feminists have emphasized *equality of result.*[21] There is a strong sense that just treatment means treating individuals and groups in ways necessary to produce equal results. This has meant, as we will see below, a willingness to accept differential treatment for Quebec and the First Nations. It has also meant that those women-centred evaluations of federalism which do exist tend to be based on an analysis of *results* rather than first principles.

In terms of results, first one must examine some baseline comparative data. From a woman-centred perspective, federalism does seem to be a brake on women's attempts to gain just and equal treatment. An OECD-based comparison circa 1990 of 17 industrialized countries shows that three out of five "laggards" in providing social-protection programs were federal states (Canada, the United States and Australia) whereas all of the top five spenders were unitary states (Sweden, France, Netherlands, Belgium and Finland). Indeed only one federal state (the old West Germany) was among the top ten social-protection spenders.[22] The differences were quite large with the laggards all spending less than 20 percent of gross domestic product (Canada 18.8 percent) while the unitary state leaders spent considerably more (Sweden 33.9 percent, France 28 percent, Finland 27.1 percent). While the Canadian data may not include regional disparity transfers, which have indirect but positive results for women, nonetheless, the picture is clear. Women living in a federal state are likely to receive lower levels of public social protection, even if we cannot conclusively determine that federalism is the cause. It is for this reason that

Canada's "best-country-in-the-world" rating from the UN is seriously down-graded when women's lives are considered.

Keith Banting has concluded that federalism "constrains both rapid expansion and contraction in the scope of state activity."[23] As we will observe below, most women in Canada would agree that federalism constrains the expansion of state activity but as low-level public employees and those most dependent on state programs they would probably reject the premise that rapid contraction is equally constrained. While there are no figures on comparative shrinkage, Doris Anderson's 12-country study suggests that defensive mobilization is easier in unitary states.[24]

Alberta political scientist Linda Trimble analyzed Canadian federalism from a woman-centred perspective which focused on the feminization of poverty and the barriers federalism poses to effective efforts to deal with it. First Trimble argues that "the obsession with federalism obscures other sources of conflict, prevents non-territorial issues from being addressed in political debates and resolved with public policy, and even restricts the definition of 'politics' itself."[25] Trimble's analysis deals with three aspects of Canadian federalism: (i) the division of jurisdictions and authority between two levels of government; (ii) federalism as an attempt to reflect geographically organized diversity; and (iii) federalism as an institutional arrangement for the accommodation of geographically organized differences.

Trimble identifies *fiscal federalism* and *executive federalism* as two practices of the federal state in Canada that significantly harm women's interests. Canada's system of fiscal federalism, in her view, is noted by an expansion of provincial areas of activity and jurisdiction but in a context of limited provincial taxation powers: "In other words, provinces can develop social welfare policy but they cannot pay for it."[26] As a consequence, both levels of government are involved in policy development and delivery but often with ideologically opposed agendas. Further municipal governments also play an important role "leading to multiple and overlapping jurisdictions."[27]

For women's groups the costs in human and other resources to be effective and lobby at all three levels is extremely demanding given women's greater family responsibilities and smaller economic resources. She outlines how shelters for battered women and children must deal with provincial and municipal governments and with the federal Canada Assistance Plan (CAP) for their funding. She concludes: "Shelter operators must be aware of opportunities, rules and structures at three levels of government."[28] Trimble notes that *in theory* having multiple access points to influence policy and obtain funding could benefit women organized to achieve change or needing services. She notes that Sandra Burt in a 1984 survey of women's groups concluded that, in practice, most groups found government officials were "unable or unwilling to help them; one of the reasons cited for this was the federal-provincial division of responsibility."[29] She concluded that governments use jurisdictional over-laps to "pass the buck" and use "marble-cake federalism" as an excuse for territorial skirmishes.

Many of the services women need to avoid poverty, seek employment or participate in politics exist only because they have been created by women and are only slowly and grudgingly supported by governments. The federal system has resulted in constant obfuscation as to whose responsibility particular pro-grams actually are. Trimble concludes that the current practice of federalism keeps women poor by evasion, territorial warfare, buckpassing, and a lack of clear responsibility on which political actions could be taken. She also notes, however, that: "There is nothing about the formal division of powers in the constitution which prevents governments from addressing issues like the feminization of poverty."[30] It is the practice of federalism that permits resis-tance to women's demands, then, not the actual constitutional principles, in her view.

Trimble also argues that, while federalism in Canada is effective in reflecting and accommodating some geographically organized forms of diversity (espe-cially of the francophone community in Quebec), it represses other major forms of diversity, including some that are geographically but not provincially organ-ized. So federalism does not effectively express or accommodate the diverse needs and values of the many racial, ethnic, and linguistic minority communi-ties. Most important to Trimble is the fact that the major institutional arrange-ments developed to accommodate the forms of diversity and conflict valorized by federalism are the practices of *executive federalism*. To Trimble, this "government by conference" largely excludes women, since women are grossly underrepresented as political elites in this arena and since there are few public points of access.[31] She also notes the exclusion of minority women. I would note that aboriginal women have become a presence in some sessions of executive federalism although probably not in many of the estimated 1,000 annual intergovernmental conferences.

Trimble illustrates that, at best, the exclusion of women results in a lack of coordination between the two levels. Ultimately, however, federalism is por-trayed as a set of institutions and practices favourable to the powerful, espe-cially those within governments and bureaucracies, and grossly disadvantaging to the poor and powerless, a disproportionate number of whom are women, of minority race or otherwise marginalized. Nonetheless, Trimble, like most anglophone feminists, accepts it as part of Canada's historical "furniture."

By contrast, most francophone feminists conclude a similar analysis by advocating the end of federalism or the adoption of an extremely decentralized form. Chantal Maille, a political scientist at Concordia University, explores these issues by examining the women's health movement in Quebec. Her central theme is that: "the women's health movement has been an important agent of change for women because of the autonomy negotiated by the Quebec provincial government in the definition and administration of its policies and programs." Maille's analysis of women's circumstances parallels the others cited above. Women are poorer, more likely to experience abuse and also more often the providers of unpaid and informal health-care services for children, the elderly, the disabled, etc. She concludes that "women have a unique relationship to the health care system, partly because of their reproductive capacities, but also because of their multiple social roles."[32]

The women's health-care movement in Quebec and in English Canada believes that "woman's needs are best served by a health care system with a preventive, *community-based*, caring approach."[33] In Quebec, the women's health movement has been particularly active around abortion, violence (battering and sexual assaults), the humanization of delivery (midwives), and mental health. From the 1970s, the Quebec state stopped enforcing the old criminal law against abortion in some centres. In Quebec, francophone feminists have felt closer to the provincial government and have negotiated step-by-step with that government which, Maille concludes, "made it possible to reach the principle of grass-roots decision-making."[34]

Maille also believes it is easier to initiate changes at the provincial level than at the federal level. This insight, similar to Pierre Trudeau's advice to socialists[35] to establish provincial beachheads first as in the case of medicare, is hotly contested by many anglophone women faced with persuading at least nine provincial governments. Maille's argument is that "it is easier to initiate change and to gain influence over issues in a small-scale context, i.e. a province, than to initiate a pan-Canadian change, where huge discrepancies between provinces and regions make it difficult clearly to establish a consensus."[36] To Maille, woman-centred models of health and social service delivery require decentralization and local control. To her, decentralization to the local region where women can have some say requires prior decentralization of the key powers first to Quebec.

It has been important for women in Canada outside francophone Quebec to understand that *decentralization* is a positive value for progressive francophone women in Quebec. While all such francophone women would not see shared jurisdictions as inevitably reflecting, in the words of Diane Lamoureux, "une irresponsabilite partagee,"[37] most would see shared jurisdictions as something to be eliminated in order to attain woman-centred goals. [38] Maille's theme that women are best served by a decentralized system of service delivery and decisionmaking flows coherently from the values of contemporary feminism. It is necessary, therefore, to probe more fully the reasons why most women's groups outside Quebec and many non-francophone groups in Quebec favour a strong federal presence.

Anne McLelland has argued that the inclusion in the constitution of something like an enforceable social charter would make women outside Quebec less fearful of decentralization.[39] That is, women's experiences with provincial states have led them to value the leverage of shared jurisdictions and the federal spending power, so that when women have faced provincial governments resistant to their equality claims they have been able to put pressure on the federal government. It is clearly situation rather than language or culture that shapes this view since the Federation nationale des femmes canadiennes-francaises in a 1992 text "The Voice of Francophone Women Living in Minority Situations in the Constitutional Debate" shared the view I have here associated with English-Canadian women, that is a desire for some instrument to ensure comparability of benefits, legal conditions, and support programs wherever in Canada they might be living. That is, women other than Quebec francophones also value decentralization to the extent that it allows women to participate more easily in decisionmaking and allows programs to be shaped to their needs *with their* consent. But most believe that the luxury of that decentralization is impossible outside Quebec (and perhaps the First Nations) since without the federal presence they fear many provincial governments would dismantle programs and revoke rights central to women's equality-seeking.

Constitutional lawyer and vice-president of the National Action Committee on the Status of Women (NAC) Shelagh Day argues that Canadian women outside Quebec and the First Nations have had enough experience with provincial governments over the past two decades to "fear, rather than welcome, powers being devolved" to their provinces. She argues that everyone in Canada "disadvantaged by disability, poverty, racism, age and homophobia have a common interest in the federal spending power."[40] Nor does she believe that they will be better off if federal powers were "disentangled" to eliminate duplication. She concludes: "For those who are disadvantaged, even though we feel as though we are running in circles, resort to another level of government or another forum is always useful. This many *not* be efficient, but it is nevertheless the reality that women in the rest of Canada cannot depend on any one elected government to hear or address our problems."[41]

In summary, women's views about federalism primarily have been shaped by their experiences as consumers of government social programs. While this is important for the reasons I have already outlined, it is important also to understand women's values as political actors. In the final section of this chapter, therefore, I will explore some emerging feminist ideas about how federalism could be reconceptualized.

TOWARDS A WOMAN-CENTRED UNDERSTANDING
OF FEDERALISM

In recent decades, organized women's groups in Canada have been exploring federalism through the lens provided by their shared understanding of equality. To again quote Shelagh Day, "equality is not a question of same treatment or different treatment, but a question of whatever treatment is necessary to put a group which has historically been disadvantaged on an equivalent footing with the dominant group in society."[42] Because Canadian women have struggled to develop an idea of equality that can embrace difference, their groups have attempted to understand how the desires of the francophone community in Quebec and of the First Nations can be accommodated while satisfying the desire (and perceived need) of the majority of women for a strong federal presence and comparable programs from province to province.

In its brief to the Standing Committee on Human Resource Development on 25 February 1994, NAC stated its most recent and its most mature conception of the possible nature of the Canadian federation. Like other women's groups, it advanced an understanding of individual and collective citizenship aimed at equal results through appropriate but not identical treatment. The brief is worth quoting at length to illustrate the point:

> Social programs are valued by all Canadians. At the same time, Canada's consti-
> tutional debates have demonstrated that English-speaking Canadians, aboriginal
> peoples and the people of Quebec have distinct perspectives on the role of
> particular governments in the management and delivery or social programs. A
> restructuring of social programs must respect these differences and not attempt to
> impose a formula which meets the needs of one national community onto the
> others. With respect to English-speaking Canada, this means respecting the desire
> of most Canadians outside of Quebec to have the Canadian government play a
> strong role in social programs. With respect to Quebec, this means recognizing
> that the majority of Quebecers look to the Quebec government for the management
> and delivery of their social programs. With respect to aboriginal peoples, this
> means respecting their desire for self-government which includes control of social
> services. Furthermore, the multi-racial and multi-cultural makeup of Quebec and
> the rest of Canada must be recognized in the design and delivery of anti-racist and
> culturally appropriate social services.[43]

This has been described by some as support for asymmetrical federalism, although it is described as a "three nations" position in debate within NAC. As a political position it was hard won as differently located women came to realize that, despite often shared substantive policy goals, their circumstances led them to different strategic judgements about how Canadian federalism ought to be organized (or reorganized). Perhaps the most important intuition I have identi-fied in the NAC debates about Canada's "three nations" is that many women conceive of there being three national communities in Canada but that these communities are not primarily territorial in character. Certainly, few women, other than Quebec francophones, see any great political relevance in the territorial division of Canada into provinces. This is not to suggest that there are not "regional" conflicts within women's organizations. Rather, it suggests the lack of fit between most political identities and the current provincial-territorial geography.

Canada has been described by some as the first post-modern country in which multiple nations co-exist within a common political entity. The NAC vision conceptualizes the parties as peoples and communities and does not advance a primarily territorial concept of the elements to be accommodated. This reflects the view widely held among some anglophone and most racial/cultural minority women that the provinces do not represent units which they especially value or seek to preserve. This disaffection from provincial governments outside Quebec is stronger in some cases than in others. In part, it reflects long periods of non-progressive governments in some provinces and the strong client relationship developed by the federal Liberal government in the 1960s, 1970s, and early 1980s with women's groups. It also reflects the fact that most provinces are simply too large to permit women much more opportunity to participate than at the federal level. As Anne McLellan has argued, many women "have viewed provincial governments as less tolerant and receptive to their claims for equality than the national government."[44] Especially appealing to her, however, is the greater practicality, the efficiency in lobbying, and the possibilities for becoming involved in only one government. In her view, "once the federal government is convinced of the need of a program or initiative, it can ensure its availability on a national basis."[45]

In fact, the NAC vision is of three national communities, each of which contains minorities requiring special standing.[46] These communities do not correspond to the current geography of Canada since part of the aboriginal community is within Quebec and part of it is not territorially bounded (the urban aboriginal population). Finally, the decentralized program-administration and decisionmaking so attractive to many women occurs now primarily in the units of local governments which constitutionally have few powers, but are the locale for much of women's most effective political activity. Part of their attempt to re-vision Canadian federalism, then, also reflects a desire to combine pan-Canadian standards with responsive, local administration.

CONCLUSION

If we ask what place federalism occupies in a woman-centred conception of the Canadian political system, the answer is variable. Most politically active women experience frustration about a form of politics that can only really "see" territorially—organized needs and issues and those only at the far-from-home levels. Although I have focused in this text on social policy and welfare-state programs, women's frustration with federalism also infuses their discussions of economic policy, educational policy, and environmental policy. While a few feminist observers like Day value federalism for pragmatic reasons such as the multiple access points it provides, none have seen in it a state system that effectively protects individual rights or protects them against the abuses of power by governments and their agents. From a woman-centred perspective, federalism has not been a protector of rights nor a guardian against abuses of power.

Nonetheless, Canadian women value diversity and have thought about its meaning in considerable detail. Woman-centred conceptions of how different national communities can receive equal results from their citizenship point the way to a new vision of federalism less tied to geographic boundaries. Such a vision imagines that people would receive the services and programs that they need from governments and that people from all of the different communities would be able to play a role in decisionmaking. That is, it is a vision of politics organized "as if people mattered," and for their benefit. Women's suspicion is that too often the principles of federalism are invoked to represent the interests of governments and governors. It is too early in the development of woman-centred approaches to federalism to know if there are virtues as yet uncovered. It is also unclear if women have the capacity to achieve changes that would develop more responsive practices of federalism. Nonetheless women should be interested in federalism; and woman-centred analyses of federalism can shed light on aspects of its operation too little studied.

NOTES

I wish to acknowledge the support of the SSHRC for the research on which this chapter is based.

1.   Mr. Justice Subba Rao of the Supreme Court of India quoted in Philip Resnick, *The Masks of Proteus: Canadian Reflections on the State* (Montreal and Kingston: McGill-Queen's University Press 1990), p. 232.

2.   By a *woman-centred perspective* I mean an analysis that takes women's political behaviour as the norm not men's. This means questioning all of the political structures, processes, theories, and behaviours created by men in the period when women were excluded from participation (as recently as the 1950s for Quebec women and the 1960s for on-reserve aboriginal women and men). For a more detailed analysis see Jill Vickers, Pauline Rankin and Christine Appelle, *Politics As If Women Mattered* (Toronto: University of Toronto Press, 1993).

3.   *Femocrat* is a term developed in Australia to describe women who entered the public service to work in the machinery developed because of the pressure from the women's movement to advance an understanding of women's interests and needs when all government policy is being considered.

4. Anne McLellan, "Women and the Process of Constitution-Making" in David Schneiderman, ed., *Conversations Among Friends <<>> Entre Amis: Proceedings of an Interdisciplinary Conference on Women and Constitutional Reform* (Edmonton: Centre for Constitutional Studies, University of Alberta, 1991), p. 9.

5. Carolyn Andrew, "Women and the Welfare State," *Canadian Journal of Political Science* 27,4 (December 1984): 667-683.

6. Helge Hernes, ed., *Welfare State and Women Power* (Oslo: Norwegian University Press, 1987).

7. I have developed this idea in various sources describing the stance adopted by English-Canadian feminists as *radical liberalism* as distinct from radical or cultural feminism with its U.S. influenced antistatism. As Micheline Dumont and Micheline de Séve have pointed out to me, however, francophone women in Quebec have been more divided on this matter. Further, this majaritarian operational code has had dissenters. In particular, those involved in grassroots, anti-violence, anti-porn groups and those influenced by U.S. radical feminism tended to be antistatist. See Micheline Dumont, "The Origins of the Women's Movement in Quebec," in Constance Backhouse and David H. Flaherty, eds., *Challenging Times: The Women's Movement in Canada and the United States* (Montreal and Kingston: McGill-Queen's Press, 1992).

8. National Action Committee on the Status of Women (NAC) *ACTION NOW!* May 1994, pp. 1-2. Founded in 1972, NAC represents over 600 women's groups, mainly from English Canada but widely representative of Canada's racial and (other) cultural diversity.

9. Richard Simeon and Ian Robinson, *State, Society and the Development of Canadian Federalism* (Toronto: University of Toronto Press, 1990), p. 14.

10. Diane Lamoureux, "Une Majorité Encore Oubliée," in Schneiderman, *Conversations Among Friends*, p. 59.

11. Linda Trimble, "Federalism, The Feminization of Poverty and the Constitution," in Schneiderman, *Conversations Among Friends*, p. 87.

12. The areas were: human rights, aboriginal women's rights, family law, economic policies, education, political representation, income security, health and welfare, criminal law, immigration, administration of justice, communications, cultural policy, housing and the environment. (See Trimble, ibid., p.87). Trimble's evaluation of education as divided into jurisdictions probably reflects federal involvement in French-language education in English Canada.

13. Canadian Advisory Council on the Status of Women (CACSW), "Brief to the Special Joint Committee of the Senate and of the House of Commons on the 1987 Constitutional Accord." Ottawa, 1987, p. 22.

14. Ibid., p. 87.

15. Ginette Busque, "Why Women Should Care About Constitutional Reform?" in Schneiderman, *Conversations Among Friends*, p. 14.

16. Ibid

17. Geoffrey Sawer, quoted in Resnick, *The Masks of Proteus*, pp. 232-3.

18. Elisabeth Gidengil, "A Different Voice? Gender and Political Behaviour in Canada," paper presented to the CPSA Meetings, Charlottetown, P.E.I., May 1992.

19. Jill Vickers, "The Canadian Women's Movement and a Changing Constitutional Order," in *International Journal of Canadian Studies* (Spring/Fall, 1993) pp. 7-8.

20. Feminist groups sought a childcare policy structure that would have made it public, an extension of the education system and of even quality in all jurisdictions. This would require use of the federal spending power in a policy structure comparable to that developed for health care. There is little likelihood of such a system being developed now. In unitary states, France for example, such systems are well developed.

21. The concepts of equality evident in the theory and practice of federalism are varied. On the one hand, the *equality of provinces* approach focuses rigidly on the equality of treatment despite the unequal (and unfair) results which are the consequence. The conception of *equal treatment* between two founding nations likewise results in unequal (and unfair) results, especially for First Nations, other Aboriginal Peoples and immigrants. The practice of the equalization of resources among provinces, however, reflects an *equality of results* approach comparable to that developed by Canadian feminists.

22. Canadian Centre for Policy Alternatives, *CCPA Monitor*, Ottawa: Canadian Centre for Policy Alternatives, May 1994, p. 5.

23. Keith Banting, *The Welfare State and Canadian Federalism,* 2d ed. (Montreal and Kingston: McGill-Queen's University Press, 1987), p. 206.

24. Doris Anderson, *The Unfinished Revolution: The Status of Women in Twelve Countries* (Toronto: Doubleday Canada, 1991).

25. Trimble, "Federalism," p. 87. Many observers have noted that territorial cleavages overwhelm other issues in Canadian politics (notable Alan Cairns and Donald Smiley). What they lack is a power analysis of the consequences for major sections of the population such as women.

26. Timble, "Federalism," p. 87.

27. Ibid.

28. Ibid., p. 88.

29. Ibid.

30. Ibid.

31. Ibid., p. 89.

32. Chantal Maille, "The Women's Health Movement in Quebec: An Analysis for the Purpose of the Constitutional Debate," in Schneiderman, *Conversations Among Friends*, p. 78.

33. Anita Fochs Heller, *Health and Home: Women as Health Guardians* (Ottawa: CACSW, 1986), cited in Maille, ibid.

34. Maille, ibid., p. 79.

35. "Federalism must be welcomed as a valuable tool which permits parties to plant socialist governments in certain provinces from which the seeds of radicalism can slowly spread," P.E. Trudeau, "The Practice and Theory of Federalism" in *Federalism and the French Canadians* (Toronto: MacMillan of Canada, 1968), p. 127.

36. Maille, "The Women's Health Movement in Quebec," p. 80.

37. Diane Lamoureux, "Une Majorité Encore oubliée," p. 60.

38. Féderation des Femmes du Québec, *Mémoire présenté à la Commission sur l'avenir politique et constitutionnel du Québec*, Nov. 1990; FFQ, *Pour un Québec féminin pluriel: Dossier de consultation*, March 1992; Clair Bonenfant, "Presentation de notre mémoire à la commission Bélanger-Campeau," *Le féminisme en revue* 4, 2 (1991).

39. McLelland, "Women and the Process of Constitution-Making," p. 11.

40. Day, Shelagh, "Constitutional Reform: Canada's Equality Crisis" in Schneiderman, *Conversations Among Friends*, p. 98.

41. Ibid.

42. Ibid., pp. 96-97.

43. NAC, "Brief to the Standing Committee on Human Resource Development," 25 February 1994, pp. 3-4.

44. McLellan, "Women and the Process of Constitution-Making," p. 10.

45. Ibid.

46. Women Within NAC have expressed concern about non-traditional aboriginal women seeking Charter protection within self-governing First Nations.

8

The Charter and Federalism: Revisiting the Nation-Building Thesis

Janet Hiebert

Lorsque la Charte fut enchâssée dans la constitution, plusieurs prédirent que cela aurait un effet centralisateur sur les politiques publiques, ce qui minerait le pluralisme fondé sur le territoire tel que le conçoit le fédéralisme canadien. Quoique l'on ne puisse nier le fait que la Charte a un effet sur le fédéralisme en imposant des contraintes sur la capacité des provinces de faire la promotion de valeurs communautaires fondées sur des priorités différentes de celles des autres juridictions, il est prématuré de conclure que la Charte préviendra l'apparition de différences fondées sur le territoire et mènera à l'homogénisation des politiques canadiennes. Autant la jurisprudence de la Cour suprême en matière de fédéralisme et d'enjeux reliés aux droits que la structure de la Charte fournissent aux provinces de bonnes raisons de s'élever contre une interprétation uniforme ou universelle de ce qui est une réconciliation adéquate des valeurs individuelles et collectives. Bien que la clause dérogatoire constitue la façon la plus directe pour qu'une province puisse faire la promotion de valeurs particulières à son sens des priorités, l'hostilité largement répandue à l'égard de la clause dérogatoire, notamment à l'extérieur du Québec, fera qu'il sera difficile pour les leaders politiques d'y avoir recours. Les limites imposées par l'article 1 constitueront plus probablement le cadre de l'argumentation voulant que la Charte soit interprétée dans un contexte fédéral permettant des diversités fondées sur le territoire.

Much has been said of the *Charter of Rights and Freedoms*'s nation-building effects for Canada, particularly in transforming citizen identities from passive spectators to assertive rights-bearers in constitutional debates.[1] What has not received the same attention, however, is the institutional side of the nation-building thesis. When entrenched rights were first included in the constitution many predicted that the Charter would have a centralizing effect on public policy that would undermine the territorial-based pluralism contemplated by Canadian federalism.[2] Yet little has been done to test the thesis in light of more than a decade of Charter jurisprudence.[3] Moreover, despite expectations that the Charter would promote national standards, in that rights' entitlements would undermine provinces' capacity to promote regional or community values and policy preferences, little discussion exists in the literature on the normative question of whether protected rights should at all times be interpreted as constraints against territorial-based differences.[4]

This chapter will revisit the issue of whether and how the Charter frustrates the territorial pluralism of Canadian federalism by examining both Supreme Court jurisprudence on the Charter-federalism relationship and the structure of the Charter. The Charter contains two clauses that might allow for provincial diversity in the administration of federal laws and, more importantly, in the pursuit of policies that conflict, *prima facie*, with the protected rights in the Charter. One of these, the limitation clause of section 1, is judicially determined while the other, the legislative override of section 33, is politically initiated. Depending both on judicial and political wills, these clauses could enable the provinces to promote territorially based diversities in how individual rights are reconciled with collective values. The chapter will argue that both clauses are important from a federalism perspective: to allow provinces, under some circumstances, to promote policies that reflect community or collective values different from the priorities of other jurisdictions. This argument will not assume that protected rights can be easily or casually dismissed because of community or majority preferences. Rather, it holds that what is required is to find "principled ways to mediate the tensions within Canada's distinctive ... form of liberalism."[5]

THE CHARTER AND NATION-BUILDING

The Charter has been characterized as a centralizing force in Canada not because it confers any additional powers on the federal Parliament but because it imposes constraints on the extent to which the provinces can promote community values based on a set of priorities different from other jurisdictions. In this sense the Charter strengthens "Canadian as against provincial identities."[6] The *Charter of Rights and Freedoms* clearly has implications for federalism, attributable in large part to Canada's hierarchical judicial system in which the Supreme Court's jurisprudence is binding on all other courts. By establishing an authoritative role for courts in evaluating the constitutionality of legislative and executive decisions, the Charter is expected to encourage national standards on the parameters of protected rights and the justification of governmental initiatives that impose limits on these rights. While the articulation of rights is expected to constrain the policy choices of both provincial legislatures and the federal Parliament, the Charter's effects are expected to be greater at the provincial level. This is because provinces, which are less heterogenous than the broader Canadian society, are more apt to promote particularities that diverge from national norms and conflict with protected rights.[7] In a more specific way the Charter affects federalism in that it has transformed what traditionally has been a matter of provincial jurisdiction — minority education language policy — to an entrenched right that is national in scope. Tension between federalism and the Charter has been particularly acute among political leaders in Quebec. Given the importance to Quebec of provincial autonomy it is hardly surprising that the Charter, which will be interpreted by a national (i.e., federal) court and whose members are appointed at the discretion of the prime minister and federal justice minister, has been viewed in that province with scepticism and criticism.[8] Concerns about the Charter arise largely from its influence on Quebec's ability to determine its own cultural policy: in particular, language policy. Language policy has been a vital part of Quebec's political agenda since the Quiet Revolution, not in a narrow linguistic sense but in its connection to Quebec nationalism and culture.

It is not difficult to see why the entrenchment of minority education language rights in section 23 raises concerns in Quebec. Its technical precision, which reads more like a statutory instrument than a constitutional provision, suggests that this clause was intended to challenge directly Quebec's minority education language provisions in Bill 101, *The Charter of the French Language*. Bill 101, which allowed English school instruction only to children with at least one parent who had received all of his or her elementary education in Quebec in English, children of newcomers whose parents were living in Quebec when the law was passed but who had been educated in English outside the province, and children with older brothers or sisters already enrolled in an English-language school,[9] was more restrictive than the Charter's section 23. Section 23 guarantees public primary and secondary education in English or French to the children of citizens whose first language learned and still understood, or whose primary school instruction in Canada, was in the language of the English or French linguistic minority population of the province in which they reside.[10]

This inclusion of minority education language rights in the Charter could be interpreted in Quebec as a direct intervention into exclusive provincial autonomy over education as well as an assault on the ability of the Quebec government to promote cultural values through the primacy of the French language. Indeed, this was the effect of section 23 of the Charter; an outcome that allowed no legislative redress for Quebec.[11] The Supreme Court, in one of its earliest Charter cases, ruled that the provisions in Quebec's Bill 101 restricting access to English Schools violated the right in section 23 to minority education language rights and constitutionally were not justified.[12]

Conflicts between the Charter and policies intended to promote Quebec's cultural objectives have not been confined to school language instruction. In one of the most anxiously awaited Supreme Court decisions the Court, in an unsigned judgement, ruled that Quebec legislation that required public signs, commercial advertising, and firm names be in French only was an unjustified restriction on the constitutional guarantee of freedom of expression.[13]

Based on these decisions in which rights-based claims have provided the justification for setting aside aspects of Quebec's cultural policy, it is understandable why the Charter is seen by some in Quebec as frustrating the capacity of the Quebec state to promote cultural policies. Given that policies affecting education and commercial practices are within provincial jurisdiction, the Charter is undermining the federalism principle of allowing for provincial autonomy over matters local in nature.

While there is no denying that the Charter has constrained Quebec's ability to control its language policy it may be premature to assume that on other matters the Charter will necessarily undermine the federalism principle. Much of the rationale for federalism in a culturally diverse nation like Canada has been to allow provinces to promote community or local rather than national perspectives and preferences. The Charter has neither superseded federalism nor altered its logic and rationale for Canada. To conclude that province-based diversities historically authorized by federalism are now precluded by the Charter disregards community differences and dismisses, unnecessarily, the potential for a federalist interpretation of the Charter — one that recognizes legitimate provincial differences both in the priorities that are attached to conflicting values and in the configuration of how legislative objectives are reconciled with protected rights.

SUPREME COURT AND CHARTER/FEDERALISM JURISPRUDENCE

Federal laws have been struck down more often than provincial ones.[14] Furthermore, the Supreme Court has indicated a greater sensitivity to federalism concerns, to allow provinces to address problems and issues in different ways, than may be indicated in the nation-building literature. The Court's willingness to interpret the Charter in a federalism context has occurred both in the interpretation of substantive rights as well as in the assessment of whether legislative objectives impose reasonable limits on protected rights. Review of Charter cases generally assumes two stages: whether a protected right has been infringed and, if so, does the legislation represent a reasonable limit under section 1 which is demonstrably justified in a free and democratic society. At both stages the Supreme Court has been receptive to arguments that the Charter should not be interpreted in a manner that disregards federalism.

The first indication that members of the Court were sympathetic to federalism concerns when interpreting the Charter arose in *R. v. Edwards Books and Art Ltd.*[15] At issue was whether the requirements under the *Retail Business Holidays Act* that Ontario retail businesses close on Sunday for a secular common pause day violates freedom of religion. A majority found that the Act did violate freedom of religion of Saturday worshippers but was reasonable under section 1. A majority of the Court held that when attempting to reconcile the legislation with protected rights, there is no constitutional obligation on a province to adopt the same legislative arrangement used elsewhere.[16] This is because these choices require an in-depth knowledge of all circumstances and are choices that must be made by the particular legislature in question: "The simple fact is that what may work effectively in one province (or in a part of it) may simply not work in another without unduly interfering with the legislative scheme."[17]

In three cases the Court has rejected arguments that province-based differences constitute an abridgement of equality rights. In two of these the issue was whether provinces can administer federal laws in diverse ways, while the third case involved the question of whether differences between provincial and federal legislation on a similar issue infringes equality.

The first of these equality-based challenges was *R v. Turpin*[18] in which an accused, charged with murder, argued that differential interpretations by provinces of the federal Criminal Code violate the Charter. The code provides that for certain indictable offences an accused in all provinces but Alberta shall be tried by a court composed of a judge and jury. In this case, the accused, who preferred to be tried by a judge alone but who lived in Ontario and therefore was not eligible, argued that this distinction violated equality. The unanimous decision held that this difference in treatment did not constitute a violation of equality.[19]

The Court has interpreted equality in two stages: the first is to determine whether an individual has been denied equality before the law and the second is to assess whether this denial results in discrimination. Discrimination arises, in the Court's view, when distinctions are made for reasons based on the enumerated grounds in section 15 — race, national or ethnic origin, colour, religion, sex, age or mental or physical disability — or analogous categories. The distinction in this case, the Court held, could not be considered discrimination.[20]

A second challenge based on the different applications of federal legislation, *R. v. S.(S.)*,[21] involved the *Young Offenders Act* which allows provinces to designate "alternative measures" to deal with a young person alleged to have committed an offence instead of judicial proceedings under the Act. At issue was Ontario's decision not to designate alternatives. In rejecting the argument that equality was denied because of the different treatments between provinces the Court, in an unanimous judgement, offered its most explicit statement on the need to recognize and protect province-based diversities in a federal system. In arguing that differential applications of federal law in provinces can be a legitimate means of promoting and advancing the values of a federal system,[22] the Court warned that to assume that interprovincial distinctions constitute discrimination for equality purposes would undermine seriously the federal system.[23] It would, the Court argued, "potentially open to Charter scrutiny every jurisdictionally permissible exercise of power by a province, solely on the basis that it creates a distinction in how individuals are treated in different provinces."[24] The Court elaborated on the tension between federalism and the Charter and indicated it would be reticent to interpret the Charter in a manner that is not cognisant of the diversities authorized by federalism:

> There can be no question ... that unequal treatment which stems solely from the exercise, by provincial legislatures, of their legitimate jurisdictional powers cannot be the subject of a s. 15(1) challenge on the basis only that it creates distinctions based upon province of residence.... To find otherwise would be to completely undermine the value of diversity which is at the foundation of the division of powers.[25]

The most recent defence of federalism in Charter review is the *Haig* case[26] which questioned whether the absence in federal referendum legislation of provisions to respond to the different residency requirements for the Quebec referendum, which had the effect of disenfranchising newcomers to Quebec from elsewhere in Canada, violated freedom of expression, the right to vote, and equality. Both the federal and Quebec referenda were held 26 October 1992 and put to the electorate identical questions about approval of the Charlottetown Accord. On enumeration day for the federal referendum Mr. Haig was no longer a resident in Ontario and having lived in Quebec for less than six months he did not meet Quebec's eligibility requirements. As a result he was not enumerated and could not vote.

At issue was whether the Charter extends an entitlement to vote even if one does not meet the enumeration requirements of either the federal or Quebec referendum.[27] The claim before the Court was that the Charter litigant should not have lost his residence status for the purpose of voting in the federal referendum until he had qualified as an elector in Quebec.[28] The Court rejected this claim on two grounds: (i) the right to vote in section 3 is limited to the elections of provincial and federal representatives and does not extend to a referendum,[29] and (ii) this interpretation would undermine provincial autonomy and the federalism principle.

> The appellants are asking the Court to conclude that ordinary residence under the *Referendum Act* (Canada) cannot be lost until one is entitled to vote under the *Referendum Act* (Quebec).... Such a conclusion would strike a blow at the autonomy and independence of legislative bodies in a federal system. It is clear that, carried in different settings, such an interpretative approach would have incredible and untenable consequences.[30]

The Court not only rejected the claim that a federal referendum should contain provisions to enumerate individuals in provinces where they do not meet a provinces' eligibility criteria but also that a federal referendum should be national in scope and apply to all provinces.[31] The Court argued that unlike national elections, a referendum is a consultative process that does not have to be held in all jurisdictions.[32] In coming to this conclusion, the majority opinion disagreed with the suggestion, implicit in the claim of a national referendum, that the federal government "allowed" Quebec to administer part of what really was a "national" referendum. Mr. Haig had claimed that "the differential application of federal law to the provinces can only be tolerated if it is 'legitimate' and advances the values of a federal system." In his view, the decision to hold a referendum in only nine provinces did not advance these values. To this claim the Court replied:

> Though the federal government may well have taken note of the results of the Quebec referendum, it would be unfounded in law to suggest that the federal government "allowed" Quebec to administer part of what was really a "national" referendum. Quebec did not need the authorization of the federal government to hold its referendum, and the Quebec referendum legislation was not within federal control or authority. Had the federal government wished to hold a "national" referendum, it could have included Quebec in the proclamation. Though it had every right to do so, it chose not to, as it also had the right to do.[33]

While the previous federalism cases considered provincial differences in administering federal law, the Court implied in *Haig* that this principle is also applicable to differences between federal and provincial laws. It indicated that the mere fact of difference between similar provincial and federal laws does not constitute a violation of equality. To presume otherwise would undermine the division of powers in the federal system: "Section 15(1) of the Charter, while prohibiting discrimination, does not alter the division of powers between governments."[34]

One exception to the Court's willingness to allow for provincial diversity is the *R. v. Morgentaler* decision.[35] A majority of the Court ruled that the federal abortion law, section 251 of the Criminal Code, which had prohibited the procurement or performance of an abortion without prior approval from a therapeutic abortion committee at an accredited hospital, violates the principles of fundamental justice in section 7. The majority opinion was that the procedure required to obtain approval for a legal abortion imposed undue burdens on women that resulted in a danger to health. The decision touched on the issue of provincial diversity. Then Chief Justice Brian Dickson, who wrote one of the three separate judgements on the majority side, referred to an earlier decision in which La Forest J. had urged the Court to ensure that provinces are given sufficient opportunity to make choices regarding the type of administrative structure that will suit their needs unless the provincial structure itself is "so manifestly unfair, having regard to the decisions it is called upon to make, as to violate the principles of *fundamental* justice."[36] The abortion policy, in the opinion of Dickson CJ., is precisely the kind of arrangement that contradicts the principles of fundamental justice. His difficulty in allowing for provincial diversity is that the differences within and between provinces in providing for therapeutic abortions ensures that many women may not be able to have access to medical procedures necessary for their health.

> [T]he structure [of the abortion law] — the system regulating access to therapeutic abortions — is manifestly unfair. It contains so many potential barriers to its own operating that the defence [to criminal prosecution] it creates will in many circumstances be practically unavailable to women who would prima facie quality for the defence, or at least would force such women to travel great distances in order to benefit from a defence that is held out to be generally available.[37]

The majority's rejection of varying levels of access to therapeutic abortions is seen as contradictory to the intent of the 1969 law which, as Christopher Manfredi argues, responded to a complex legislative objective — to liberalize access to abortion in a manner that would allow local authorities to control access to ensure that the policy accords with a community's moral views.[38] Local autonomy was recognized, implicitly, in the law's failure to explicitly define health or require that all hospitals establish therapeutic abortion committees, and by leaving enforcement of section 251 to the provinces. While these aspects of the legislation "virtually guaranteed unequal access to abortions both among and within provinces"[39] Manfredi argues that the Court's decision to nullify the procedural scheme of section 251 was tantamount to the Court rejecting, as a legitimate policy objective, local diversity in the application of a national abortion policy.[40]

Four of the five preceding cases provide compelling reasons to question assumptions that Charter jurisprudence will necessarily result in pan-Canadian or uniform interpretations of rights that are insensitive to regional differences. While this author is not arguing that the Charter imposes no constraint on the provinces' capacity to promote values rooted in community values, customs or culture, the jurisprudence provides strong indication that the Court is receptive to federalism concerns that provinces be given some latitude to enact policies that are different from other jurisdictions or to administer federal policies in different ways. In *Morgentaler*, where the Court disallowed provincial diversity in the administration of federal policy, it did not dismiss the importance of federalism but expressed a qualification on provinces' abilities to differ in how they administer a federal law: that local, community or provincial standards do not undermine the principles of fundamental justice.

Where the Charter generally poses the greatest constraint on provincial autonomy is where legislation is in direct conflict with a protected right that is specific in its definition. This was the case in the conflict between Quebec's Bill 101 and the minority education language rights of section 23 of the Charter. However, unlike minority education language rights, the majority of protected rights are stated in vague and abstract terms. The constraint in this instance on Quebec's capacity to determine school language instruction policy should not serve as the basis for a general proposition that the pursuit of cultural objectives or community values by provinces will inevitably be invalidated by the Charter. To do so would be to assign an overly narrow interpretation of the Charter that assumes a single or uniform interpretation of rights equally applicable to all jurisdictions.

In the remainder of this chapter, this author will argue that the structure of the Charter should signal caution to those who claim, in the absence of more jurisprudence, that the Charter will inevitably undermine federalism by promoting the homogenization of Canadian public policy. The limitation clause of section 1 is sufficiently broad that courts will be called upon to assess the justification of a range of policies or values, that do not necessarily reflect enumerated rights, which Parliament or the provincial legislatures believe are justifiable limits on protected rights. The legislative override of section 33 allows for the direct limitation of protected rights without judicial scrutiny. Both these clauses confer upon Parliament and the provincial legislatures opportunities to promote policies that reflect provincial or community rather than national objectives.

LIMITATION CLAUSE OF SECTION ONE

The first of these clauses, the limitation clause of section 1, both establishes many of the rights and freedoms of fundamental importance in Canada yet provides constraints on their exercise. This dual purpose of both recognizing the fundamental importance of values and allowing limits upon them is one of the ways the Charter can be reconciled with federalism. Many may find it difficult to reconcile conceptually the ideas of protecting rights and allowing for limits on them or entrenching rights but interpreting them in a federalism context. This difficulty is due, in large part, to the tendency to think of the Charter as ushering in a completely new political regime, one characterized by the primacy of rights over limits and principles over policies.[41] The question of how much discretion governments should retain to impose limits on protected rights invites controversy precisely because questions of limits on rights lie at the heart of debates about the relationship between citizens and the state and individuals and the community. The assumption that protected individual rights should be paramount to other societal objectives or values has roots in liberal theory which posits, as central tenets, the interrelated principles that the state should not advance a particular normative conception of the preferred way of life and, as a necessary condition, should respect that individual rights take precedence over collective goals. One consequence of this assumption is that legislative objectives that cannot be easily accommodated within the language of the Charter are deemed of insufficient importance to limit a protected right. This is because these objectives are seen not as protecting rights but merely as promoting policy objectives, likely characterized as the utilitarian or self-interested considerations of governments or, alternatively, the illiberal or repressive wishes of a legislative majority or community. Consequently, those who assume that the Charter gives primacy to individual rights argue that the only collective values that should be recognized as constitutional entitlements are those that are specifically enumerated or derivative of protected individual rights.[42]

This view has obvious implications for federalism. It denies the legitimacy of provinces promoting other community or cultural objectives if these affect adversely protected individual rights. Notwithstanding the rhetorical force of appealing to "principles" as opposed to "policies" in assessing conflicting values, the assumption implied in this claim is problematic. This is the idea that recourse to the Charter will and should provide the exclusive basis for resolving rights-based conflicts. While some may argue that the only justification for limiting rights is to protect other enumerated rights this view is not compelling. Given the contested nature of the standard for limiting protected rights — a free and democratic society — there is little reason to assume that:

- democratic values are confined to those particular rights entrenched in the Charter;
- democratic values are exclusively individual in nature;
- section 1 evokes a single standard for evaluating the justification of policy objectives; or
- given that federalism is a fundamental pillar of Canadian political institutions, the Charter authorizes an exclusively national standard for justifying reasonable limits on protected rights.

The constitution itself will often fail to provide a single authoritative answer to rights-based conflicts. It has become abundantly clear from Supreme Court jurisprudence on the Charter that section 1 is incapable of providing determinate answers to constitutional conflicts.[43] This indeterminacy is due not only to the vagueness of the section 1 standard — a free and democratic society — but also because of the policy-laden task that courts must assess whether the impugned legislative scheme is reasonable. Courts, in other words, must assess the merits of the legislation in terms of whether better, or less restrictive means, are available. But the complexity of policy development makes it extremely difficult for courts to recognize whether legislative alternatives, which impose a less substantial impairment of a protected right, are practical or effective. It further encourages the Court, in many instances, to accept legislative explanations for why policies are reasonable.[44]

Given the indeterminacy of the section 1 standard for justifying limits on protected rights it could be argued that section 1 enlarges rather than defines the scope of permissible values that warrant limiting protected rights. In doing so it provides provinces and the federal government the opportunity to assert that non-enumerated or community values are worthy of constitutional accommodation, that they fulfil important democratic objectives that justify limiting protected rights. The Supreme Court itself has recognized that the values essential to a free and democratic society are not confined to those specifically enumerated in the Charter.

> Obviously, a practical application of s. 1 requires more than an incantation of the words "free and democratic society." These words require some definition, an elucidation as to the values that they evoke. To a large extent, a free and democratic society embraces the very values and principles which Canadians have sought to protect and further by entrenching specific rights and freedoms in the Constitution, although the balancing exercise in s. 1 is not restricted to values set out in the Charter ...

> Undoubtedly, these values and principles are numerous, covering the guarantees enumerated in the Charter and more. Equally, they may well deserve different emphases, and certainly will assume varying degrees of importance depending upon the circumstances of a particular case.[45]

In deciding whether impugned legislative objectives warrant constitutional protection — whether they are "of sufficient importance to warrant overriding a constitutionally protected right or freedom"[46] — the Court has recognized the justification of a range of policy objectives and values that impose limits on protected rights and which represent collective or community values that cannot be said to constitute specific enumerated rights. These include the objective of ensuring that retailers, who are predominantly women, enjoy a common pause day;[47] the protection of children from manipulative advertising,[48] the promotion of public safety on roads and highways;[49] the insulation of identifiable groups from the wilful promotion of hatred literature;[50] and the avoidance of harm resulting from antisocial attitudes influenced by exposure to obscene materials.[51]

The Court's willingness to accept, under section 1, collective or community values reflects that Canada's political culture diverges in important ways from the unencumbered primacy of individualism. There has been in Canada little counterpart to the theorizing by early American thinkers of how best to limit government and strike a balance between republican values and individual rights, principally property.[52] Whether Canada's failure to embrace a strictly individualistic political culture can be attributed to the inheritance of tory and socialist influences[53] the influence of federalism and its objective of promoting community values, or the need for the state to assume a role in developing a foundling economic and industrial base,[54] Canada's political culture(s) has never represented, and arguably still does not reflect, a liberal monolith.

The Court's reception to federalism concerns also reflects that while Canadians share in common commitment to basic rights and freedoms, important differences exist within Canada, and within a liberal tradition, on the relationship between individual rights and community values. As Charles Taylor argues, while there are only minimal divergences between French and non-French segments of Canada on what constitutes fundamental values, for example, commitment to equality, non-discrimination, the rule of law and the mores of representative democracy, important differences nevertheless exist on the relationship between individual rights and collective goals. These differences are not an indication that French Quebecers are likely to embrace an illiberal or undemocratic polity. Rather, the different assumptions of the relationship between individual rights and collective goals are best understood as a preference for a different model of liberal society.[55]

The capacity under section 1 for Parliament and the provincial legislatures to promote values other than those specifically enumerated helps to overcome the narrowness of the Charter in recognizing fundamental rights and freedoms. The Charter is overwhelmingly an individual rights document. While the Charter gives limited recognition to collective rights the extent to which collective values are protected by the Charter should not be overstated. The collective rights that are entrenched, most notably minority education rights, can be thought of both as collective and individual rights; they are entitlements conferred on individuals but that can be called upon only in a collectivity (where numbers warrant). Minority education language rights can be distinguished, conceptually, from other collective rights such as aboriginal or association rights (collective bargaining and striking) that reflect a collective orientation that is not dependent on or derivative of an individual right. The extent to which the Charter embraces collective values that cannot be reduced to an individual right is minimal. Multicultural rights, for example, do not constitute substantive entitlements of their own but rather offer an interpretive guide for other protected rights. Aboriginal rights also do not represent new substantive entitlements and offer an interpretive guide for judges in light of earlier aboriginal treaty or pre-Charter rights. The extent to which other protected rights in the Charter will embrace collective values depends largely on judicial assumptions about the philosophical content of these.

Having argued that the limitation clause is a way of conferring constitutional recognition on community or collective values that are not specifically enumerated, it is important to emphasize that not all community values may justify limiting protected rights. The justification for community or collective values should not be that these reflect the preferences of a legislative majority. Rather, the justification should be that these values represent compelling democratic objectives and that they do not impose unnecessary or excessive burdens on protected individual rights. As Charles Taylor argues, communities must be mindful of how collective values affect individuals who are not willing members:

> A society with strong collective goals can be liberal ... provided it is also capable of respecting diversity, especially when this concerns those who do not share its goals, and provided it can offer adequate safeguards for fundamental rights. There will undoubtedly be tensions involved, and difficulties, in pursuing these objectives together, but they are not uncombinable, and the problems are not in principle greater than those encountered by any liberal society that has to combine liberty and equality, for example, or prosperity and justice.[56]

When considering whether collective or non-enumerated values should be tolerated under the Charter, it is helpful to keep in mind the distinction Peter Russell has made between core values and more peripheral claims. One of the more difficult tasks of a democratic policy, Russell argues, is determining the appropriate limits that can be imposed upon them.[57] The reason this is so difficult is that as we move away from the central core of those values that reflect ideals common to all contemporary liberal democracies (political freedom, religious toleration, due process of law and social equality) we incur considerable dilemmas in determining what limits are appropriate for less universal and more contested values.

> As we move out from the central core of these values, we encounter restrictions and limits on each, and considerable controversy about the right limits ... It is in the way we deal with [questions about the appropriate limits on protected values] that the Charter will have its main effect. A constitutional charter guarantees not that there will be no limits to rights and freedoms but that a change will be made in the way our society makes decisions about these limits.[58]

The Supreme Court itself has begun constructing a hierarchy of rights in which the difficulty of limiting a protected right will depend on whether the infringed right relates to a core or universal right as opposed to a more marginal or peripheral claim. The principal effect of the core-periphery distinction has been to lessen the burden a legislature has to satisfy to justify impugned policies as a reasonable limit on a protected right. Where the legislative action affects a rights-based claim that is not central or core to the essence of a protected right, the burden for demonstrating the justification of the objective is lessened.[59]

The distinction the Court makes is useful in determining how collective or non-enumerated values should be assessed. Where policies seek to promote values that impose serious constraints on a core element of a fundamental right or freedom, these policies should be difficult to justify. Where, on the other hand, the effect is on a more peripheral aspect of a protect right, justification should not be as difficult. Take, for example, Quebec's signs law policy. The effect of the policy was to impair the ability to engage in commercial advertising. Arguably, this claim of entitlement is not related to the core of free speech — the right to express views on political or social issues.[60] As such, this policy should be easier to justify than if a government sought to promote collective or cultural objectives by prohibiting the expression of contrary views. Because this hypothetical policy would attack the very core of freedom of expression it should be extremely difficult, if not impossible, to justify.

LEGISLATIVE OVERRIDE OF SECTION 33

Like the limitation clause of section 1, the legislative override has generated divergent responses to the appropriate relationship between individual rights and community values and to questions of whether enumerated rights should be given priority over non-enumerated values. From a federalism perspective, the debate becomes: Can provinces promote policies that have a differential effect on protected rights than other provinces? And can provinces promote collective values that may adversely affect protected rights?

In the original debates over the drafting of the Charter some analysts were critical of the proposed limitation clause. Their concerns have been placated to a great extent by the final text of the Charter that makes it considerably more difficult for Parliament and the provincial legislatures to impose limits on protected rights.[61] But while section 1 has received greater acceptance, critics have not similarly warmed to section 33. The legislative override continues to be characterized as being incompatible with entrenched rights. While many predicted that the popularity of the Charter and public sentiment would ensure that it would be difficult for governments to use the override, the language of rights has so captivated our public discourse that section 33 has now, except for the francophone majority in Quebec, generally assumed the mantle of being constitutionally illegitimate. This became particularly clear following Quebec's decision to enact the legislative override in order to exempt new legislation from potential judicial review in response to the Supreme Court's decision that its signs law policy violates the Charter.

Not only did Quebec's use of the override renew criticisms that section 33 is inconsistent with entrenched rights but the enactment of the override, at a time when the proposed Meech Lake amendments dominated the national constitutional agenda, reinforced criticisms of the distinct society clause in the failed Meech Lake constitutional reforms. While rarely analyzed in conjunction with each other,[62] the distinct society clause and legislative override were intricately related, particularly in the context of how the Quebec government views its political responsibilities for promoting French culture in light of the Charter.

Critics of the distinct society clause argued that not only did the clause prescribe a shift away from the pan-Canadian model but[63] it also represented a turning away from our newly enacted "Charter regime." By failing to provide explicitly for the Charter's exemption from the distinct society clause, many critics feared that the clause would undermine equality and minority language rights and would remodify the political system to the extent that some decisions about limiting rights, particularly in Quebec, would effectively remain in the hands of politicians.[64]

The distinct society clause became even more controversial when it became clear that Premier Bourassa regarded it in a similar light as he did section 33: as a way of accommodating and promoting Quebec culture despite the protected rights in the Charter. It was not only the decision to invoke the override but the justification Bourassa gave for his decision that prompted widespread controversy. Bourassa suggested that had the distinct society clause and Meech Lake Accord been ratified, the use of the override would not have been necessary.[65] Bourassa's explanation and his subsequent statement about the need for collective values to prevail in this instance, underscored the concerns of many that the distinct society clause could be used to give priority to collective over individual rights:

> When two fundamental values clash, someone has to make a choice, and find a balance between both. An unavoidable arbitration has to take place. Anywhere else in North America, the arbitration would have been made in favour of individual rights...

> At the end, when a choice had to be made between individual rights and collective rights, I arbitrated in favour of collective rights, by agreeing to invoke the notwithstanding clause.

> I am the only head of government in North America who had the moral right to follow this course, because I am, in North America, the only political leader of a community which is a small minority.

> Who can better, and who has more of a duty to protect and promote the French culture if not the Premier of Quebec? ... I chose to do what seemed to me to be vital for the survival of our community.[66]

The use of the override evoked widespread political[67] and public reaction throughout the country. Tension between French-speaking Quebec and English-speaking Canada goes a long way towards explaining the overwhelming critical response levied at Bourassa's use of the override. With the Charter, critics could express their dislike for Quebec's language policies in the powerful rhetoric of rights. They could, as Roger Gibbins suggests, "Wrap themselves in the flag of the Charter and come charging forward in defence of universal human rights."[68]

But there is more to the explanation than long-standing grievances based on ethnic, language, and regional factors. The answer also lies in how the relationship between entrenched rights and limits is viewed by the academics, the media, politicians, and the public at large. Public debate ensuing after

Bourassa's use of the override renewed suggestions that the Charter is insufficient as long as it contains the override.[69] Underlying these concerns is the belief that protected rights are too important to be subject to the discretionary decisions of political leaders who may wish to promote the values of a community or legislative majority that undermine individual rights. The debate over the override also signalled fundamental disagreement about the importance of the right to expression in the signs law issue. One view is that the ability to advertise in one's preferred language on signs is a vital aspect of free speech. It relates to one's identity and autonomy and is an essential condition of mobility so that an individual can be free to live and establish a business anywhere in the country. Therefore, this right should not be circumscribed for any reason. A second perspective is that the right to advertise is not a core aspect of speech and therefore can be justifiably limited for compelling reasons. The ability to advertise in one's preferred language on commercial signs does not relate to the ability to express opinions on political issues. Given the importance of protecting and promoting Quebec's culture, this right can justifiably be limited. Further, the Charter is not generally concerned with economic issues; organized labour has not been granted economic rights and therefore business interests should not be protected under the Charter.

Despite these differences of opinion, the public and political debates emphasized the first view with little regard for the second and contrary perspective. Quebec's decision to use the override to promote its culture was portrayed in the rest of Canada as a threat to fundamental rights. The use of the override, seen as an unwelcome and residual element of parliamentary supremacy, was deemed illegitimate because it contradicts the belief that the virtue of entrenched rights lies in the fact that decisions about limiting rights are removed from the political process. As Peter Russell states:

> In the hue and cry which then arose outside Quebec we could hear how the rhetoric of constitutional rights invests political discourse with a deep sense of moral rectitude.... There was no need to give any heed to French Quebecers' beliefs about what was necessary for the survival of their culture. Clifford Lincoln's words, "Rights are rights and will always be rights," brought tears to his own and to English Canada's eyes. Freedom to advertise in the language of one's choice was now elevated to the status of a fundamental human right that must override any other human right or social interest. The Meech Lake Accord must die because its recognition of Quebec's distinct culture posed too severe a threat to fundamental rights.[70]

What is interesting about this difference in opinion in the legitimacy of sections 1 and 33 is that conceptually the two clauses serve similar purposes. This might seem a strange statement to make given that the nexus between sections 1 and 33 has not generally been discussed. Rather than being viewed as inconsistent with entrenched rights, the override should be viewed as a similar, although more extreme, form of limiting protected rights. Just as limitations on protected rights may be justified to pursue important democratic objectives — to pursue polices, for example, that promote compelling general welfare concerns or pursue justifiable collective or community values — the override can similarly be considered as a way of conferring constitutional protection on collective or non-enumerated values. The difference between the two clauses falls primarily in how justification of policies is assessed. While courts evaluate the justification of policies that pursue collective or non-enumerated values under section 1, the public scrutinizes the merits of objectives enacted through the use of section 33. The override requires renewal in five years to ensure an opportunity for public scrutiny in an election. Some who defend the override have argued, persuasively, that although the concept is itself consistent with entrenched rights, it should be more difficult to use: the threshold for legislative approval should be higher;[71] the override should not be used preemptively before the Court has ruled on the issue of whether the impugned legislation is a reasonable limit on a protected right;[72] and public consultation should occur whenever it is used.[73]

Just as care must be taken when reviewing legislative decisions under section 1 to ensure that community or general welfare values do not unduly transgress important fundamental rights and freedoms, the same concern exists for the override. The justification of the override should not be to allow legislative majority preferences to veto protected rights but rather to preserve the capacity of the public, through debate within and beyond its representative institutions, to make difficult decisions about the priorities that should be attached to conflicting values.[74] Occasionally the justification may be to reverse a judicial decision but this should happen only after the Supreme Court has ruled on the dispute under section 1 and only then when a policy has been pursued in the course of meaningful and rigorous debate about its justification and effects on protected rights.

The importance of debate is not to validate policy decisions that conflict with protected rights. The presence of robust parliamentary and legislative debate would not justify policies that exact an unnecessary rights-burden on some. Nor would a robust debate validate a majority's or community's demand, interest or preference that results in a serious deprivation of a core right and which, itself, does not represent a compelling democratic value. In short, the mere fact of robust debate cannot justify "bad" policies that are incongruent with the fundamental values of a free and democratic society. The importance of debate is to contribute to, reflect on, and evaluate critically legislative obligations under the Charter and to assess whether decisions that impose limits on protected rights are justified, given the nature of the affected right and in the face of claims of compelling societal values and interests.

The lack of public debate prior to the use of the override by Bourassa may have contributed to the overwhelmingly critical response this action received. Prior debate was negated largely because Bourassa chose to invoke the override as a preemptive measure rather than encourage debate in the National Assembly about whether the legislation represented a reasonable limit under section 1. What is ironic about Bourassa's use of the override in the context of Bill 178, and the role it played in the Meech Lake debate, is that the constitutional validity of the signs policy may not have required the override.

The Supreme Court's ruling in the *Ford* case, which found the policy an unreasonable limit on freedom of expression, was based on the province's earlier unilingual policy and not on Bill 178. In making its decision, the Court did not find that the objective itself was unreasonable, only that the means of accomplishing it were. Far from being an unqualified victory for the primacy of the Charter over federalism, the Court's decision was receptive to federalism concerns. The Court went a long way towards reading a distinct society interpretation into the limitation clause. The Court agreed with the Quebec government's claim that a rational legislative approach to the survival of the French culture was the protection of the French language to assure that the "reality of Quebec society is communicated through the 'visage linguistique'."[75] This approach extended section 1 protection to the collective cultural values promoted by the Quebec government even though these values are not readily identifiable in the Charter.

What troubled the Court, however, was the means by which the objective was sought. In the Court's view, while the Quebec government's objective was a serious and legitimate one, the requirement of French-only was unjustified. The Court speculated about alternative forms of the legislation that would impose a less severe restriction on the freedom to advertise in other languages and indicated that two alternative means would be to require the predominant display of the French language or the requirement that French be in addition to any other language.[76]

One could argue that Quebec's policy under Bill 178, which required that public signs be in French only on the outside of stores while allowing for the use of other languages on signs inside stores,[77] might be interpreted by the Court as a reasonable attempt to ensure that the promotion of the policy objective does not impose an overly severe restriction on freedom of expression. Arguably, the inside-outside distinction in Quebec's policy is consistent with the Court's own suggestion that an acceptable approach would require the predominant display of the French language.

Quebec, however, chose to use the override preemptively rather than to argue the merits of the legislation under section 1. And in doing so it encouraged, perhaps unnecessarily, claims that the province was disregarding the protected rights in the Charter. Given the context of the constitutional debate at the time, in which Bourassa was under pressure within his own province to demonstrate that the proposed constitutional reforms went far enough, this helps explain why, for political purposes, Bourassa chose to use the override. By using the override it served to bolster his claim that the distinct society clause, when combined with the override, would allow Quebec to promote its cultural policies despite the emphasis in the Charter on individual rights. Further, given pressures from nationalists, Bourassa would understandably have been reluctant to give the appearance of being uncertain about the province's legal capacity to promote its signs law policy by waiting for a renewed Charter challenge and the opportunity to argue that the policy imposed a reasonable limit on speech.

CONCLUSIONS

While there is no disputing the fact that the Charter affects federalism by imposing constraints on the extent to which the provinces can promote community values based on a set of priorities different from other jurisdictions, it is premature to assume that the Charter will prevent territorially based differences and result in the homogenization of Canadian policies. The structure of the Charter provides strong incentives for the provinces to promote community values and to argue against a uniform or universal interpretation of the proper reconciliation between these values and protected rights. While the legislative override provides the most direct way for a province to promote values that are peculiar to its sense of priorities, widespread hostility towards the legislative override clause, particularly outside Quebec, will make it difficult for political leaders to use this clause. The limitation clause of section 1 will provide the more likely context for arguments that the Charter should be interpreted in a federalism context to allow for territorially based diversities.

While the Court has not encountered many cases in which federalism questions arise directly, the small body of jurisprudence that addresses the relationship between the Charter and federalism should be seen with cautious optimism by those who would argue against the assumption that the Charter presumes a singular interpretation of the Charter — one that transcends provincial differences. This does not mean that provinces can or should escape the requirement that they respect protected rights. Provinces have an obligation to justify why the values they pursue warrant constitutional protection and why alternative and less restrictive means have not been adopted.

While it is too soon to predict how much latitude the Supreme Court will confer on provinces to pursue divergent priorities, what this jurisprudence does suggest is that provinces retain a measure of discretion to pursue policies that represent values not specifically enumerated, provided that they can justify these in democratic and reasonableness terms. It also suggests that provinces that choose to enact policies in a manner different from other jurisdictions or to apply federal provisions differently do not risk, solely on the basis of difference, implicating equality rights.

Opposition to the distinct society clause in the Meech Lake Accord gave rise to strong reservations about protecting and promoting collective values in Canada. While many are concerned that collective or community values are simply a way of promoting the preferences of legislative majorities over the rights of minorities that the Charter is intended to protect, it is wrong to assume that Quebec, as the one province most willing to promote collective values, lacks respect for individual rights. Charles Taylor's reflections on our shared values — in which minimal divergences exist between French and non-French segments of Canada on what constitutes fundamental values — is demonstrated in extensive survey research that found both in English and French Canada a high level of support for the fundamental values of political freedom, due process of law, and social equality.[78] As Peter Russell argues, "so far as civil liberties are concerned, Quebec is not a distinct society."[79]

One other reason for questioning the view that the Charter has fundamentally compromised federalism is that it implies that without a Charter provinces would be free of all rights-based constraints. Increased public sensitivity to equity issues and the plight of vulnerable groups in society suggest that it is a mistake to presume that the Charter represents the only constraint on provinces' capacity to pursue community values within the jurisdiction authorized by federalism. Moreover, one cannot presume that without a Charter provinces would be free of all judicially-imposed constraints in their pursuit of collective or community values. The Supreme Court's record in the 1950s reveals how, despite the constraints of "parliamentary supremacy," Supreme Court justices have been willing to engage in creative means to set aside provincial legislation that seriously transgressed fundamental or core rights even in the absence of a constitutional Charter.[80]

NOTES

1.   Alan Cairns, *Disruptions: Constitutional Struggles, from the Charter to Meech Lake,* (Toronto: McClelland & Stewart, 1991).

2.   Rainer Knopff and F.L. Morton, "Nation-Building and the Canadian Charter of Rights and Freedoms," in Alan Cairns and Cynthia Williams, eds., *Constitutionalism, Citizenship and Society in Canada* (Toronto: University of Toronto Press. 1985); Peter H. Russell, "Political Purposes of the Charter," *Canadian Bar Review* 61 (1983); Peter Hogg, "Federalism Fights the Charter of Rights," in David P. Shugarman and Reg Whitaker, eds., *Federalism and Political Community: Essays in Honour of Donald Smiley* (Toronto: Broadview Press, 1989); Alan C. Cairns, *The Charter Versus Federalism: The Dilemmas of Constitutional Reform* (Montreal: McGill-Queen's University Press, 1992).

3. An exception is the work of F.L. Morton et al. which has examined the judicial nullification of statutes in the Supreme Court's first 100 Charter cases. Sees F.L. Morton, G. Solomon, I. McNish and D.W. Poulton, "Judicial Nullification of Statutes under the Charter of Rights and Freedoms, 1982-1988," *Alberta Law Review* 28 (1990). See also F.L. Morton, Peter H. Russell and Michael J. Whitey, "The Supreme Court's First One Hundred Charter of Rights Decisions: A Statistical Analysis," *Osgoode Hall Law Journal* 30 (1992). Alan Cairns also revisits the issue of the Charter's nation building effects in Alan Cairns, "Reflections on the Political Purposes of the Charter," in Gerald A. Beaudoin, ed., *The Charter: Ten Years Later* (Cowansville, PQ: Editions Y. Blais, 1992).

4. One exception in the scholarly literature is Denis Robert, "La signification de l'Accord du lac Meech au Canada anglais et au Québec francophone: Un tour d'horizon du débat public," in Peter M. Leslie and Ronald L. Watts, eds., *Canada: The State of the Federation 1987-1988* (Kingston: Institute of Intergovernmental Relations, Queen's University, 1988).

5. This phrase is taken from Robert Vipond, *Liberty & Community: Canadian Federalism and the Failure of the Constitution* (Albany: State University of New York Press, 1991), p. 3.

6. Peter Hogg, "Federalism Fights the Charter of Rights," in David P. Shugarman and Reg Whitaker, eds., *Federalism and Political Community*, p. 249.

7. Knopff and Morton, "Nation-building and the Canadian Charter," p. 148.

8. See for example, Pierre Fournier, "The Future of Quebec Nationalism," in Keith Banting and Richard Simeon, eds., *And No One Cheered: Federalism, Democracy & The Constitution Act* (Toronto: Methuen, 1983), p. 159.

9. Alain Gagnon and Mary Beth Montcalm, *Quebec: Beyond the Quiet Revolution* (Scarborough, ON: Nelson, 1990), p. 183.

10. The right of citizens of Canada to have their children receive publicly paid primary and secondary school instruction in the language of the English or French linguistic minority population of a province is subject to where numbers warrant.

11. Minority education language rights of s. 23 are one of the few rights and freedoms in the Charter that cannot be subject to the legislative override of s. 33.

12. *A.G. Quebec v. Quebec Association of Protestant School Boards* [1984] 2 S.C.R. 66.

13. *Ford v. Quebec (Attorney General)* [1988] 2 S.C.R. 712.

14. In the first decade of Supreme Court jurisprudence, 23 federal statutes were nullified while 18 provincial statutes were declared invalid. F.L. Morton, Peter H. Russell and Troy Ridell, "The First Decade of the Charter of Rights, 1982-1992: A Statistical Analysis of Supreme Court Decisions," paper presented at the annual meeting of the Canadian Political Science Association, University of Calgary, 12-14 June 1994.

15. *R. v. Edwards Books and Art Ltd.* [1986] 2 S.C.R. 713.

16. Ibid. at 782.

17. Ibid. at 802.

18. *R v. Turpin* [1989] 1 S.C.R. 1296.

19. Ibid. at 1329-1333.
20. Ibid. at 1332-1333
21. *R. v. S.(S.)* [1990] 2 S.C.R. 254.
22. Ibid. at 289-92.
23. The Court did not reject the possibility that some interprovincial differences in how federal laws are administered might constitute an infringement on equality. But these distinctions should be assessed on a case-by-case basis and in the context of a principled approach that recognizes explicitly the importance in Canada of federalism:

> It is necessary to bear in mind that differential application of federal law can be a legitimate means of forwarding the values of a federal system. In fact, in the context of the administration of the criminal law, differential applications is constitutionally fostered by ss. 91(27) and 92(14) of the *Constitution Act, 1867*. The area of criminal law and its application is one in which the balancing of national interests and local concerns has been accomplished by a constitutional structure that both permits and encourages federal-provincial cooperation. A brief review of Canadian constitutional history clearly demonstrates that diversity in the criminal law, in terms of provincial application, has been recognized consistently as a means of furthering the values of federalism. Differential application arises from a recognition that different approaches to the administration of the criminal law are appropriate in different territorially based communities. (Ibid., at 289-290).

24. Ibid. at 285.
25. Ibid. at 287-288.
26. *Haig v. Canada (Chief Electoral Officer)* [1993] 2 S.C.R. 995.
27. An additional claim was that the federal Chief Electoral Officer should have used the discretion of his office to extend the entitlement to vote for those persons who were not residents on the enumeration date in a province or territory where the federal referendum was held. The majority decision rejected this claim. Ibid. at 1028.
28. Ibid. at 1022.
29. Ibid. at 1033.
30. Ibid. at 1024-1025.
31. Ibid. at 1029. An argument made by the Charter claimant was that the *Referendum Act* (Canada) and the *Canada Elections Act* were inadequate because they did not make provision for all Canadians to vote in a *national* referendum.
32. Ibid. at 1029-30. The Court also held that even if there was a right to vote in referenda, Mr. Haig's claim that a "national" referendum confers the right to vote, even if an individual is not enumerated, was flawed because there was no "national" referendum but rather two referenda.
33. Ibid. at 1030.
34. Ibid. at 1046-1047.
35. *R. v. Morgentaler* [1988] 1 S.C.R. 30.

36. *R. v. Jones*, [1986] 2 S.C.R. 284 at 304, cited by Dickson in *Morgentaler* at 70. (Emphasis in original).

37. *Morgentaler* at 73.

38. Christopher P. Manfredi, *Judicial Power and the Charter: Canada and the Paradox of Liberal Constitutionalism* (Toronto: McClelland & Stewart, 1993), p. 163.

39. Ibid., p. 119.

40. Ibid., p. 163. Manfredi observes that ironically, in the absence of a national abortion law, the Court's decision has resulted in even greater diversity as the provinces are regulating access to abortion under provincial health-care laws. See pp. 258-259, note 23.

41. See in particular, Lorraine E. Weinrib, "The Supreme Court of Canada and Section One of the Charter." *Supreme Court Law Review* (1988) and David Beatty, *Talking Heads and the Supremes: The Canadian Production of Constitutional Review* (Toronto: Carswell, 1990).

42. Ibid., p. 496.

43. Janet Hiebert, "The Dilemma of the Charter: Is Judicial Deference Appropriate?" paper prepared for CPSA 66th Annual Meeting in Calgary, 12-14 June 1994.

44. Ibid.

45. *R. v. Keegstra* [1990] 3 S.C.R. 697 at 736-737.

46. *R. v. Oakes*, [1986] 1 S.C.R. 103 at 138-139.

47. *R. v. Edwards Books and Art Ltd.*, [1986] 2 S.C.R. 713.

48. *Irwin Toy v. A.G. Quebec* [1989] 1 S.C.R. 927.

49. See the unanimous decisions in *R. v. Thomsen*, [1988] 1 S.C.R. 640; *R. v. Hufsky*, [1988] 1 S.C.R. 621; and *R. v. Whyte* [1988] 2 S.C.R. 3.

50. *R. v. Keegstra.*

51. *R. v. Butler* [1992] 1 S.C.R. 452 at 491.

52. See Jennifer Nedelsky, *Private Property and the Limits of American Constitutionalism: The Madisonian Framework and Its Legacy* (Chicago: Chicago University Press, 1990).

53. G. Horowitz, "Conservatism, Liberalism and Socialism in Canada: An Interpretation," *Canadian Journal of Economics and Political Science* 32, 2 (May 1966).

54. See, for example, H.V. Nelles, *The Politics of Development: Forests, Mines & Hydro-Electric Power in Ontario, 1849-1941* (Toronto: MacMillan, 1974).

55. Charles Taylor, "Shared and Divergent Values," in *Reconciling the Solitudes: Essays on Canadian Federalism and Nationalism* (Montreal: McGill-Queen's University Press, 1993).

56. Ibid., pp. 176-177.

57. Russell, "Political Purposes of the Canadian Charter," p. 43.

58. Ibid., pp. 43-44.

59. *R. v. Keegstra* [1990] 3 S.C.R. 697 at 760-761; *R. v. Butler* [1992] 1 S.C.R. 452 at 500.

60. In the signs law case, the Quebec Attorney General claimed that there is nothing fundamental about commercial expression and argued that American decisions recognizing a degree of First Amendment protection for commercial speech, which the Supreme Court was examining, must be interpreted in the context of a constitution that protects the rights of property. The Attorney General also reminded the Court of its earlier reasons for refusing to give constitutional protection for striking — that economic interests were not protected by the Charter — and argued that to extend freedom of expression beyond political expression, and possibly artistic and cultural expression, would trivialise it.

61. For a discussion of political debates surrounding the evolution of the limitation clause, see Janet Hiebert, "The Evolution of the Limitation Clause in the Charter," *Osgoode Hall Law Journal* 28 (Winter 1990).

62. An exception is F.L. Morton, "Judicial Politics Canadian-Style: The Supreme Court's Contribution to the Constitutional Crisis of 1992," in Curtis Cook, ed., *Constitutional Predicament: Canada after the Referendum of 1992* (Kingston: McGill-Queen's University Press, 1994), pp. 138-146.

63. Critics who view the distinct society clause in this manner ascribe little significance to the pan-Canadian aspects of the clause; specifically, the recognition in s. 2(1)(a) of French-speaking Canadians present outside Quebec and the English-speaking Canadians present in Quebec, which are part of the fundamental characteristic of Canada.

64. This view presumed that courts would have been given a generous interpretation of the distinct society clause which would have granted the Quebec government significant latitude to enact limits on protected rights to promote cultural values.

65. "New Quebec policy to require French on outside signs," *The Globe and Mail*, 19 December 1988, pp. A1, A3.

66. "Bourassa's use of Charter clause shows his vision of distinct Quebec," *The Globe and Mail*, 22 December 1988, pp. A1, A5.

67. The most significant reaction in terms of the future of the Meech Lake amendments came from Manitoba Premier Gary Filmon who, not a party to the original agreement, abruptly withdrew his minority government's support for the Accord in response to Bourassa's use of the override. Manitoba had agreed in principle to support the Meech Lake proposals under the then NDP government leader Howard Pawley whose party was defeated before the legislature had debated the amendment.

68. Roger Gibbins, "Constitutional Politics in the West and the Rest," in Robert Young, ed., *Confederation in Crisis* (Toronto: James Lorimer, 1991), p. 23.

69. The belief that rights are only meaningful if politicians cannot tamper with them has been fuelled, particularly at the popular level, by continued attacks on the override by public officials of the highest order. Then Prime Minister Mulroney, for instance, suggested that the Constitutional Accord proclaimed in 1982 is virtually worthless because, aside from dividing the nation, it fails to protect Canadians' rights. (*Ottawa Citizen*, 7 April 1989, pp. A1-2.)

    However, conflict arose within Mulroney's Cabinet on the virtue of the override. Then Secretary of State Lucien Bouchard endorsed publicly the role of the override, claiming that it is "essential for the survival of certain fundamental Quebec values." These differences were downplayed by Mulroney who implied that they amounted merely to nuances and were not a breach of Cabinet solidarity. Bouchard quoted in *La Presse*, as cited in Hansard, 20 December 1988, p. 425. See also Hansard, 22 December 1988, p. 619; "Fight looms over opting-out clause: Bourassa disputes PM," *The Globe and Mail*, 7 April 1989, pp. A1-A2.

70. Peter H. Russell, "Political Purposes of the Charter," in Philip Bryden, Steven Davis, and John Russell, eds., *Protecting Rights & Freedoms: Essays on the Charter's Place in Canada's Political, Legal, and Intellectual Life* (Toronto: University of Toronto Press, 1994), p. 36.

71. Christopher Manfredi argues that the threshold for using the legislative override should be three-fifths of Parliament. Manfredi, *Judicial Power and the Charter*, p. 209.

72. Ibid.

73. Peter Russell argues that the legislative override should be subject to two separate enactments, both before and after an election. Peter H. Russell, "Standing Up for Notwithstanding," *Alberta Law Review* 29 (1991): 301-302.

74. Ibid., pp. 299-300.

75. *Ford v. Quebec (Attorney General)*, (1988) 2 S.C.R. at 778-779.

76. Ibid., at 779-780.

77. Many of the controversial aspects of Bill 178 have been rescinded by Bill 86, *An Act to Amend the Charter of the French Language*, passed in June 1983. The Quebec government decided against renewing use of the legislative override. In the amended law, public signs, posters, and commercial advertising must be in French but may also include another language provided that French is markedly predominant. However, the government reserves the ability to determine, by regulation, the places, conditions or circumstances where public signs must either be in French only or where French need not be predominant.

78. Paul M. Sniderman, Joseph F. Fletcher, Peter H. Russell and Philip E. Tetlock, "Political Culture and the Problem of Double Standards: Mass and Elite Attitudes Toward Language Rights in the Canadian Charter of Rights and Freedoms," *Canadian Journal of Political Science* 22 (June 1989). See also by the same authors, "Liberty, Authority and Community: Civil Liberties and the Canadian political Community," paper presented at the annual meeting of the Canadian Political Science Association, Windsor, Ontario, 9 June 1988.

79. Russell, "Political Purposes of the Charter," p. 35.

80. These techniques included: a redefinition of sedition, one that was narrower than earlier common law interpretations, in a case in which the Quebec government had prohibited the distribution of religious pamphlets which were "expressive of a seditious intention" (*Boucher v. R.*, [1951] S.C.R. 265); an interpretation of the preamble of the *Constitution Act* which requires freedom of discussion and debate to set aside provincial legislation that required that newspaper presentation of the provincial policy satisfy the government's criteria of accuracy (*Reference re Alberta Statutes* [1938] 2 S.C.R. 100); federalism grounds, to set aside Quebec legislation which sought to prohibit the propagation of communist ideology in the

9

Prospects for Intergovernmental Harmonization in Environmental Policy

Kathryn Harrison

À la fin des années quatre-vingts et au début des années quatre-vingt-dix, l'arène environnementale était lourde de tensions intergouvernementales. Pendant cette période, le gouvernement fédéral est devenu de plus en plus actif dans le secteur de l'environnement, autant de sa propre volonté que sur l'ordre des environnementalistes et des tribunaux. L'affirmation fédérale croissante a provoqué des objections de la part des provinces, sur la défensive à l'égard de leurs propres programmes en matière d'environnement et, ce qui est peut-être plus important, de leur autorité sur l'orientation du développement des ressources naturelles. Toutefois, au cours des deux à trois dernières années, les deux niveaux de gouvernement ont fait des efforts concertés afin de ramener l'harmonie qui caractérisait auparavant les relations fédérales-provinciales dans le secteur de l'environnement. Les premiers efforts ont mis l'accent sur le besoin de coordonner les programmes fédéraux et provinciaux en matière d'environnement qui se chevauchaient, alors que des efforts plus récents cherchent à rationaliser les programmes fédéraux et provinciaux en éliminant le dédoublement et le chevauchement. Ce chapitre passe en revue cette évolution et offre une explication des efforts actuels visant à rétablir l'harmonie. Notamment, la tendance à la rationalisation s'explique par des pressions fiscales et commerciales, des dividendes électoraux décroissants pour une affirmation du fédéral au plan de sa juridiction, de même que par la position de force qu'occupent les provinces au sein du Conseil canadien des ministres de l'Environnement. Le chapitre se conclut par une réflexion sur les avantages et les désavantages de la rationalisation.

In the late 1980s and early 1990s, the environmental arena was one of heightened intergovernmental tensions. The federal-provincial conflicts of this period were primarily the result of greater federal involvement in the environmental field, which prompted provincial objections that a stronger federal role was not only unnecessary in light of well-established provincial environmental programs, but an unwarranted intrusion in provincial jurisdiction over natural resources. Intergovernmental conflict was especially pronounced with respect to environmental assessment, an area where the federal government was forced by judicial decisions to exercise its substantial environmental authority.

In response to these developments, both orders of government have made concerted efforts in the last two to three years to restore the harmony that previously characterized federal-provincial relations in the environmental field. Through the forum of the Canadian Council of Ministers of the Environment (CCME), the federal government and the provinces have moved from the unilateralism that incited recent intergovernmental conflicts, to partnership, and now towards rationalization of federal and provincial roles in environmental protection.

The following section will provide an overview of recent trends in federal-provincial relations in the field, from the late 1980s to date. Thereafter, an effort will be made to explain these developments, in light of both societal and institutional forces. This chapter will conclude with reflections on the desirability of recent efforts to restore intergovernmental harmony.

TRENDS IN FEDERAL-PROVINCIAL RELATIONS

Federal-provincial relations in the environmental field were characteristically cooperative from the early 1970s to the late 1980s.[1] The mutually agreeable division of labour between federal and provincial governments that evolved during this period involved the federal government conducting research on environmental problems and control technologies, and setting a limited number of national standards in consultation with the provinces. It was the provinces that took the lead role in environmental protection: setting their own standards, monitoring source performance, and taking responsibility for enforcement of both their own and federal regulations. Harmonious intergovernmental relations prevailed largely because the federal government deferred to provincial authority and declined to test the limits of its own jurisdiction.[2] The resulting situation was one of "provincial control of environmental matters being exercised against a background of minimum federal interference."[3]

This stable pattern of federal-provincial roles and relations was disrupted in the late 1980s, when the federal government began to take a broader view of its environmental jurisdiction. Developments since then can be divided into three phases — unilateralism, partnership, and rationalization — each of which will be discussed in turn. It bears emphasis that these three phases overlap, since in each case responses to developments in federal-provincial relations emerged before the momentum of those developments was spent.

UNILATERALISM

Beginning in the mid-1980s, public opinion polls indicated growing public concern for the environment, culminating in a dramatic peak in 1989, when the environment was most often identified by survey respondents as "the most important problem in Canada."[4] Support for *federal* intervention was especially strong.[5] In response to this growing public demand, both federal and provincial governments became more active in the environmental field, passing new laws and regulations and stepping up enforcement of existing ones. While the higher level of activity at both levels created the potential for conflict, it was especially the federal government's move from a deferential to an assertive posture vis à vis the provinces that provoked opposition.

The first source of dissension among environment ministers was the federal government's proposal to revamp its *Environmental Contaminants Act*. The resulting *Canadian Environmental Protection Act* (CEPA), proclaimed in 1988, signalled the federal government's intent to play a larger role in the environmental field.[6] CEPA offered the prospect of new federal regulations for dozens of toxic substances, while an accompanying compliance policy promised a more active federal role in the enforcement of those regulations.[7] In presenting the legislation, the federal minister, Tom McMillan, stressed the essential role of the federal government in setting national standards, and departed from his immediate predecessors' deference in stating: "In the final analysis, the federal government has to act. Even though it may be an area of overlapping jurisdiction in some instances, we do have authority and the federal government intends to exercise it. We do not intend to do it by committee."[8]

Objections to CEPA were raised by some provinces in the closed forum of the Canadian Council of Resource and Environment Ministers (the predecessor to CCME). The larger provinces, in particular, argued that a stronger federal role amounted to unnecessary duplication of their efforts at best, and created the potential for conflict between federal and provincial approaches at worst. Quebec objected most strongly, depicting the proposed federal law as an unjustified intrusion in provincial jurisdiction. In response to provincial proposals, the federal government amended its bill to allow Cabinet to declare that federal regulations would not apply in a province where it was agreed that provincial regulations met certain standards of "equivalency." Both opposition members and environmentalists criticized the equivalency amendment, depicting it as a sellout to the provinces that would result in a patchwork of inconsistent standards across the country.[9] It is noteworthy, however, that although the basic approach was proposed by Quebec and supported by other provinces, most if not all provinces took exception to the statutory conditions associated with equivalency that emerged in the final legislation. Quebec, in particular, vowed never to sign an equivalency agreement.

The next federal environmental proposal to disrupt intergovernmental relations was the Green Plan. Already bruised by CEPA, the same provinces complained of inadequate consultation by the federal government during the protracted development of the Green Plan. Some provinces feared the prospect of federal interference in their environmental programs and, more importantly, in their economies, with Alberta especially anxious about the prospect of a carbon tax. Although the provinces' worst fears turned out to be unfounded when the Green Plan was released in December 1990,[10] the sense of exclusion from the drafting process proved a lasting source of resentment in many provinces.

The intergovernmental tensions provoked by CEPA and the Green Plan paled in comparison to those that subsequently emerged in the environmental assessment field. Unlike previous irritants, which emerged as a result of the federal government's greater assertiveness with respect to its environmental jurisdiction, in the case of environmental assessment, a more activist role was thrust upon a reluctant federal government by environmentalists and the courts.

The question of environmental assessment rose to prominence in 1989, when the federal Court accepted environmentalists' arguments that the federal government was compelled to perform an environmental assessment of the Rafferty-Alameda dam project in Saskatchewan under the terms of its own Environmental Assessment and Review Process (EARP) Guidelines Order.[11] The Court effectively ruled that in using non-discretionary language (i.e., "the Minister shall") in a formal regulation, the federal government had regulated itself, however unintentionally, and thus must abide by its own regulation. In the wake of the decision, environmentalists across the country eagerly turned to the courts to force the federal government to perform assessments of dozens of other major projects.

The EARP litigation brought to the fore the potential tension between the federal regulatory role in environmental policy and provincial control of natural resource development. Individual provinces reacted angrily as the federal government undertook belated reviews of dozens of projects that had already received provincial approvals, some of which were already under construction. Not surprisingly, the provinces most concerned were those with major projects on their economic agendas. Even more contentious was the fact that the provinces themselves were the proponents of some of the most highly contested projects, including the James Bay development in Quebec, the Oldman dam in Alberta, and the Rafferty-Alameda dams in Saskatchewan.

There were important obstacles to intergovernmental accommodation in the environmental assessment case. First, in interpreting the Guidelines Order as non-discretionary, the courts had granted environmental groups substantial leverage over the federal agenda. As one provincial official active in intergovernmental relations complained at the time, "As it now stands, it's no longer a matter between us and them. It's up to third parties who walk in off the street and demand an environmental impact assessment."[12] Second, the Rafferty-Alameda and subsequent EARP decisions were handed down at the height of public concern for the environment. Although the option of amending the regulation to include more discretionary language (e.g., substituting "mays" for "shalls") was technically available, and strongly advocated by the provinces, it was clear from the reception of the CEPA equivalency amendment that such an approach would be widely depicted as a federal evasion of responsibility. The federal government chose instead to hasten development of a new environmental assessment act to replace the controversial EARP regulation.

The result was the *Canadian Environmental Assessment Act* (CEAA), which received royal assent in June 1992. With the new law, the federal government recaptured a measure of control of its own agenda from the courts by replacing the general language of the Guidelines Order with regulations listing specific projects and decisions requiring assessments. However, in many respects CEAA retains and even strengthens the language of the predecessor Guidelines Order.[13] As under the EARP Guidelines Order, environmental assessments will be mandatory in the case of federal projects, federally financed projects, and projects on federal lands. The non-discretionary language of the Act will still afford ample opportunities for citizen lawsuits should the government fail to abide by the Act and its accompanying regulations. For the same reasons that it was politically untenable to amend the EARP regulation in the face of unprecedented public concern for the environment, it would have been equally difficult for the federal government to retreat legislatively from its new activist role in environmental assessment.

It is thus not surprising that the new Act did little to assuage provincial objections to the federal regulation. From the provinces' perspective, CEAA promised to entrench statutorily a regime of federal interference in provincial resource management decisions. As one Alberta minister stated, "We fought hard for control of the resources of this province, and we're against the federal government coming into this process through the side door."[14]

Unlike CEPA, which provoked dissent primarily from the largest provinces, the provinces were united in their objections to the proposed *Canadian Environmental Assessment Act*. Quebec was no longer participating in the Canadian Council of Ministers of the Environment (CCME) in the wake of the failure of the Meech Lake Accord. However, the Quebec minister clearly conveyed his objections to the proposed legislation in a series of letters to his federal counterpart. The other nine provincial ministers, acting under the leadership of Alberta, proposed amendments to the parliamentary committee considering the bill, including a form of equivalency that would authorize the federal government to satisfy its statutory obligations with a provincial assessment.[15] The provinces' proposals were rejected by the committee. When the bill was passed by the House of Commons, the Quebec government staged a last ditch effort to prevent its passage in the Senate. When that effort failed, the Quebec environment minister, Pierre Paradis, vowed "judicial guerilla warfare" in the future.[16] However, as of June 1994, the war had yet to begin; CEAA has not been proclaimed pending finalization of essential regulations.

The first of the three recent phases of intergovernmental relations in the environmental field thus drew to a close with the passage of CEAA. During this period, federal-provincial relations were characterized by unilateralism, as both orders of government sought to respond to growing public demand for environmental protection. It bears emphasis, however, that it was *federal* unilateralism that was new and increasingly contentious, since the provinces had long operated with a significant degree of independence in the environmental field.

PARTNERSHIP

Efforts to restore intergovernmental cooperation began soon after tensions emerged in the environmental field and continue to date. The goal during the second phase was to promote coordination of the now distinct federal and provincial environmental programs. The initiative was taken by the provinces. In the landmark 1988 Crown Zellerbach decision, the Supreme Court of Canada relied on the Peace, Order and Good Government power in authorizing federal control of marine pollution.[17] The decision clearly strengthened the federal government's constitutional position in the field, and undercut provincial resistance to CEPA.[18] Thus, after the passage of CEPA, even the most jurisdictionally defensive provinces conceded the inevitability of greater federal involvement. They abandoned the strategy of trying to preclude federal interference and sought instead to at least prevent federal unilateralism. As one provincial official explained, "if some guy moves into your basement and you can't evict him, you at least try to keep him in the basement."[19] This strategy explains why one of the strongest opponents of federal environmental initiatives, Alberta, became a champion of efforts to promote intergovernmental cooperation.

In addition to jurisdictional sensitivities, there were good policy motives underlying the new intergovernmental initiatives. All ministers in CCME were keenly aware of investors' complaints about the uncertainties and delays resulting from independent and uncoordinated federal and provincial environmental assessment processes. Moreover, virtually all provinces were eager to achieve national harmonization of standards, both to avoid competition to set more stringent standards, and to prevent less aggressive provinces from undercutting their environmental standards to entice investors.

The first expression of the new will to cooperate was the revitalization of the intergovernmental council. The former Canadian Council of Resource and

Environment Ministers was renamed the Canadian Council of Ministers of the Environment in 1988, and relocated to Winnipeg with a substantially larger budget and staff. This development reflected both a recognition that CCME was the most obvious forum for resolution of existing grievances, and a desire by some provinces to establish CCME as a "national" alternative to "federal" actions.

To a large extent that has occurred. In recent years, CCME has been transformed from little more than a small secretariat making logistical arrangements for annual meetings to a significant national policymaking body. Through coordination of federal and provincial efforts, CCME has undertaken a number of ambitious national programs, including the VOC/NOx plan to control ground level ozone, a national packaging reduction strategy, and a joint federal-provincial program to clean up orphan hazardous waste sites.

During this period, the watchword in federal-provincial relations became "partnership." The first formal expression of that partnership was the Statement on Interjurisdictional Cooperation (STOIC), which was signed by federal and provincial environment ministers in 1990.[20] The text is primarily a statement of aspirations, promising consultation and coordination, but offering little by way of specifics.[21] STOIC was followed by a similarly lofty statement of environmental assessment principles, which was adopted by CCME in 1991 with the intent of promoting coordination of and consistency among federal and provincial environmental assessment processes.[22]

In anticipation of more specific bilateral federal-provincial agreements, CCME developed prototype bilateral agreements for equivalency, environmental assessment, and CEPA administration. These multilateral efforts have only recently begun to bear fruit. A Canada-Alberta agreement concerning environmental assessment was signed in August 1993. It was followed in May 1994 by a Quebec-Canada agreement concerning administration of federal pulp and paper regulations. In June 1994 the governments of Canada and Alberta concluded an administrative agreement concerning pollution provisions of the *Fisheries Act.* Also in June 1994, the first CEPA equivalency agreement, which will suspend the effect of federal regulations for pulp mills, lead smelters, and vinyl chloride plants in Alberta, was signed.[23] Numerous other bilateral administrative agreements are under negotiation.[24] The one exception to this pattern of bilateralism is the so-called Atlantic Accord, signed in May 1994 by environment ministers from the federal government and the four Atlantic provinces.[25]

It is not possible to review each of these agreements and accords within the space of this chapter. However, two general observations can be offered. First, while still largely aspirational in tone, these agreements represent what Kennett has called a hardening of federal-provincial "soft law." From multilateral statements of principles to bilateral framework agreements to more specific annexes, there has been a gradual movement from broad principles to more specific commitments. As such agreements become increasingly specific and quasi-contractual in form, there is a greater likelihood that they will be granted legal status by the courts.[26] However, the enforceability, whether by signatory governments or third parties, of even the most detailed of recent agreements remains unclear.

Second, the agreements now emerging all express a commitment to a "single window" approach. In recent years, regulated industries have lobbied hard for a return to the single window of the 1970s, in which one level of government, the provinces, was responsible for administering and enforcing both federal and provincial standards. The most detailed recent agreements, the Canada-Alberta *Fisheries Act* administrative agreement and the Canada-Quebec pulp and paper administrative agreement, both suggest that it will be the provinces that again staff the single window. A noteworthy departure from past practice, however, is the federal commitment in the case of the Canada-Quebec agreement to transfer a sum of $300,000 per year to the province to cover the costs of provincial administration of federal regulations. This sets a clear precedent for future federal-provincial administrative agreements.[27]

The second of the three phases is drawing to a close with the completion of various bilateral agreements based on previous multilateral efforts within CCME. A crucial difference between the first and second phases lies in the degree of provincial acceptance of federal involvement in the field. Efforts by the provinces to preempt federal interference were replaced in the early 1990s by an attempt to preclude unilateralism and promote coordination of federal and provincial efforts through formal agreements.

RATIONALIZATION

Even as a bewildering number of bilateral and multilateral accords are just beginning to emerge, CCME has moved in a new direction. In November 1993, the ministers announced that harmonization would be the Council's top priority in the coming two years. While harmonization was already a clearly stated goal of the Statement on Interjurisdictional Cooperation, the term is now being used more broadly. It includes the obvious goal of promoting consistency of standards between federal and provincial governments and across provinces, an effort that has met with little success to date despite the good intentions of STOIC. However, a second goal of minimizing overlap and duplication while maintaining or enhancing current levels of environmental protection also has been identified. Interviews with federal and provincial officials indicate that, to date, much greater emphasis has being placed on the second goal than the first.

A task group of federal and provincial officials was created and mandated to pursue harmonization according to an ambitious schedule. The first track is the development of work plans for harmonization in five critical policy areas: pulp and paper, environmental assessment, international environmental agreements, parliamentary review of CEPA, and trade policy. The second, and arguably more significant, track is to develop a new "Environmental Management Framework," to clarify and rationalize federal and provincial roles and responsibilities concerning environmental protection. The task group of federal and provincial officials first developed a "Purpose, Objectives, and Principles" document, which was approved by the Ministerial Council in June 1994.[28] They were directed to prepare a draft framework document for review by the ministers at their November meeting. The intent is to circulate the document for public comment thereafter and to finalize it at the CCME meeting in the spring of 1995.

The harmonization initiative represents a dramatic change of direction. The emphasis on eliminating duplication and overlap contrasts with the implicit acceptance of overlap in STOIC and other recent CCME documents. It is clear that more ambitious changes are being considered than embodied in recent multilateral and bilateral agreements. The proposed framework has been described by the ministers themselves as nothing less than "a new environmental management regime for Canada."[29] The ministers have given the task group considerable scope short of constitutional reform. Ironically in light of the absence of the environmental jurisdiction issue in recent constitutional proposals, environmental protection is among the policy sectors where the federal government and the provinces could accomplish significant reform within the current constitutional framework. There is no need for constitutional amendments to eliminate overlap, since either order of government can simply agree not to exercise its jurisdiction.

While STOIC and subsequent bilateral agreements were prompted by the provinces, the harmonization initiative emerged as a result of what both federal and provincial officials described as a "dramatic" change of heart by the federal government.[30] In the summer of 1993, federal officials, serving a new minister and deputy minister under the Campbell government, conveyed to their provincial counterparts in CCME a new commitment to eliminate the overlap that had emerged in recent years, and to work together to rationalize federal and provincial roles in the field. The olive branch was initially received with considerable scepticism by provincial representatives. Indeed, the emergence of several bilateral agreements in 1994 can be seen as a response to the provinces' demand for evidence that the federal government was acting in good faith.

While the process of drafting the Framework for Environmental Management is just beginning, there are some indications of the direction the initiative is moving. The task group has shown considerable interest in the model of the

Australian Intergovernmental Agreement on the Environment, signed by the Commonwealth, state, and territorial governments in May 1992 with a similar intent of minimizing overlap and duplication.[31] Of particular interest is the Australian model of Commonwealth accreditation of state programs, which enables the Commonwealth to withdraw from a program while granting "full faith and credit" to a comparable state program. Accreditation is, in a sense, a more flexible and far reaching version of equivalency.

Although specific proposals for federal and provincial roles have yet to emerge, a more narrowly defined federal role seems inevitable.[32] The move towards "one window" monitoring and enforcement by the provinces in recent bilateral agreements offers an early indication. Most provinces already have substantial enforcement teams in place, and they are eager to maintain their role in managing natural resources. The federal government, on the other hand, is just beginning to confront the reality of implementing its newly adopted laws and regulations with inadequate resources.

The prospects for continued federal involvement in national standard setting are clouded. There is clearly a will among the provinces to harmonize standards across the country. However, provincial officials are adamant that what is needed are "national," as opposed to "federal" standards; many hope to see national standards set by CCME, rather than the federal government. There is some evidence that the federal Liberal government is receptive. Unlike former Conservative environment minister, Tom McMillan, who stressed that the fundamental role of the federal government was to establish national standards, unilaterally if necessary, the current federal minister, Sheila Copps, recently stated: "[A]cid rain is a regionalized problem ... that requires regional approaches.... Rather than the national government coming in with national regulations, we're trying to ensure we have harmony in application and standards that will be developed across the country by consensus."[33]

Discussions thus appear to be moving "back to the future." The federal government could once again conduct research ("out of the gumboots and back in the lab where they belong" in one provincial official's words), manage federal lands and oceans, take the lead in negotiating international agreements (with extensive provincial consultation), and facilitate the development of consensual national standards. The provinces, in contrast, could set their own standards with national standards as their guide, issue permits, monitor source performance, and enforce both their own and any federal regulations.

Among the many difficult unresolved issues is how to reconcile the very different needs and capabilities of small and large provinces. Historically, smaller provinces have been more open to federal involvement, both because they lack human and capital resources to undertake major regulatory initiatives on their own, and also because their weaker economies make them reluctant to regulate unilaterally. The question thus arises whether rationalization demands different roles for the federal government in different provinces. At this point, the preferred alternative is "capacity building," which would entail the federal government transferring resources to smaller provinces rather than playing a direct role itself. The rationale offered is that it would be inefficient for the federal government to maintain capacity to perform certain functions in only a few provinces. However, there is also concern among the larger provinces that a federal government that retained such capacity for the sake of small provinces would be tempted to intervene in other provinces as well.

The third phase in intergovernmental relations concerning the environment thus has just begun, with the most difficult issues remaining to be resolved. The harmonization initiative departs from previous intergovernmental efforts, which sought compatible coexistence through multilateral and bilateral agreements. Overlap is now the enemy, and in a policy arena fraught with overlap, success could entail quite dramatic changes. It is significant, however, that the harmonization initiative is proceeding in a spirit of federal-provincial cooperation. Both orders of government are strongly committed to rationalizing federal and provincial environmental roles.

EXPLAINING RECENT DEVELOPMENTS

Conflict and cooperation in federal-provincial relations in the environmental field have closely followed trends in federal jurisdictional assertiveness. Intergovernmental tensions emerged in the late 1980s, when in response to growing public demand, the federal government proposed to re-enter the environmental field. The first effort to restore intergovernmental harmony was predicated on agreement to forego unilateralism, particularly on the federal government's part. And the present effort to harmonize federal and provincial roles was prompted by the federal government's willingness to entertain withdrawal from contentious functions.

The recent decline in federal assertiveness in the environmental field can be explained by societal and institutional forces in the environmental field, and spillover effects from other policy arenas. After reviewing factors that collectively account for the return to intergovernmental harmony, several countervailing forces will be considered that could sustain or renew federal-provincial conflict despite ongoing efforts to achieve harmonization.

SOCIETAL FORCES: TRENDS IN PUBLIC OPINION

Just as the growing federal assertiveness of the late 1980s coincided with the rising salience of environmental issues, so does the decline in federal assertiveness coincide with declining salience. With the onset of the recession, the environment fell precipitously from its position at the top of public opinion polls. For instance, while the environment was the top ranked problem nationally, cited by 16.5 percent of respondents as "the most important problem" facing Canada in July 1989, it was cited by only 3.8 percent in December 1990 (7th place), and less than 1 percent in January 1994.[34] While discrete environmental controversies, such as Clayoquot Sound and Hydro Quebec's Great Whale project, persist on the front pages in some provinces, the number and scope of environmental stories has declined nationally. Indeed, the few newspaper stories concerning the environment during the 1993 election focused on the near invisibility of environmental issues during the campaign.[35]

Despite the decline of the environment among Canadians' top priorities, the level of concern expressed in response to closed-ended questions (e.g., "How concerned are you about the quality of the environment?") has remained very high. The "most important problem" question could exaggerate trends in public opinion, since abrupt changes in Canadians' highest priorities could mask relative stability among second-tier concerns. Some have argued that persistently high levels of concern indicate that the environment has become a "core value," and that exaggerated trends in response to the "most important problem" question therefore are less relevant.[36] This perspective suggests that governments retreat from environmental commitments at their peril.

That argument would be more compelling had Canadians objected more strenuously in the early 1970s to federal and provincial governments' retreat from earlier commitments in the face of very similar trends in public opinion.[37] In many respects, the recent wave of public concern for the environment was a replay of an earlier green wave that crested in 1969-70. Growing public concern at that time also prompted federal and provincial responses in the form of legislative and regulatory initiatives. Federal threats to venture into a field previously left to the provinces elicited intergovernmental conflicts in the early 1970s very similar to those recently experienced. However, when the visibility of environmental issues declined abruptly, the provinces remained defensive of their jurisdiction, while the federal government declined to test the limits of its own environmental authority, thus facilitating the prolonged period of intergovernmental harmony in the 1970s and early 1980s.

The public's complacency in the face of declining governmental enthusiasm for the environment during the 1970s and early 1980s, despite surveys indicating persistently high levels of environmental concern, offers support for Dunlap's alternative explanation that the environment tends to be a subject of "permissive consensus."[38] While the public expresses very real concerns when cued to environmental threats by pollsters, most of the time they are not paying close attention to what governments are actually doing to address environmental problems.

One would anticipate a shift in the relative influence of interest groups advocating and opposing environmental controls in response to declining salience of environmental issues. During peak periods, governments should be more responsive to environmental groups, which they perceive to speak for the broader public. Objections from regulated industries are likely to carry increasing weight, however, as the prominence of environmental issues declines, and they are replaced in the polls by "bread and butter" concerns like jobs and the economy. The concerns of business — the costs of overlapping monitoring and reporting requirements, and the lack of national harmonization of standards — clearly were influential in prompting both the federal government's 1993 overture to the provinces and CCME's harmonization initiative.[39] It is noteworthy that governments were less receptive to those same concerns when overlapping statutes and regulations were being promulgated at the height of public attention to environmental issues.

As the salience of environmental issues declines, one would also expect the provinces to lose interest in pressing the limits of their environmental jurisdiction. How, then, can one account for the provinces' persistent jurisdictional defence? A critical difference between federal and provincial environmental authority is that the provinces' constitutional jurisdiction is inextricably tied to their control of natural resources and economic development.[40] Provincial jurisdictional defensiveness thus may owe less to a desire to protect the environment than to manage provincial economies. As one provincial official explained in the context of federal-provincial disagreements over environmental assessment, "The bottom line is not environmental protection here, but economic development."[41]

INSTITUTIONAL FORCES: CCME

Although CCME was created only in 1988, the federal-provincial ministerial council previously had existed as the Canadian Council of Resource and Environment Ministers (CCREM) since 1970 and before that as the Canadian Council of Resource Ministers since 1961. The existence of a well-established forum for resolution of federal-provincial differences would be expected to hasten resolution of intergovernmental tensions.

Several authors have emphasized the role of the Council in contributing to the intergovernmental cooperation that preceded the late 1980s.[42] It has been argued that the permanence of the Council facilitated the emergence of "trust ties,"[43] among federal and provincial ministers and officials. Officials in the harmonization task group emphasize the high degree of trust that has emerged after years of working together on CCME committees. The confidential nature of CCME discussions also facilitates candid discussion and compromise among jurisdictions.

Of particular interest is the relative strength of federal and provincial governments within CCME. CCME is unique among intergovernmental institutions in having both an independent secretariat, and a Chair that rotates annually among the 11 federal and provincial ministers. Within CCME, the provinces thus are in a relatively strong position to resist federal proposals. The Council's long-established norm of consensual decisionmaking also strengthens the provinces' ability to constrain federal involvement, particularly in joint initiatives. These features can help to explain why revitalization of the Council was consciously pursued by some provinces as a means to establish a credible alternative to federal policymaking.

SPILLOVER EFFECTS

Environmental policymaking does not exist in a vacuum. In addition to social and institutional forces in the environmental policy arena, there are spillover effects from other policy areas. The most influential spillover issue has been the deficit. Growing public concern with the deficit and government inefficiency has led federal and provincial governments alike to pursue aggressive spending cuts in the last two years. In turn, budgetary restraint has created pressure on individual departments to rationalize their programs, since they are pressed to deliver the same services with fewer resources. Federal and provincial officials place the greatest emphasis on this factor in explaining recent intergovernmental efforts to eliminate duplication in the environmental field.

The desire to rationalize appears to have affected federal and provincial governments differently, however. The federal government, which is forced to confront the costs of implementing its new programs at a time of budgetary restraint and declining public attention to environmental issues, has shown increasing interest in provincial monitoring and enforcement. Yet while provincial officials interviewed expressed at least as much interest in improving efficiency, there is no evidence that the provinces are seeking to reduce their administrative costs by shifting program delivery to the federal government. When provinces seek "one window" implementation, they invariably envision themselves staffing the window. The defence of provincial jurisdiction appears to prevail over the desire to evade costly administrative responsibilities.

A second spillover issue that helped prompt the harmonization initiative is free trade. NAFTA, GATT, and the internal free trade initiative all make it increasingly difficult for individual ministers to justify inconsistent standards across jurisdictions. Environmental departments face criticism from within their jurisdictions that strong process regulations (e.g., discharge standards) hinder competitiveness, and criticism from other jurisdictions that strong product regulations (e.g., packaging restrictions or recycling requirements) are merely trade barriers in disguise. The trade issue thus presents an external threat to federal and provincial environmental ministers, which serves to unite them in defence of their common jurisdiction.

COUNTERVAILING FORCES

Since the harmonization initiative is still at an early stage, it is worth reviewing countervailing forces that could sustain or renew intergovernmental tensions. The first factor is a societal one. Canadian environmental groups are clearly in a much stronger position to counteract the declining salience of environmental issues and waning governmental commitment than they were in the early 1970s, when most environmental groups were just being established. Environmental groups thus may be able to mobilize latent public concern to oppose any back-tracking by federal and provincial governments. Moreover, the success of recent efforts by environmental groups to influence consumer demand suggests that governmental action in the future may be less critical to environmental protection. In campaigns against the environmental impacts of the Great Whale hydro project in Quebec and against pulp mills using chlorine bleaching, environmentalists have bypassed governments and lobbied Canadian and international consumers directly, with considerable success.

With respect to the harmonization initiative, it is noteworthy that Canadian environmentalists have typically advocated a strong federal role in environmental protection to counteract provincial preoccupation with resource development.[44] It is no accident that some of the greatest victories of Canadian environmental groups in recent years were predicated on forcing federal overlap of provincial efforts in the environmental assessment field. The federal and provincial governments thus can expect scepticism, if not resistance, from environmentalists to their forthcoming harmonization proposals. Already, environmentalists on a national advisory group established by the harmonization task force have expressed reservations.

If environmentalists are successful in depicting harmonization as a retreat by either order of government from environmental responsibilities, they may be able to generate opposition to forthcoming proposals for rationalization. However, they will need to counteract governments' efforts to frame the issue in terms of improving government efficiency, which also holds considerable popular appeal. Moreover, while environmentalists have had dramatic recent successes in mobilizing public opposition on discrete environmental issues — more than 800 people were arrested in 1993 protesting logging in Clayoquot Sound — it will be much more difficult to rally a constitutionally-fatigued public's interest in abstract jurisdictional and administrative questions.

Two institutional constraints could preclude more radical harmonization proposals. First, the federal government must contend with its own statutory and regulatory legacy of the last few years. Having spent several years building the foundations for a strong federal role in environmental protection, it will be difficult to withdraw from certain functions now. It is particularly noteworthy that the new statutes, CEPA and CEAA, are less discretionary than the first generation of federal environmental laws passed during the 1970s. In the face of inevitable lawsuits demanding federal environmental assessments under CEAA, and citizens' statutorily authorized requests for investigations under CEPA, it will be difficult for the federal government to defer to the provinces. Thus, more radical harmonization proposals will almost certainly require legislative amendments to extend opportunities for delegation of administration to the provinces and possibly to relax the definition of equivalency now in CEPA and establish a comparable mechanism in CEAA.[45]

A second source of institutional resistance is likely to come from within the federal government. Reservations concerning Environment Canada's harmonization activities have already been expressed within Cabinet, both from departments like National Defence, which fear provincial intrusion in their activities, and those like Fisheries and Oceans that are eager to maintain a strong federal role. One might also anticipate resistance within the federal department of Environment from public servants concerned about losing their jobs, particularly those involved in monitoring and enforcement activities in regional offices.

Finally, the change in government after the 1993 federal election can be viewed as a temporal spillover, which could sustain federal involvement in the environmental field. It could be particularly difficult for a new party in government to withdraw from certain environmental functions after having repeatedly criticized its predecessors for not being aggressive enough. While there is evidence of the Liberals' intentions to follow-through on Red Book commitments,[46] at the same time, the government-wide effort led by Marcel Massé to "renew the federation" by eliminating overlap and duplication strongly reinforces the harmonization initiative launched by the Conservative government. Moreover, the efficiency of the federation undoubtedly will assume increasing importance in coming debates in Quebec.

The trend towards rationalization thus can be explained by fiscal and trade pressures, declining electoral incentives for federal jurisdictional assertiveness, and the relatively strong position of the provinces within CCME. However, environmental group resistance to harmonization, statutory constraints, and resistance from within the federal government may yet present obstacles to harmonization.

IS HARMONIZATION DESIRABLE?

The restoration of federal-provincial cooperation in the environmental field clearly has intuitive appeal. Incidents such as the federal-provincial legal clash in the Rafferty-Alameda case only serve to discredit politicians at both levels.[47] However, cooperation is not the end in itself, at least not the only end. What are the implications of recent trends in federal-provincial relations for protection of the environment?

The current harmonization initiative, if successful, offers three significant advantages. The first is the potential to save money, or more aptly, to cope with declining resources by eliminating unnecessary duplication. It may well be possible to deliver the same level of environmental protection more efficiently by dividing tasks between federal and provincial governments according to their strengths. Second, in addition to savings for governments, there are potentially significant savings for regulated firms if overlapping reporting and assessment requirements can be eliminated. Finally, rationalization of federal and provincial roles in the field holds the promise of enhancing accountability. The constitution itself is far from clear concerning which level of government is responsible for what, and it is questionable whether the plethora of complex bilateral and multilateral agreements now emerging serves to clarify lines of accountability for the general public. A sharper delineation of federal and provincial responsibilities thus could limit opportunities for intergovernmental buck passing.

Rationalization also entails serious risks, however. While overlap can be costly, it creates the potential for backup enforcement — if one level does not do the job, maybe the other will — and for federal and provincial oversight of each other's activities. Full or partial federal withdrawal from standard setting and enforcement would leave critical environmental decisions in the hands of provincial governments, which tend to be more directly involved in resource-driven economic development. In setting and enforcing environmental standards, provincial governments, by virtue of their smaller size, must contend to a greater degree than the federal government with the risk of placing local industries at a competitive disadvantage by imposing greater regulatory burdens than their neighbours. While in recent years some provinces have shown admirable resolve to ensure that environmental standards are not sacrificed to short-term economic objectives, and indeed have adopted more stringent standards than both neighbouring provinces and the federal government, others have been less aggressive.

Much depends on how it is proposed to set national standards in the future. Historically, CCME has operated by consensus. Such a decision rule risks generating national standards at the lowest common denominator, since the least aggressive province is in a position to resist efforts to strengthen national standards.[48] Members of the harmonization task group are considering alternative decision rules to overcome this problem.

The prospects for national standards also depend on whether provinces will be bound to adopt them. Acceptance of collective standards necessarily involves a loss of autonomy for individual governments. Some ministers have already expressed reservations concerning the task group's proposal for an enforceable agreement, and reluctance is likely to grow as more concrete proposals emerge.[49]

Finally, even if strict national standards are established, their impact can be undermined by non-enforcement. In this regard, the track record of most provinces during the 1970s and early 1980s is not reassuring.[50] During that period, the federal government withdrew from enforcement on the condition that the provinces adhere to consensual national standards. The fact that the federal government showed little inclination to intervene, despite evidence of widespread non-compliance with national standards, suggests that overlap is no panacea. Effective rationalization thus will demand clear mechanisms to promote accountability of governments not only to each other but to their electorates.

NOTES

I would like to thank the federal and provincial officials and interest group representatives who generously gave their time for interviews.

1. O.P. Dwivedi, R. Brian Woodrow, "Environmental Policy-Making and Administration in a Federal State: The Impact of Overlapping Jurisdiction in Canada," in William M. Chandler and Christian W. Zollner, eds., *Challenges to Federalism: Policy-Making in Canada and the Federal Republic of Germany* (Kingston: Institute of Intergovernmental Relations, Queen's University, 1989).

2. Donna Tingley, "Conflict and Cooperation on the Environment," in Douglas Brown, ed., *Canada: The State of the Federation 1991*, (Kingston: Institute of Intergovernmental Relations, Queen's University, 1991), p. 132.

3. Andrew R. Thompson, *Environmental Regulation in Canada: An Assessment of the Regulatory Process* (Vancouver: Westwater Research Centre, 1980), p. 25.

4. Gallup Canada poll 907-1, July 1989.

5. Doug Miller, in House of Commons, *Minutes of Proceedings and Evidence of the Standing Committee on the Environment*, September 1991, 6A:18.

6. Alastair Lucas, "The New Environmental Law," in R. Watts and D. Brown, eds., *Canada: State of the Federation 1989*, (Kingston: Institute of Intergovernmental Relations, Queen's University, 1989).

7. Environment Canada, "Canadian Environmental Protection Act: Enforcement and Compliance Policy" (Ottawa, 1987.

8. House of Commons, *Minutes of Proceedings and Evidence of the Legislative Committee on Bill C-75*, 3 February 1988, 14:18.

9. See, for instance, Charles Caccia in House of Commons, *Debates*, 26 April 1988, 14821; and Richard D. Lindgren, "Toxic Substances in Canada: The Regulatory Role of the Federal Government," in Donna Tingley, ed., *Into the Future: Environmental Law and Policy for the 1990s*, (Edmonton: Environmental Law Centre (Alberta) Society, 1990).

10. George Hoberg and Kathryn Harrison, "It's Not Easy Being Green: The Politics of Canada's Green Plan," *Canadian Public Policy* 20 (1994): 119-137.

11. Canadian Wildlife Federation Inc. v. Minister of the Environment, *Canadian Environmental Law Reporter* 3 [1989]: 287.

12. Confidential interview.

13. Joseph de Pencier, "The Federal Environmental Assessment Process: A Practical Comparison of the EARP Guidelines Order and the Canadian Environmental Assessment Act," *Journal of Environmental Law and Practice* 3 (1993): 329-343.

14. *Western Report*, "Fjordbotten: No means No," 25 December 1989, p. 30.

15. The provinces' proposals were presented twice by successive Chairs of CCME. See, for instance, House of Commons, Legislative Committee on Bill C-13, *Minutes of Proceedings and Evidence*, 19 November 1991, 10:10.

16. Peter O'Neil, "Senate bucks pressure from Quebec and passes environmental bill," *Vancouver Sun*, 24 June 1992, p. A4.

17. *R. v. Crown Zellerbach Canada Ltd.*, N.R. 84 [1988]: 1-68.

18. The subsequent Oldman decision similarly undercut provincial resistance to the *Canadian Environmental Assessment Act.* ["Re: Friends of the Oldman River Society and The Queen in right of Alberta et al.; Attorney-General Saskatchewan et al., Intervenors," *Dominion Law Reports* 88 (1992): 1-60.] More recently, in the 1994 Grand Council of Cree decision, the Court interpreted environmental authority associated with the trade and commerce power broadly. ["The Grand Council of the Crees (of Quebec) and the Cree Regional Authority, appellants v. The Attorney General of Canada, the Attorney General of Quebec, Hydro-Quebec and the National Energy Board, respondents," 24 February 1994.] While this series of decisions greatly strengthens the federal government's constitutional position, the mere fact of constitutional clarification does not compel the federal government to demand a stronger role in the environmental field.

19. Confidential interview.

20. Canadian Council of Ministers of the Environment, "Statement of Interjurisdictional Cooperation on Environmental Matters," March 1990.

21. Steven A. Kennett, "Hard Law, Soft Law and Diplomacy: The Emerging Paradigm for Intergovernmental Cooperation in Environmental Assessment," *Alberta Law Review* 31 (1993): 644-661, at 657.

22. Canadian Council of Ministers of the Environment, "Cooperative Principles for Environmental Assessment," May 1991.

23. Canada-Alberta Agreement for Environmental Assessment Cooperation, August 1993; "Entente Entre le Gouvernement du Québec et le Gouvernement du Canada sur l'Application au Québec de la Réglementation Fédérale sur les Fabriques de Pâtes et Papiers," May 1994; "Canada-Alberta Administrative Agreement for the Control of Deposits of Deleterious Substances under the Fisheries Act," June 1994; and "An Agreement on the Equivalency of Federal and Alberta Regulations for the Control of Toxic Substances in Alberta," June 1994. The equivalency agreement will not be final until it is published in Canada Gazette II.

24. These include pulp and paper administrative agreements between the federal government and the provinces of British Columbia and Ontario, environmental assessment agreements between the federal government and Newfoundland,

Manitoba, Saskatchewan, and British Columbia, and a Canada-Saskatchewan Fisheries Act administrative agreement.

25. "Federal/Provincial Framework Agreement for Environmental Cooperation in Atlantic Canada," June 1994. The accord establishes a general framework for more detailed agreements that will follow.

26. Kennett, "Hard Law, Soft Law," pp. 653-658.

27. Agreement in principle has been reached on a similar transfer under the Canada-Alberta agreement concerning the *Fisheries Act*.

28. Canadian Council of Ministers of the Environment, "Rationalizing the Management Regime for the Environment: Purpose, Objectives and Principles," June 1994.

29. CCME, "Rationalizing the Management Regime."

30. Confidential interviews.

31. *Intergovernmental Agreement on the Environment*, 1 May 1992.

32. Confidential interviews with federal and provincial officials.

33. Canadian Council of Ministers of the Environment, "Environment/Energy Air Pact Signed," *Envirogram* 2 (1993): 2.

34. Data are from Gallup Canada polls 907-1 (July 1989), and 012-1 (December 1990); and *The Gallup Poll*, 31 January 1994.

35. "Whatever happened to the environment?" *Toronto Star*, 20 October 1993, p. A21; "Is the environment a forgotten issue? (Election 93)," *Montreal Gazette*, 8 October 1993, p. A9.

36. Miller, *Minutes of Proceedings and Evidence*.

37. Kathryn Harrison, "Passing the Buck: Federalism and Canadian Environmental Policy," unpublished PhD thesis, University of British Columbia, 1993, chap. 5.

38. Riley E. Dunlap, "Public Opinion and Environmental Policy," in James P. Lester, ed., *Environmental Politics and Policy* (Durham: Duke University Press, 1989).

39. Confidential interviews.

40. For a review of federal and provincial sources of environmental jurisdiction, see Alastair R. Lucas, "Natural Resources and Environmental Management: A Jurisdictional Primer," in Tingley, *Environmental Protection and the Canadian Constitution*.

41. Confidential interview. Similarly, provincial testimony concerning the 1977 amendments to the *Fisheries Act* suggests that the provinces resisted federal regulations because they feared that overzealous federal officials would close vital local industries. See Harrison, "Passing the Buck," p. 206.

42. See, for instance, Grace Skogstad and Paul Kopas, "Environmental Policy in a Federal System: Ottawa and the Provinces," in Robert Boardman, ed., *Canadian Environmental Policy* (Toronto: Oxford University Press, 1992).

43. J. Stefan Dupré, "Reflections on the Workability of Executive Federalism," in Richard Simeon, ed., *Intergovernmental Relations* (Toronto: University of Toronto Press, 1985).

44. See, for instance, Anne McIlroy, "Environmentalists fear power shift to provinces," *Vancouver Sun*, 25 March 1990, p. A6.

45. The legislative review of CEPA recently launched and the new federal government's proposals to revise CEAA may offer windows of opportunity. It is noteworthy that Environment Canada's regulatory review recently proposed relaxation of CEPA equivalency criteria. (Environment Canada, "Environment Canada Regulatory Review — Environmental Protection Program: A Discussion Document," November 1993, p. vii.)

46. For instance, the new government reportedly is working to "green" the CEAA regulations proposed by their predecessors by lengthening the list of conditions under which environmental assessments will be required.

47. In that case, Canadians witnessed the spectacle of federal and provincial ministers challenging each other's version of a backroom deal in court. See Ross Howard, David Roberts, "De Cotret denies making deal with Saskatchewan on dams," *The Globe and Mail*, 26 October 1990, p. A1; and David Roberts, "Minister 'didn't care' if dam panel quit," *The Globe and Mail*, 2 November 1990, p. A1.

48. On the other hand, during a period of relaxation of environmental standards, the most aggressive provinces would be in a position to block efforts to relax consensual standards.

49. Confidential interview.

50. Kathryn Harrison, "Is Cooperation the Answer? Canadian Environmental Enforcement in Comparative Context," *Journal of Policy Analysis and Management*, forthcoming 1995. It is noteworthy that a reference to "legal standards" in the final draft "Purpose, Objectives, and Principles" document was changed to "standards" in the final version. The omission of "legal" opens the door to voluntary, non-regulatory approaches.

Part IV

10

Chronology of Events July 1993 – June 1994

Anne Poels

An index of these events begins on page 233

5 July 1993
Justice

A federal-provincial report, commissioned by Kim Campbell in 1990, concludes that the male-dominated justice system discriminates against women — leaving them vulnerable to violence, poverty, and unequal treatment. The report recommends improvements in the way courts deal with female victims and offenders, tougher anti-pornography laws and a change in the way women are portrayed in advertising.

7 July 1993
Labour – Ontario

Ontario's social contract legislation, affecting the province's 900,000 public sector employees, passes in the Ontario legislature. The bill is designed to cut $2 billion in spending through a three-year wage freeze and unpaid leave days. Public sector employees will be offered incentives and are urged to conclude non-legislated settlements before the deadline of 1 August.

8 July 1993
Social Assistance – Ontario

Ontario's minister of community and social services, Tony Silipo, announces that the Ontario government "is going to scrap the province's welfare system as we know it." Welfare was the primary source of income for 1.2 million people in Ontario last year, costing the provincial government $6.1 million. A program called "Job Link" will create more than 100,000 places a year in educational institutions and apprenticeship programs for welfare recipients. People on welfare who fail to enroll in job training programs will be penalized. Ontario will also replace its existing welfare programs with two new ones. The Ontario Child Benefit will provide monthly cheques to parents with low incomes to provide basic needs for their children. The Ontario Adult Benefit will provide a single monthly cheque to help needy adults while they look for new jobs.

14 July 1993
Fiscal Policy –
Alberta

Alberta's Treasurer Jim Dinning announces cuts to hospital funding and welfare in an attempt to reduce the province's huge deficit. Health-care spending is cut by $67.5 million and welfare by $24.5 million. More reductions are expected.

19 July 1993
Maritime/Atlantic
Provinces
– Cooperation

Canada's Maritime premiers meet in Charlottetown and agree to cooperate in order to save money on health-care. Health ministers of Prince Edward Island, New Brunswick, and Nova Scotia will now look at areas that could be merged into regional operations aimed at avoiding costly duplication of services.

22 July 1993
Federal-Provincial
Relations – Ontario

Ontario's Premier Bob Rae meets with Prime Minister Kim Campbell in Toronto. Rae strongly expresses his dissatisfaction with the way Ottawa continues to take more from the "have" province of Ontario — in order to give to poorer provinces — without recognition for its present economically weakened state.

26 July 1993
Aboriginal Peoples

Ovide Mercredi opens the annual meeting of the Assembly of First Nations by charging that Ottawa is using the defeat of the Charlottetown constitutional accord as an excuse to bury issues such as aboriginal self-government. He calls on all natives to fight in order to get their concerns back on the national agenda.

1 August 1993
Labour – Ontario

The Ontario government's deadline for social contract settlements with its public sector workers passes with more than one-third of its 900,000 employees failing to reach a deal. The province's public sector workers who do not endorse cost-cutting agreements face an automatic three-year wage freeze and up to 12 days of unpaid annual leave.

3 August 1993 *Manpower –* *Quebec*	Prime Minister Kim Campbell and Quebec Premier Robert Bourassa announce an agreement in principle between the federal government and Quebec that appears to turn over control of manpower training to the province much as had been planned in the failed Charlottetown Accord. Campbell denies the agreement means a transfer of powers.
18 August 1993 *Aboriginal Peoples* *– Land Claims*	Ontario and the Teme-Augama Anishnabai Indian Band reach a tentative settlement aimed at resolving a long-standing native land claim dispute. The tentative accord gives the band exclusive title to 300 square kilometres of land and provides $15 million in compensation.
18 August 1993 *Aboriginal Peoples*	The Royal Commission on Aboriginal Peoples releases an interim report *Partners in Confederation*. The report affirms that the inherent right of self-government was never extinguished and is constitutionally protected. This is significant as it implies that the right of native self-government does not have to be sanctioned by a constitutional amendment.
19 August 1993 *Social Assistance –* *New Brunswick*	The federal and New Brunswick governments agree to cooperate on employment and training programs. The agreement announced in Fredericton involves coordinating unemployment insurance services, workforce training, and social services.
27 August 1993 *Premiers – Annual* *Conference*	Canada's ten provincial premiers and two territorial leaders meet in Baddeck, Nova Scotia for a two day annual conference. The premiers call for a first ministers' conference on the economy and voice their concerns regarding cuts to federal transfer payments that are having an impact on health care and education. The premiers also urge the federal government to resume negotiations for aboriginal self-government. Native leaders attend the final session of the two-day conference.
31 August 1993 *Fisheries –* *East Coast*	The federal government announces a further moratorium on the cod fishery of the east coast. The announcement is expected to put 12,000 people out of work, bringing to 42,000 the number of people who have lost their jobs since Ottawa imposed a ban on cod fishing last July in order to save dwindling fish stocks. A $190,000 million

compensation package will be available to help displaced workers until May 1994.

6 September 1993
Aboriginal Peoples – Land Claims

The Sahtu Dene and Metis of the Northwest Territories sign a comprehensive land-claim agreement with the federal government. The particulars of the agreement were worked out in January. The deal gives the natives claim to 41,437 square kilometres of land including 1,813 square kilometres with subsurface rights. In addition, Ottawa will pay $75 million over 15 years as well as a percentage of resource royalties. As well, the deal provides for native participation in management of land, water, renewable resources, and environmental reviews.

8 September 1993
Elections – Federal

Prime Minister Kim Campbell announces that Canada's 35th general election will take place 25 October.

8 September 1993
Budgets – Alberta

Alberta releases a mini-budget in which treasurer Jim Dinning places the provincial deficit at $3.77 billion for 1992-93 fiscal year. No new taxes or cuts in program spending are announced. Dinning is optimistic that the government can still meet its 1993-94 deficit target of $2.5 billion by implementing $700 million in previously announced spending cuts.

13 September 1993
Throne Speech – Nova Scotia

Nova Scotia's Premier John Savage paints a bleak picture of the provincial economy in his throne speech opening the fall legislature, following the June 1993 election that brought the Liberals to power. The province's total debt stands at $6.8 billion. The speech promises changes but provides few specifics.

14 September 1993
Party Leadership – Quebec

Premier Robert Bourassa announces his resignation as leader of the Liberal Party of Quebec. He will stay on until a Liberal convention chooses a new leader in order to ensure an orderly transfer of power before next year's provincial election.

27 September 1993
Trade – Ontario-Quebec

Ontario minister of economic development and trade, Frances Lankin announces that Ontario will impose trade barriers against Quebec in retaliation for that province's discrimination against Ontario construction workers. Quebec regulations prevent Ontario contractors from obtaining a licence to work in Quebec and from bidding on government contracts. New Brunswick has already imposed barriers against Quebec in a similar dispute over construction labour.

28 September 1993
Fiscal Policy –
Fiscal Stabilization
Plan – Quebec

The Quebec government submits a claim to Ottawa for $282 million. Finance Minister Gerard D. Levesque says Quebec is entitled to the money under the fiscal stabilization plan which compensates provinces that experience a decline in revenue due to economic downturn. Ontario, Prince Edward Island, and Saskatchewan have already received some compensation from the federal government for the 1991-92 fiscal year.

30 September 1993
Budgets –
Nova Scotia

The Nova Scotia Liberal government introduces its first budget. It is expected to raise an additional $78 million through tax increases. The provincial sales tax will rise to 11 from 10 percent and will apply to more services, including professional fees and recreation. Nova Scotia's Finance Minister Bernie Boudreau says that further spending cuts may be expected as, in spite of the tax increases, the province will raise less money than last year.

3-4 October 1993
Elections – Federal

Televised debates are held between major party leaders in the federal election campaign. Most observers agree that there is no clear winner in either the French or English debate.

8 October 1993
Transportation –
Prince Edward
Island

Financial agreements are signed in Charlottetown finalizing the deal with Strait Crossing Development Inc. to build a bridge linking Prince Edward Island to the mainland. Under the terms of the agreement Strait Crossing must finance the operation. Ottawa agrees to pay the consortium $42 million a year for 35 years, a sum equivalent to the cost of operating the federally owned ferry service between New Brunswick and Prince Edward Island.

25 October 1993
Elections – Federal

Canadians vote in a general election and elect a majority Liberal government. Jean Chrétien and his Liberals win 177 seats. The Progressive Conservatives suffer an unprecedented defeat going from 157 seats to two. Prime Minister Kim Campbell fails to retain her seat. The New Democrats lose 35 of their 44 seats, electing only nine members. The big winners, besides the Liberals, were the Bloc Québécois with 54 seats and the Reform Party with 52 seats. In terms of the popular vote the Liberals take 42 percent, Reform 18 percent, PCs 16 percent, BQ 14 percent and NDP 7 percent.

Members elected by province/territory and party:

	Lib	BQ	Ref	NDP	PC	Ind
Newfoundland (7)	7	0	0	0	0	0
P.E.I. (4)	4	0	0	0	0	0
Nova Scotia (11)	11	0	0	0	0	0
New Brunswick (10)	9	0	0	0	1	0
Quebec (75)	19	54	0	0	1	1
Ontario (99)	98	0	1	0	0	0
Manitoba (14)	12	0	1	1	0	0
Saskatchewan (14)	5	0	4	5	0	0
Alberta (26)	4	0	22	0	0	0
British Columbia (32)	6	0	24	2	0	0
Yukon/NWT (3)	2	0	0	1	0	0
Totals (295)	*177*	*54*	*52*	*9*	*2*	*1*

	1993	*1988*	*1984*
Liberals	177	83	40
Bloc Québécois	54	0	0
Reform Party	52	0	0
New Democratic Party	9	43	30
Progressive Conservatives	2	169	211
Independent	1	0	1
Totals	*295*	*295*	*282*

29 October 1993
Fiscal Policy –
Equalization
Payments

Canada's seven poorest provinces are told to expect a $1 billion cut in federal equalization payments as a result of the narrowing gap in their economic performance and that of the traditionally "have" provinces of Ontario, Alberta, and British Columbia. Manitoba will lose $230 million, Saskatchewan $225 million, Quebec $110 million, New Brunswick $186 million, Nova Scotia $169 million, Newfoundland $18 million, and Prince Edward Island $23 million.

4 November 1993
Elections – Federal

Jean Chrétien becomes Canada's twentieth prime minister. The new Cabinet includes ten ministers from Ontario, five from Quebec, two from Alberta, and one from each of the remaining provinces except Prince Edward Island. Just hours after being sworn in Chrétien cancels the controversial $4.8 billion contract for 43 EH-101 helicopters.

6 November 1993
Party Leadership – British Columbia

Grace McCarthy becomes leader of the Social Credit Party in British Columbia. She wins on the third ballot by more than 14,000 votes.

11 November 1993
Aboriginal Peoples

Canada's Minister of Indian Affairs Ron Irwin agrees to draft a political accord with the country's chiefs to recognize the inherent right of self-government. The accord would also incorporate other Liberal election promises.

12 November 1993
Interprovincial Trade – Quebec

Quebec introduces legislation that would ease restrictions on out-of-province construction workers. The bill would eliminate the requirement that companies have a place of business in Quebec.

19 November 1993
Maritime/Atlantic Provinces – Cooperation

The Atlantic premiers meet in Gander, Newfoundland and agree to coordinate drug purchases to cut down on health costs. The premiers also agree to create a joint film and video classification system in the three Maritime provinces.

24 November 1993
Fiscal Policy – Ontario

Two major financial firms cut Ontario's credit rating. Standard and Poor of New York downgrades the province to double A minus from double A while Toronto's Dominion Bond Rating Service cuts its rating from double A minus to a single A. Ontario had a triple A credit rating when the New Democrats came to power in 1990.

24 November 1993
Fiscal Policy – Alberta

Alberta announces that it will cut the salary portion of provincial grants for hospitals, school boards, and universities by 5 percent next year. In his quarterly report Treasurer Jim Dinning says Alberta's deficit this year will be $2,435 billion, $9 million less than originally projected.

25 November 1993 *Premiers – Western* *Provinces*	Four western premiers and territorial leaders meet in Canmore, Alberta. They call on Ottawa not to cut transfer payments to the provinces and urge the federal government to expand its $6 billion infrastructure program to include environmental protection, skills training, communications networks, and other technological advances.
26 November 1993 *Fiscal Policy –* *Quebec*	Quebec's finance department announces that the provincial deficit will be $375 million more this year than expected. The 1993-94 deficit will reach at least $4.5 billion, almost 10 percent more than the $4.15 billion forecast in May's provincial budget. The increase is being blamed on a $450 million decline in projected revenue.
28 November 1993 *Party Leadership –* *Ontario*	Ontario's Premier Bob Rae receives a vote of confidence from 300 delegates to the NDP's provincial council meeting in Toronto. The delegates overwhelmingly reject a resolution calling for an early leadership review.
29 November 1993 *Fisheries –* *East Coast*	The federal government's Atlantic Fisheries Resource Conservation Council presents a report that says that the east-coast fishery is not recovering and thousands more Atlantic Canadians will likely lose their jobs. The report concludes that the conservation measures that have left 42,000 unemployed in the past 18 months are not enough.
30 November 1993 *Economy – Quebec*	Quebec Premier Robert Bourassa announces a three year, $1 billion economic recovery plan designed to reduce the province's unemployment. The plan is expected to create 47,000 new jobs over the three-year period. Areas targeted for job creation are regional development, industrial and technological innovation, help for business to adapt to export markets, retraining of welfare recipients, and entrepreneurship support.
2 December 1993 *Fiscal Policy –* *Federal-Provincial*	Provincial finance ministers meet in Halifax and call on the federal government not to cut or freeze transfer payments in order to finance its share of the $6 billion infrastructure program.
2 December 1993 *Trade – NAFTA*	Prime Minister Jean Chrétien agrees to implement the North American Free Trade Agreement 1 January in spite

of failing to secure changes he said were vital for Canada's approval. Chrétien is unsuccessful in renegotiating the issue of energy exports but settles instead for a unilateral declaration stating that Canada would not give up the right to energy security in times of shortages.

3 December 1993
Transportation

Prime Minister Jean Chrétien cancels a deal that would hand over Pearson International Airport in Toronto to a private consortium. The $700 million deal to privatize Terminals 1 and 2 was initiated by the former Conservative government.

6 December 1993
Fisheries –
East Coast

The Task Force on Incomes and Adjustment in the Atlantic Fishery, chaired by Richard Cashin, releases its report. The report, entitled *Charting a New Course: Towards the Fishery of the Future*, says the depleted state of fish stocks has made a major reorganization of the industry a matter of extreme urgency. It calls for a reduced fishery of professional fishermen and processors who would be certified and registered based on competence and experience. The report recommends that current relief programs for laid-off fishermen and processors be maintained for now, but urges the federal and provincial governments to start work immediately on the restructuring process.

8 December 1993
Taxation – Ontario

The Ontario government introduces legislation for a minimum corporate tax. Finance Minister Floyd Laughren says the tax will bring in $10 million in 1994 and $100 million annually when it is fully phased-in in 1996. The rate will rise from 2 percent of profits in 1994 to 4 percent in 1996. Introduction of the legislation is part of a series of tax reforms the government is planning in order to make the provincial system more fair.

9 December 1993
Health Policy –
Alberta

Alberta publishes a controversial report dealing with ways to reduce health-care costs in the province. The report recommends a two-tiered system that would guarantee basic services while making it possible for those who want to pay to get access to a wider range of medical assistance. The government says the restructuring is necessary to cut $900 million from Alberta's health-care budget over the next three years as part of its goal of eliminating the annual budgetary deficit by 1997.

9 December 1993 *Justice – Ontario*	Ontario passes employment equity legislation which will force companies in the province to develop plans to hire and promote more women, minorities, natives, and disabled people. The bill requires employers to set numerical goals and timetables for making their workforces more reflective of the surrounding community within three years of proclamation.
10 December 1993 *Environment –* *British Columbia*	First Nations and the government of British Columbia sign a logging accord in Victoria. Under the agreement members of five First Nations will manage logging in two forested regions of Clayoquot Sound — Clayoquot River Valley and Flores Island. The program will cost $1.25 million over three years and will train natives to manage the logging and to work as forest workers, environmental inspectors, and auditors.
14 December 1993 *Party Leadership –* *Federal*	Jean Charest becomes interim leader of the Progressive Conservative Party, replacing Kim Campbell. Charest, who lost the leadership race to Campbell in June, is one of two conservatives elected to the House of Commons in the 25 October federal election.
14 December 1993 *Party Leadership –* *Quebec*	Daniel Johnson is acclaimed as leader of the Quebec Liberal Party. He will take over from Premier Robert Bourassa 11 January.
14 December 1993 *Social Assistance –* *Newfoundland*	Newfoundland makes a proposal to restructure unemployment insurance and welfare in order to target resources towards the most needy. Premier Clyde Wells wants Ottawa's cooperation to change the way the province spends the $2 billion annual federal contribution for social security. Newfoundland is offering to accept much stricter rules on unemployment insurance in exchange for an innovative guaranteed annual income system for its poorest residents.
16 December 1993 *Constitutional* *Reform*	In an interview Prime Minister Jean Chrétien says the federal government will not be holding any constitutional discussions with Quebec even if the province opts for sovereignty.
20 December 1993 *Fisheries –* *East Coast*	Federal Fisheries Minister Brian Tobin closes most of the east-coast groundfish fishery. The fishing ban is necessary because bottom dwelling groundfish such as

cod, haddock, and redfish have dwindled to record lows. Newly unemployed workers will be eligible for $28 million in aid until next May when an ongoing relief package worth $1billion ends. Ottawa is currently trying to determine how to replace the fund. Tobin also announces an indefinite ban on fishing northern cod off the northeastern coast of Newfoundland and suggests it may last as long as six years.

21 December 1993
Federal-Provincial Relations – First Ministers' Conference

In Ottawa, Prime Minister Chrétien meets with the provincial premiers and territorial leaders. Agreement is reached on a national public works program. Tax reform as well as restructuring of social services is discussed. The premiers accept the federal government's proposal for splitting the cost of the proposed $6 billion two-year infrastructure program equally among Ottawa, the provincial governments, and municipalities. Chrétien does not promise that transfer payments to the provinces for social programs will not be frozen next year. The ministers agree to complete talks on a new five-year agreement on transfer payments by next spring. The leaders also agree to eliminate interprovincial trade barriers by June 1994 as well as to replace the GST and harmonize federal and provincial consumption taxes in the near future.

21 December 1993
National Infrastructure Program

Based on population and provincial unemployment rates, under the proposed national infrastructure program, the provinces will receive the following funds from Ottawa:

Ontario	– $722 million or 36.4	percent
Quebec	– $527 million or 27.2	percent
British Columbia	– $225 million or 11.2	percent
Alberta	– $173 million or 8.8	percent
Nova Scotia	– $ 69 million or 3.9	percent
Manitoba	– $ 68 million or 3.6	percent
Saskatchewan	– $ 58 million or 2.9	percent
New Brunswick	– $ 51 million or 2.6	percent
Newfoundland	– $ 49 million or 2.5	percent
Prince Edward Island	– $ 12 million or .69	percent

22 December 1993 *Bank of Canada*	Finance Minister Paul Martin announces that Gordon Thiessen will be the new governor of the Bank of Canada, replacing the current governor John Crow.
24 December 1993 *Trade –* *Ontario-Quebec*	Ontario and Quebec end their trade war and sign an agreement committing both governments to removing barriers in construction contracting and labour mobility, government procurement, and municipal bus purchasing. The agreement is signed, in Hull, by Ontario Minister Frances Lankin and Quebec Minister Gerald Tremblay.
1 January 1994 *Trade – NAFTA*	The North American Free Trade Agreement comes into effect bringing Mexico into partnership with Canada and the United States to create the largest free trade zone in the world. The three countries will continue negotiations over the next two years to settle issues such as rules on subsidies and dumping as well as an acceleration of tariff cuts.
11 January 1994 *Party Leadership –* *Quebec*	Daniel Johnson is sworn in as Premier of Quebec. Johnson promises to work closely with Ottawa to create jobs and streamline government.
14 January 1994 *National* *Infrastructure* *Program*	The federal government signs formal funding agreements with four provinces under the $6 billion infrastructure program. The agreements commit Ottawa to a one-third share of projects in Nova Scotia ($69 million), New Brunswick ($51 million), Manitoba ($68 million) and Saskatchewan ($57.7 million) over the next two years. The other two-thirds of the funds will come equally from provinces and municipalities.
18 January 1994 *Throne Speech –* *Federal*	In the throne speech opening the 35th Parliament, the new Liberal government promises to replace the GST, restore trust in public officials, and reform social programs. Cutting the deficit remains a priority but the speech reassures Canadians it will not be done at the expense of the unemployed.
18 January 1994 *Budgets – Alberta*	Alberta's Premier Ralph Klein announces new budget cuts of $1.5 billion to health, welfare, and education. The province will also phase out $113 million in operating grants to municipalities forcing them to rely on property taxes for their revenue.

21 January 1994
Fiscal Policy –
Equalization
Payments

Finance Minister Paul Martin announces an increase in equalization payments to the seven poorest provinces in the amount of $900 million over the next five years. Martin's announcement means that equalization payments, paid to all provinces except Ontario, Alberta, and British Columbia, will rise to $10.4 billion by 1998-99 from $7.4 billion this year, an increase of 5 percent a year.

24 January 1994
National
Infrastructure
Program – Ontario

Ontario signs a $2.1 billion infrastructure deal with the federal government designed to repair public buildings, roads, sewers, and bridges. The federal and Ontario government will each contribute $722 million, with the rest of the money coming from municipalities, school boards, and postsecondary institutions that propose projects to be funded under the plan. The program is expected to create 25,000 jobs over the next two years.

25 January 1994
Aboriginal Peoples

The province of Saskatchewan is helping three native groups in a legal challenge of Ottawa's right to offload jurisdiction for status Indians living off reserves. The province and native groups feel that under treaties it is a federal not a provincial responsibility to pay for welfare benefits for Indians whether they live on or off reserves. The Saskatchewan government has contributed $100,000 to the native groups to help pay for legal costs.

31 January 1994
Fisheries –
East Coast

Fisheries Minister Brian Tobin announces the closing of all recreational fishery off the northeast and south coasts of Newfoundland. Major fishing unions and the provincial government have demanded such a ban because of the continuing dismal state of fish stocks and reports that fish caught for personal use are being sold on the black market.

31 January 1994
Social Assistance –
Reform

Human Resources Minister Lloyd Axworthy announces a government review of all social programs. The Liberals want to introduce legislation before the end of 1994 to link unemployment insurance and welfare, tie benefits more closely to education, and give youth more opportunities. The planned review will cost between $3 million and $4 million and is slated to be completed by 30 September 1994.

| 7 February 1994
National
Infrastructure
Program | Quebec signs a $526 million infrastructure agreement with Ottawa. Federal Finance Minister Paul Martin predicts the deal will create 20,000 direct jobs and as many as 40,000 indirect jobs in the next two years. |

7 February 1994
Throne Speech –
Saskatchewan

Saskatchewan's NDP government opens a new session of the legislature. The speech from the throne promises legislation to promote economic development, trade, and tourism, shifting the government's emphasis away from the deficit cutting measures of the previous two years.

8 February 1994
Taxation – Tobacco

In an effort to stop illegal cigarette trade, the federal government cuts taxes on cigarettes sold in Canada. At the same time the government announces a major anti-smoking campaign targeting young people in an effort to convince them not to smoke. The plan will cost $600 million, including an estimated $300 million in lost tax revenue, $150 million in tax rebates on existing stocks of cigarettes and $150 million for police and customs enforcement. Following the federal announcement Quebec also cuts taxes. The result of reduced federal and Quebec taxes reduces by half the price of a carton of cigarettes in the province from $47 to $23. New Brunswick follows suit, cutting cigarette prices by about $16 to $39. Other provinces, however, show little enthusiasm for cutting taxes and are critical of the impact cheap tobacco will have on health programs.

9 February 1994
Health Policy –
Reform

Provincial, territorial, and federal health ministers meet in Ottawa. They approve a plan for a radical restructuring of Canada's blood supply system. The plan would give more control over the blood system to the provinces and less to the Canadian Red Cross Society.

10 February 1994
Throne Speech –
Alberta

In a throne speech opening a new session of the legislature, Alberta's Premier Ralph Klein commits his government to continuing tight fiscal policies designed to eliminate the province's $2.4 billion deficit in three years. The speech promises educational reform that would allow the government to amalgamate school boards and collect school taxes, a new system of grants for universities and colleges, performance incentives for government employees, and *Access to Information Act* reform.

11 February 1994
Aboriginal Peoples

Native leaders from the Assembly of First Nations agree to talk with Ottawa about setting up a system to negotiate aboriginal self-government under the existing constitution.

14 February 1994
Social Assistance –
Reform

Social services ministers meet in Ottawa and discuss experimental restructuring of programs such as unemployment insurance and welfare. New Brunswick and Ontario already have plans underway and other provinces are expected to follow suit soon. Federal Human Resources Minister Lloyd Axworthy says Ottawa will try to help finance new provincial efforts to help people reduce their income assistance.

15 February 1994
Throne Speech –
New Brunswick

In a throne speech the government of New Brunswick promises no new taxes and no major program cuts. Latest figures indicate the province will have a 1993-94 deficit of $140 million, about $100 million more than projected in last spring's budget. Premier Frank McKenna promises to make New Brunswick the first pay-as-you-go province with a balanced operating budget for 1994-95.

16 February 1994
Transportation –
Prince Edward
Island

Parliament approves a proposal to build a bridge over Northumberland Strait to connect Prince Edward Island to the mainland. The issue must still go before the Island legislature before any construction on the $840 million project can begin.

17 February 1994
Budgets –
Saskatchewan

Saskatchewan NDP government introduces a new budget with no new taxes or spending cuts. Finance Minister Janice MacKinnon forecasts a deficit of $188.7 million in fiscal year 1994-95, down from $294 million last year. The budget does include $23.4 million in cuts to provincial grants for municipalities, school boards, and hospitals as announced in last year's budget.

18 February 1994
Elections –
British Columbia

Grace McCarthy loses an important by-election, in the Fraser Valley riding of Matsqui, to Liberal candidate Mike de Jong, by 66 votes. In spite of the loss British Columbia's Social Credit caucus unanimously endorses McCarthy as party leader. Standings in the B.C. legislature now are: 51 Liberal, six Social Credit, two Progressive Democratic Alliance and one independent.

18 February 1994
National
Infrastructure
Program – British
Columbia

British Columbia signs a $675 million infrastructure agreement with the federal government. Ottawa and the province will each contribute $225 million under the deal with the remaining third financed by local government and private partners. The joint project could mean 10,000 jobs in the province.

21 February 1994
Taxation – Tobacco

The Ontario government cuts tobacco taxes saying it has no choice but to bring the price of cigarettes in the province in line with prices in Quebec. Finance Minister Floyd Laughren says he regrets the decision that will cost the provincial treasury $500 million a year in tax revenue and will lead to more tobacco-induced illness.

22 February 1994
Budgets – Federal

The federal government presents its budget. It contains no significant tax increases, and funding for unemployment benefits and defence spending is cut. Finance Minister Paul Martin projects a deficit of $39.7 billion for fiscal year 1994-95. The budget contains $17 billion in cuts to planned spending over three years but only $700 million will actually be cut in 1994-95. The Department of National Defence, which received a $7 billion cut over five years, will close 21 bases, stations, and units across the country and phase out 16,500 military and civilian employees. Two of Canada's three officer training colleges — Collège Militaire Royale in St-Jean, Que. and Royal Rhodes in B.C. — will be closed. As well, a cap of 5 percent on increases in transfer payments to Ontario, British Columbia, and Alberta for social programs will be maintained, and transfer payments to all provinces will be frozen in 1995-96.

Reaction to the budget is not favourable. Bloc Québécois Leader Lucien Bouchard criticizes Martin for ignoring job creation and targeting the poor through unemployment insurance cuts. Reform Leader Preston Manning accuses Martin of missing the boat on deficit reduction. The Atlantic provinces are upset about unemployment insurance cuts, military base closures, and reduced compensation for fishermen. Ontario's Premier Bob Rae charges that his province has been "knee capped" once again by restrictions to transfer payments.

24 February 1994
Budgets – Alberta

Alberta's Conservative government presents its budget. Spending is cut by almost $1 billion and there are no tax increases. The budget is praised by business and condemned by labour and the opposition Liberals. The budget calls for spending cuts of $956 million in 1994-95, reducing the deficit to $1.5 billion from $2.4 billion. It projects a surplus of $212 million in 1996-97 after spending is reduced by another $1.7 billion. The areas most affected by the latest cuts are health care and education.

24 February 1994
Energy –
Hydro-Québec

The Supreme Court of Canada rules that Hydro-Québec cannot build new power facilities that produce exports for the United States unless it first conducts federal environmental reviews. The 9-0 decision upholds the environmental review conditions that the National Energy Board placed on Hydro-Québec when it granted it a licence to export power to New York and Vermont in 1990. The decision is claimed as a victory by James Bay Cree long opposed to further hydro-electric development in northern Quebec.

25 February 1994
Budgets –
New Brunswick

New Brunswick introduces its new budget avoiding both tax increases and major cutbacks to programs. Public sector wages will be frozen for 1994, 600 positions will be eliminated and government offices will be closed for the Christmas holidays. Budgets for education, housing and income assistance are cut by $24 million and political parties will receive less public money. Salaries of all politicians will be frozen.

28 February 1994
Throne Speech –
Newfoundland

Faced with high unemployment and an ailing fishery, the province of Newfoundland announces a new economic agenda. New and expanding businesses can expect tax incentives and less red tape in the future. The province will continue to review its options for selling its power utility, Newfoundland and Labrador Hydro, as well as other branches of government.

28 February 1994
Aboriginal Peoples

The Native Council of Canada changes its name to The Congress of Aboriginal Peoples. Jim Sinclair, the newly elected president, signs a political accord to work with the federal government on Liberal campaign promises for off-reserve natives. The accord outlines a year-long agenda for discussions on issues such as self-government, land claims, and the eventual elimination of the Indian Affairs Department.

1 March 1994
Reducing
Duplication –
Federal-Provincial

Five provinces and Ottawa agree to find a way of ending costly duplication by cooperating in areas of job training and social program delivery. The meeting in Toronto, was between Human Resources Minister Lloyd Axworthy and his provincial counterparts. Ontario, Quebec, Alberta, Nova Scotia, and New Brunswick want to start talks immediately.

2 March 1994
Energy –
Hydro-Québec

Hydro-Québec reaches an agreement-in-principle with electrical utility Consolidated Edison to sell power to New York City between 1999 and 2018. A Hydro-Québec spokesperson says the new deal will involve only surplus energy delivered in the summer months.

8 March 1994
Throne Speech –
Prince Edward
Island

In the speech from the throne Prince Edward Island Premier Catherine Callbeck promises to replace the pension plan for MLAs and reduce the deficit. The government plans to balance the budget by the end of 1996. The provincial deficit for fiscal year 1993-94 will be $65 million.

9 March 1994
Aboriginal Peoples

Indian Affairs Minister Ron Irwin tells the Commons that his department has begun negotiations with Manitoba chiefs on transferring the department's responsibilities, including the management of federal funds, to the chiefs and bands as a pilot project for Manitoba. Irwin says he is determined to implement native self-government and eventually eliminate the need for the Indian Affairs Department.

11 March 1994
Energy –
Newfoundland

The Newfoundland legislature approves in principle a bill to privatize the province's power utility. Premier Clyde Wells suggests that privatization of Newfoundland Hydro would reduce the province's $6 billion debt by $1 billion and would make it possible for Newfoundland not to have to borrow money in the next fiscal year.

14 March 1994
Throne Speech –
British Columbia

In the speech from the throne British Columbia's NDP government promises a new forest strategy to ensure job stability as well as environmental protection. The speech reiterates Premier Mike Harcourt's promise of a three-year freeze on all taxes and a balanced budget by 1996.

17 March 1994
Budgets –
Newfoundland

The government of Newfoundland presents its budget. Teachers, provincial clerks, hospital staff, and other public sector workers will be required to give up $50 million in benefits. Finance Minister Winston Baker promises that as soon as fiscal circumstances allow, public servants will receive reasonable increases in pay. Baker projects a deficit of $24.6 million for 1994-95.

22 March 1994
Budgets –
British Columbia

The government of British Columbia tables its budget. Spending will be held to a 3.5 percent increase to $19.6 billion in fiscal year 1994-95 and limited to a 2-percent increase in the next two years. Finance Minister Elizabeth Cull promises to cut $112 million in taxes this year while reducing the deficit to $898 million and eliminating it altogether by 1996.

23 March 1994
Social Assistance –
New Brunswick

Human Resources Minister Lloyd Axworthy and New Brunswick Premier Frank McKenna introduce new and experimental social programs. The federal-provincial project offers a guaranteed annual income of about $12,000 to 1,000 unemployed workers between the ages of 50 and 65 in exchange for six months of community work. Ottawa and New Brunswick will share the cost of the voluntary program with initial funding set at $200,000. The participants will be able to earn additional money at seasonal jobs without losing their benefits.

24 March 1994
Elections –
Boundary Revisions

The Liberal government uses a form of closure to cut off debate on electoral boundary revisions. The bill, which would prevent the implementation of a new electoral map before the next election, passes second reading by a vote of 140-78. Existing legislation requires federal riding boundaries to be revised every ten years to reflect population trends. The last revision came into effect in 1987.

28 March 1994
Environment –
NAFTA

The federal government announces that the Secretariat of the North American Commission for Environmental Co-operation, established under the North American free trade agreement, will be based in Montreal. The commission will create about 30 jobs and have an annual budget of $5 million. Environment Minister Sheila

Copps says that Montreal was chosen for a variety of reasons — including its airline connections to Washington and Mexico City, its environmental record, and the relatively low cost of living.

29 March 1994
Energy –
Hydro-Québec

The New York Power Authority's board of trustees votes to cancel a $5 billion U.S. contract to buy power from Hydro-Québec. The power authority president David Freeman opposes the 20-year agreement on the basis of falling prices and local power surpluses. Freeman also suggests that the power authority does not want to be linked to environmentally controversial new power projects in Northern Quebec such as the Great Whale project.

30 March 1994
Maritime/Atlantic
Provinces –
Cooperation

The four Atlantic premiers agree to endorse public-private partnering in an effort to reduce the cost of government. Federal Public Works Minister David Dingwall announces that Ottawa is setting up a new secretariat to review and assess public-private partnership proposals.

30 March 1994
Trade –
Quebec-New
Brunswick

Quebec and New Brunswick sign an agreement for open access to government contracts between the neighbouring provinces. Construction contracts will be open to bidders from both provinces, as will health and education services contracts and those involving municipalities. The agreement will be implemented gradually over the next six months.

7 April 1994
Throne Speech –
Manitoba

In the speech from the throne the Manitoba government promises to continue a freeze on major taxes, hints at more spending cuts, and offers few specifics for the province's 61,000 unemployed. Manitoba's 1993-94 deficit is almost $461 million.

12 April 1994
Budgets – Prince
Edward Island

Prince Edward Island introduces its budget calling for a 7.5 percent cut in public sector wages and services. Public sector unions have until the end of May to decide whether to take the reduction in wages or give up other benefits such as holidays and sick leave. Education, health, and community services will have their budgets cut in an overall reduction in current-account program spending from $659 million to $625 million. Spending on economic development and tourism will rise.

| 13 April 1994
Taxation – Tobacco | Nova Scotia cuts tobacco taxes to counteract cigarette smuggling from other Maritime provinces. |

14 April 1994
Social Programs –
Reform

The federal government cancels a federal-provincial meeting scheduled for 18 April on its proposed reform of social programs after Quebec Premier Daniel Johnson refuses to take part. Quebec, along with several other provinces — including Ontario and British Columbia — has complained about the fast pace of the reform process and the lack of adequate briefing.

14 April 1994
Maritime/Atlantic
Provinces –
Cooperation

Premiers of New Brunswick, Nova Scotia, and Prince Edward Island agree to set up a common curriculum in mathematics, language arts, science, and second language programs for grades one through 12 in both French and English. Newfoundland also expects to join in but must wait until reform of its denominational education system is completed. Under the proposed system common textbooks, programs, and achievement assessments will be developed for the three provinces and phased in over the next five years.

14 April 1994
Aboriginal Peoples

Hydro-Québec releases a $1 billion agreement in principle designed to compensate the Inuit for environmental damage if the Great Whale power project is ever built in northern Quebec. The agreement in principle calls for $30 million payment once the project receives federal and provincial approval. Another $21 million will be paid over the seven-year construction period and $12 million annually, indexed to inflation, for the remaining 42 years of the pact.

18 April 1994
Environment

Environment Minister Sheila Copps announces that the federal government will spend $250 million on a six-year program to help clean up the polluted Great Lakes and the St. Lawrence River. In February the International Joint Commission warned that continued pollution of the Great Lakes will have serious health implications for people living nearby.

18 April 1994
Party Leadership –
Federal

In Ottawa, Audrey McLaughlin announces her decision to step down as leader of the federal New Democratic Party, taking full responsibility for the party's poor results in the last federal election. McLaughlin will remain as interim leader until the party renewal committee makes its report and will continue to sit as the MP for Yukon.

19 April 1994
Fisheries –
East Coast

The federal government announces a new $1.9 billion federal assistance package for Atlantic fishermen and plant workers. In St. John's, Fisheries Minister Brian Tobin says that Ottawa will no longer automatically extend assistance to people out of work because of the declining stocks of bottom dwelling fish such as cod. Under the new plan displaced fishermen and plant workers receiving compensation will have to upgrade their education or work on government-sponsored projects. Tobin says that $300 million will be spent to reduce the capacity of the fishery by 50 percent. This will involve paying workers to take early retirement or sell their fishing licences.

20 April 1994
Elections –
Boundary Revisions

Conservative Senators, who hold a majority in the Senate, suggest that they will challenge the Liberal government's bill to suspend the usual ten-year process of revising federal electoral boundaries. The Liberals used their Commons majority one day earlier to approve the bill that would suspend the redistribution process for two years. Redistribution would give four new seats to Ontario and two to British Columbia as well as change boundaries across the country to reflect population shifts.

20 April 1994
Budgets – Manitoba

Manitoba tables its budget. Spending will be cut in most departments, including health and education although overall spending will increase to $5.4 billion, $23 million more than last year. The increase is due to an extra $24 million allocated this year to cover the province's share of the national public works program, as well as the anticipated reduction in federal transfer payments. The budget projects a deficit of $296 million in 1994-95, about $40 million more than expected.

26 April 1994
Telecommunications

The Supreme Court of Canada rules that the federal government has exclusive jurisdiction over all the country's telephone companies. Parti Québécois Leader Jacques Parizeau charges that the ruling is an infringement on Quebec's cultural identity.

28 April 1994 *Health Policy –* *Ontario*	Ontario's Health Minister Ruth Grier announces that the government is reducing the amount of money it will pay for emergency hospital treatment outside Canada. The new measure is expected to save $20 million. Under the changes, to take effect 30 June, the province will pay a maximum of $100 per day for emergency hospital treatment outside Canada, down 75 percent from the current maximum of $400.
29 April 1994 *Budgets –* *Nova Scotia*	Angry demonstrators storm the Nova Scotia legislature preventing formal reading of a $3.9 billion budget expected to take yet more money from the public sector. To save $52 million a year, the province is imposing a pay freeze on about 40,000 public sector workers, a 3-percent wage rollback in November, then another freeze for three years. The budget cuts taxes by about $50 million, including $23 million imposed in last September's budget. This year's deficit is forecast at $297 million.
3 May 1994 *Quebec –* *Sovereignty*	Bloc Québécois leader Lucien Bouchard brings his message on Quebec sovereignty to western Canada, provoking a flurry of media commentary and political reaction.
3 May 1994 *Social Assistance –* *British Columbia*	The government of British Columbia announces it will spend $200 million over two years on worker training and education in an effort to reduce the ever increasing welfare rolls. Premier Mike Harcourt says more than 50,000 welfare recipients will receive training and job search coaching under the program.
3 May 1994 *Trade –* *Ontario-Quebec*	Ontario and Quebec sign a bilateral agreement in Toronto to end a long dispute over barriers imposed by Quebec against Ontario workers and companies. Under the final agreement all Quebec residency requirements for workers will be lifted by 15 June and both provinces will recognize each other's systems for assessing qualifications and experience. Government procurement for goods, services, and construction will be opened up by 15 September. The provision will be extended to municipalities and public institutions in the future.
5 May 1994 *Budgets – Ontario*	Ontario's Finance Minister Floyd Laughren tables his budget. The budget projects a deficit of $8.5 billion for 1994-95, down from $9.4 billion in the previous fiscal

year. Program spending will be cut by about $350 million this year, including $20 million from non-profit housing and $7 million from legal aid. Overhead expenditures will drop by $600 million to $6.3 billion. The province will spend $3.8 billion on capital projects such as subway lines and roads. Taxes will not increase. Opposition critics dismiss the budget as a "do-nothing" document designed to hide the true size of the deficit by not counting spending by the public sector and Crown corporations.

9 May 1994
Energy – Quebec

The federal and Quebec governments announce they will spend $34 million on a natural gas pipeline that will create 2,000 jobs. The $125 million federal-provincial project is the latest to be announced as Liberal Premier Daniel Johnson prepares for an upcoming provincial election.

10 May 1994
*Energy –
Newfoundland*

Premier Clyde Wells tells the Newfoundland legislature he plans to proceed with the unpopular plan to privatize Newfoundland and Labrador Hydro in an effort to raise money needed to prevent a serious budgetary shortfall next year. Standard and Poor, a major credit-rating agency, recently cut Newfoundland's credit rating to BBB from A minus.

10 May 1994
*Trade –
Interprovincial*

Canada's trade ministers agree on a mechanism to settle trade disputes, a critical step on the road to eliminate interprovincial barriers that cost taxpayers an alleged $7.5 billion a year. The plan, arrived at after two days of meetings in Winnipeg would allow provincial governments and private individuals access to trade dispute panels similar to those provided for in international trade agreements.

12 May 1994
Budgets – Quebec

Quebec's Liberal government tables its pre-election budget which cuts personal income taxes for low and middle income earners by $500 million and reduces the provincial sales tax from 8 to 6.5 percent. Finance Minister Andre Bourbeau projects a slight decline in the 1994-95 deficit to $4.425 billion and expects the deficit to be eliminated within the next five years. Program spending will increase by 1.7 percent to $41.7 billion. Business groups calling for significant deficit cuts are disappointed as is labour, which complains about the lack of job creation programs. The budget is expected to increase Quebec's total debt to $66 billion.

17 May 1994
Elections –
Reform-Prince
Edward Island

Prince Edward Island passes legislation to reduce the number of seats in its Legislative Assembly from 32 to 27. The bill passes by a vote of 17 to 13.

17 May 1994
Aboriginal Peoples
– Quebec
Sovereignty

Federal Minister of Indian Affairs, Ron Irwin, tells native leaders that should Quebec secede from Canada, Aboriginal Peoples could choose to remain part of Canada, including their aboriginal territory.

18 May 1994
Aboriginal Peoples

Federal and provincial ministers along with four native groups, the Inuit Tapirisat of Canada, the Metis National Council, the Congress of Aboriginal Peoples and Native Women's Association, agree to draft a national statement of principle to guide self-government negotiations across the country. Assembly of First Nations Chief Ovide Mercredi walks out of the two day meeting in Quebec City between the government and native groups saying that talks should be between Aboriginals and the federal government and should ensure constitutional protection for self-government agreements. Federal Indian Affairs Minister Ron Irwin says Ottawa and the provinces will continue to negotiate with native groups despite Mercredi's opposition.

19 May 1994
Health Policy –
British Columbia

The Government of British Columbia says it will end extra billing by doctors. Ottawa recently penalized the province $1.7 million by cutting health payments. The money, representing the amount doctors have billed their patients above medicare, was deducted from Ottawa's monthly $62 million transfer payment to British Columbia.

19 May 1994
Social Assistance –
Prince Edward
Island

The Government of Prince Edward Island announces a cut of $2.5 million from its welfare budget. Welfare benefits will be reduced, GST rebate cheques will be considered part of a calculated income, and special transportation allowances will be carefully reviewed. The province's welfare costs have risen by 66 percent since 1989.

20 May 1994 *Premiers –* *Western Provinces* *Conference*	The four western premiers end a three-day conference in Gimli, Manitoba. There is some disagreement over interprovincial trade. Alberta's Premier Ralph Klein and Manitoba's Premier Gary Filmon want all barriers to interprovincial trade removed while Roy Romanov of Saskatchewan and Mike Harcourt of British Columbia want some exceptions to remain. The premiers agree to ask Ottawa for a uniform tax on cigarettes and a greater role in a planned federal forum on health care. They also urge the federal government not to cut transfer payments to the provinces.
20 May 1994 *Social Programs*	Human Resources Minister Lloyd Axworthy announces the first phase of a youth service corps program designed for as many as 17,500 Canadians between the ages of 18 and 24 over the next three years. The program will start with 37 pilot projects involving 623 young people and lasting for six to nine months. The projects emphasize community work, skills development, and business acumen.
25 May 1994 *Prince Edward* *Island – Royal* *Commission*	Prince Edward Island Premier Catherine Callbeck establishes a royal commission to look at ways the government can improve its relationship with the province's public sector unions. The commission will be chaired jointly by Frank Ledwell and Anna Duffy.
27 May 1994 *Constitutional* *Reform*	While on a trip through western Canada Prime Minister Jean Chrétien reiterates his position regarding the continued speculation on what might happen if Quebec votes to separate from Canada. Speaking in Edmonton he says that he was elected to put Canadians back to work not to discuss a hypothetical separation that most likely would not occur. The prime minister's words "If everybody were to shut up on that, I would be very happy. The people of Canada, the people of Quebec included, are fed up with talking about the constitution."
27 May 1994 *Ontario –* *Credit Rating*	Moody's Investors Service cuts Ontario's credit rating from Aa2 to Aa3 citing the province's rising debt and slow reaction to deficit reduction.
31 May 1994 *Fiscal Policy*	Federal legislation that will cut $5.5 billion from unemployment insurance over three years and extend public service pay freeze passes in the House of Commons by

a vote of 137 to 91. The bill implementing measures introduced in the 22 February budget goes to the Senate for approval.

7 June 1994
National Unity

Before it adjourns for the summer, the House of Commons holds a one-day debate on the Reform Party's resolution regarding national unity. The debate features strongly divergent views between the Reform and BQ visions, while Chrétien blames Quebec separatists for rising interest rates.

7 June 1994
Health Policy –
Nova Scotia

Nova Scotia's Health Minister Ron Stewart announces changes in the administration of the province's health services. Under a bill introduced in the legislature, four regional health boards will replace local health boards across the province. The health boards will be responsible for determining the number and type of hospitals in each region. The province has also reached a $48 million early retirement agreement with the Nova Scotia Association of Health Organizations which represents six unions. The government of Nova Scotia plans to cut its health budget by $62 million in 1994-95.

8 June 1994
Environment

Statistics Canada reports that Canada is among the top producers per capita of industrial and household garbage, hazardous wastes, and greenhouse gases. Environment Minister Sheila Copps blames industry for not meeting government targets and promises tougher measures by September.

9 June 1994
Quebec –
Sovereignty

Reform Party Leader Preston Manning tables in the House of Commons a list of 20 questions to Prime Minister Jean Chrétien, dealing with the potential federal reaction to a vote and negotiations in favour of Quebec independence. The prime minister refuses to respond to hypothetical questions.

9 June 1994
Human Rights –
Ontario

The NDP government's controversial same-sex bill is defeated in the Ontario Legislature by a vote of 68-59. The legislation, the first of its kind in Canada, would have entitled gay and lesbian couples to spousal rights and benefits.

13 June 1994
Transportation

Transport Minister Doug Young announces that the federal government intends to cut Canada's $1.6 billion transportation subsidies. Young tells an international convention of transport officials in Toronto that governments and taxpayers can no longer afford the current overpriced system and that Ottawa is reconsidering its involvement in the St. Lawrence Seaway and Via Rail.

14 June 1994
Elections – Federal
Boundary Revisions

A revised bill ensuring that riding boundaries will be reformed before the next federal election passes in the Senate. The bill replaces an earlier version of the legislation that would have imposed a two-year delay on the normal ten-year process of adjusting ridings to reflect changes in population. The original bill was sent back to the Commons after the Conservative-dominated Senate proposed amendments.

15 June 1994
Energy –
Saskatchewan

Saskatchewan Premier Roy Romanow and federal Agriculture Minister Ralph Goodale sign an agreement in which the federal government agrees to provide $125 million to help the Government of Saskatchewan and its partner Federated Co-operatives Ltd. to restructure the province's debt-ridden New Grade heavy oil upgrader. By providing a one-time grant Ottawa will be relieved of $275 million in loan guarantees agreed to with the previous Conservative government in the province.

16 June 1994
Lobbying –
Regulation

Prime Minister Jean Chrétien announces a new ethics package aimed at restoring integrity in government. Under new rules lobbyists seeking to influence government must:

• Specify which bill or contract they are trying to influence;

• Name each government department or institution contacted and the lobbying methods used;

• Identify their true employer in cases where they are hired by subsidiaries of major companies.

Also, fees paid only if lobbying is successful will not be allowed. Chrétien appoints Howard Wilson as the new ethics counsellor.

22 June 1994
Environment –
British Columbia

British Columbia's Premier Mike Harcourt announces that new parks will be created on Vancouver Island. Harcourt says his government accepts most of the conclusions of its Commission on Resources and Environment which recommended in February that logging be limited on the island.

23 June 1994
Access of
Information Act

Federal Information Commissioner John Grace releases a report in which he recommends changes to the *Access to Information Act.* Grace's recommendations include bringing Cabinet communications under the Act, cancelling the $5 fee for access requests and penalizing departments not living up to the Act.

24 June 1994
Social Programs –
Reform

Human Resources Minister Lloyd Axworthy tours the provinces to discuss his draft plan for restructuring Canada's social programs. Axworthy promises ample opportunity for public debate in the future. While he had originally planned to publicly release his proposals next month, there are indications that this may be delayed until after the provincial election in Quebec.

28 June 1994
Trade –
Interprovincial

The federal and provincial governments make further progress towards an agreement in principle to eliminate some interprovincial trade barriers. The agreement will include more open government procurement practices, a code of conduct to stop provinces from stealing investment from one another, establishment of a dispute-settlement mechanism, and increased mobility among provinces. The provinces fail to agree on the issues of alcoholic beverages, agriculture and food, and energy, leaving them for future negotiations.

29 June 1994
Taxation –
Newfoundland

Premier Clyde Wells outlines legislation that would make Newfoundland the only province to offer new firms exemptions from all provincial taxes. In an effort to fight unemployment Newfoundland promises businesses a ten-year tax exemption in exchange for much needed jobs.

29 June 1994
Taxation

Provincial finance ministers refuse to support a national sales tax proposal put forth by federal Finance Minister Paul Martin at a two day federal-provincial meeting in Vancouver. Martin proposes a 10 percent national sales tax to replace the GST and provincial sales taxes. The ministers agree, however, to study the proposal and discuss it again in the fall.

Chronology: Index

Party Leadership 14 September 1993, 6 November 1993, 14 December 1993, 14 December 1993, 11 January 1994, 18 April 1994

Premiers 27 August 1993, 25 November 1993, 20 May 1994

Prince Edward Island 25 May 1994

Reducing Duplication 1 March 1994

Social Assistance 8 July 1993, 19 August 1993, 14 December 1993, 31 January 1994, 14 February 1994, 23 March 1994, 3 May 1994, 19 May 1994, 19 May 1994

Social Programs 14 April 1994, 20 May 1994, 24 June 1994

Taxation 8 December 1993, 8 February 1994, 21 February 1994, 13 April 1994, 29 June 1994, 29 June 1994

Telecommunications 26 April 1994

Throne Speech 13 September 1993, 18 January 1994, 7 February 1994, 10 February 1994, 15 February 1994, 28 February 1994, 8 March 1994, 14 March 1994, 7 April 1994

Trade 27 September 1993, 12 November 1993, 2 December 1993, 24 December 1993, 1 January 1994, 30 March 1994, 3 May 1994, 10 May 1994, 28 June 1994

Transportation 3 December 1993, 16 February 1994, 13 June 1994

List of Titles in Print

The Following Publications are Available From:
Renouf Publishing Co. Ltd.
1294 Algoma Rd.
Ottawa, Ontario K1B 3W8
Tel.: (613) 741-4333 / Fax: (613) 741-5439

Canada: The State of the Federation

Ronald L. Watts and Douglas M. Brown, eds., *Canada: The State of the Federation, 1993.* ($20)

Douglas Brown and Robert Young, eds., *Canada: The State of the Federation, 1992.* ($20)

Douglas M. Brown, ed., *Canada: The State of the Federation, 1991.* ($18)

Ronald L. Watts and Douglas M. Brown, eds., *Canada: The State of the Federation, 1990.* ($17)

Ronald L. Watts and Douglas M. Brown, eds., *Canada: The State of the Federation, 1989.* ($16)

Peter M. Leslie and Ronald L. Watts, eds., *Canada: The State of the Federation, 1987-88.* ($15)

Peter M. Leslie, ed., *Canada: The State of the Federation 1986.* ($15)

Peter M. Leslie, ed., *Canada: The State of the Federation 1985.* ($14)

Canada: L'état de la fédération 1985. ($14)

Conference Proceedings

2. Douglas Brown, Pierre Cazalis and Gilles Jasmin, eds., *Higher Education in Federal Systems*, 1992. ($20). French version: *L'enseignement supérieur dans les systèmes fédératifs* ($30)
1. Out of Print.

Research Papers/Notes de Recherche (Formerly Discussion Papers)

32. Robert Young, *The Breakup of Czechoslovakia*, 1994. ($12)
31. Steven A. Kennett, *The Design of Federalism and Water Resource Management in Canada*, 1992. ($8)
30. Patrick Fafard and Darrel R. Reid, *Constituent Assemblies: A Comparative Survey*, 1991. ($7)
29. Thomas O. Hueglin, *A Political Economy of Federalism: In Search of a New Comparative Perspective With Critical Intent Throughout*, 1990. ($10)
28. Ronald L. Watts, Darrel R. Reid and Dwight Herperger, *Parallel Accords: The American Precedent,* 1990. ($6)
27. Michael B. Stein, *Canadian Constitutional Renewal, 1968-1981: A Case Study in Integrative Bargaining*, 1989. ($12)

26. Ronald L. Watts, *Executive Federalism: A Comparative Analysis,* 1989. ($6)
25. Denis Robert, *L'ajustement structurel et le fédéralisme canadien: le cas de l'industrie du textile et du vêtement,* 1989. ($7.50)
24. Peter M. Leslie, *Ethnonationalism in a Federal State: The Case of Canada,* 1988. ($4)
23. Peter M. Leslie, *National Citizenship and Provincial Communities: A Review of Canadian Fiscal Federalism,* 1988. ($4)

Reflections/Réflexions

13. Daniel J. Elazar, *Federalism and the Way to Peace,* 1994. ($20)
12. Guy Laforest and Douglas Brown, eds., *Integration and Fragmentation: The Paradox of the Late Twentieth Century,* 1994. ($15)
11. C.E.S. Franks, *The Myths and Symbols of the Constitutional Debate in Canada,* 1993. ($9)
10. Out of print.
9. Donald J. Savoie, *The Politics of Language,* 1991. ($4)
8. Thomas J. Courchene, *The Community of the Canadas,* 1991. ($5)
7. Gordon Robertson, *Does Canada Matter?* 1991. ($3)
6. Thomas J. Courchene, *Forever Amber: The Legacy of the 1980s for the Ongoing Constitutional Impasse,* 1990. ($5)
5. Patrick J. Monahan, *After Meech: An Insider's View,* 1990. ($6)
4. Albert Breton, *Centralization, Decentralization and Intergovernmental Competition,* 1990. ($3)
3. Peter M. Leslie, *Federal Leadership in Economic and Social Policy,* 1988. ($3)
2. Clive Thomson, ed., *Navigating Meech Lake: The 1987 Constitutional Accord,* 1988. ($4)
1. Allan E. Blakeney, *Canada: Its Framework, Its Foibles, Its Future,* 1988. ($3)

Bibliographies

Aboriginal Self-Government in Canada: A Bibliography 1987-90. ($10)
Aboriginal Self-Government in Canada: A Bibliography 1986. ($12)
Bibliography of Canadian and Comparative Federalism, 1986. ($20)
Bibliography of Canadian and Comparative Federalism, 1980-1985. ($39)

Aboriginal Peoples and Constitutional Reform

New Releases

Douglas Brown, ed., *Aboriginal Governments and Power Sharing in Canada,* 1992. ($7)
Thomas J. Courchene and Lisa M. Powell, *A First Nations Province,* 1992. ($7)

Background Papers

16. Bradford W. Morse, *Providing Land and Resources for Aboriginal Peoples,* 1987. ($10)
15. Evelyn J. Peters, *Aboriginal Self-Government Arrangements in Canada,* 1987. ($7)
14. Delia Opekokew, *The Political and Legal Inequities Among Aboriginal Peoples in Canada,* 1987. ($7)

13. Ian B. Cowie, *Future Issues of Jurisdiction and Coordination Between Aboriginal and Non-Aboriginal Governments*, 1987. ($7)
12. C.E.S. Franks, *Public Administration Questions Relating to Aboriginal Self-Government*, 1987. ($10)
11. Richard H. Bartlett, *Subjugation, Self-Management and Self-Government of Aboriginal Lands and Resources in Canada*, 1986. ($10)
10. Jerry Paquette, *Aboriginal Self-Government and Education in Canada*, 1986. ($10)
9. Out of print.
8. John Weinstein, *Aboriginal Self-Determination Off a Land Base*, 1986. ($7)
7. David C. Hawkes, *Negotiating Aboriginal Self-Government: Developments Surrounding the 1985 First Ministers' Conference*, 1985. ($5)
6. Bryan P. Schwartz, *First Principles: Constitutional Reform with Respect to the Aboriginal Peoples of Canada 1982-1984*, 1985. ($20)
5. Douglas E. Sanders, *Aboriginal Self-Government in the United States*, 1985. ($12)
4. Bradford Morse, *Aboriginal Self-Government in Australia and Canada*, 1985. ($12)
2. David A. Boisvert, *Forms of Aboriginal Self-Government*, 1985. ($12)
1. Noel Lyon, *Aboriginal Self-Government: Rights of Citizenship and Access to Governmental Services*, 1984. ($12)

Discussion Papers

David C. Hawkes, *The Search for Accommodation*, 1987. ($7)

Position Papers

Inuit Committee on National Issues, *Completing Canada: Inuit Approaches to Self-Government*, 1987. ($7)

Martin Dunn, *Access to Survival, A Perspective on Aboriginal Self-Government for the Constituency of the Native Council of Canada*, 1986. ($7)

Workshop Report

David C. Hawkes and Evelyn J. Peters, *Implementing Aboriginal Self-Government: Problems and Prospects*, 1986. ($7)

Bibliographies

Evelyn J. Peters, *Aboriginal Self-Government in Canada: A Bibliography 1987-90.* ($10)

Evelyn J. Peters, *Aboriginal Self-Government in Canada: A Bibliography 1986.* ($12)

Final Report

David C. Hawkes, *Aboriginal Peoples and Constitutional Reform: What Have We Learned?* 1989. ($7)

The Following Publications are Available From:
The Institute of Intergovernmental Relations
Queen's University
Kingston, Ontario K7L 3N6
Tel.: (613) 545-2080 / Fax: (613) 545-6868

Institute of Intergovernmental Relations, *Annual Report to the Advisory Council, 1991-92*/Institut des relations intergouvernementales, *Rapport annuel au Conseil consultatif, 1991-1992.* (Charge for postage only)

William M. Chandler and Christian W. Zöllner, eds., *Challenges to Federalism: Policy-Making in Canada and the Federal Republic of Germany*, 1989. ($25)

Peter M. Leslie, *Rebuilding the Relationship: Quebec and its Confederation Partners/Une collaboration renouvelée: le Québec et ses partenaires dans la confédération*, 1987. ($8)

A. Paul Pross and Susan McCorquodale, *Economic Resurgence and the Constitutional Agenda: The Case of the East Coast Fisheries*, 1987. ($10)

Bruce G. Pollard, *Managing the Interface: Intergovernmental Affairs Agencies in Canada*, 1986. ($12)

Catherine A. Murray, *Managing Diversity: Federal-Provincial Collaboration and the Committee on Extension of Services to Northern and Remote Communities*, 1984. ($15)

Peter Russell et al., *The Court and the Constitution: Comments on the Supreme Court Reference on Constitutional Amendment*, 1982. (Paper $5, Cloth $10)

Allan Tupper, *Public Money in the Private Sector: Industrial Assistance Policy and Canadian Federalism*, 1982. ($12)

William P. Irvine, *Does Canada Need a New Electoral System?* 1979. ($8)

The Year in Review

Bruce G. Pollard, *The Year in Review 1983: Intergovernmental Relations in Canada.* ($16)

Revue de l'année 1983: les relations intergouvernementales au Canada. ($16)

S.M. Dunn, *The Year in Review 1982: Intergovernmental Relations in Canada.* ($12)

Revue de l'année 1982: les relations intergouvernementales au Canada. ($12)

S.M. Dunn, *The Year in Review 1981: Intergovernmental Relations in Canada.* ($10)

R.J. Zukowsky, *Intergovernmental Relations in Canada: The Year in Review 1980, Volume I: Policy and Politics.* ($8) (*Volume II not available*)

Discussion Papers

22. Robert L. Stanfield, *National Political Parties and Regional Diversity*, 1985. (Charge for postage only)
21. Donald Smiley, *An Elected Senate for Canada? Clues from the Australian Experience*, 1985. ($8)
19. Thomas O. Hueglin, *Federalism and Fragmentation: A Comparative View of Political Accommodation in Canada*, 1984. ($8)
18. Allan Tupper, *Bill S-31 and the Federalism of State Capitalism*, 1983. ($7)
17. Reginald Whitaker, *Federalism and Democratic Theory*, 1983. ($7)
16. Roger Gibbins, *Senate Reform: Moving Towards the Slippery Slope*, 1983. ($7)
14. John Whyte, *The Constitution and Natural Resource Revenues*, 1982. ($7)